I0520944

The Pipe Family Letter Collection

Volume 2

The Promise of America in Their Own Words

Joan Naomi Steiner, PhD

SCENERY HEIGHTS
Publishing

Neenah, Wisconsin (USA)

The Pipe Family Letter Collection, Vol. 2

The Promise of America in Their Own Words

First Edition

Disclaimer
The author and other contributors to this work have made every effort to focus on factual accuracy. We ask your forgiveness for any potential errors. In the event you use any of the information in this book for yourself, which is your constitutional right, the author and the publisher assume no responsibility for your actions.

ISBN: 979-8-9865709-4-5

Front cover images: (Left to right) Thomas Pipe, Elizabeth Johnson Pipe, Edwin Pipe, and John (Jack) Stickland Pipe

(Privately held by Marlene Anderson Sannes, Amherst, Portage County, Wisconsin, USA)

Back cover image: The Pipe Family Farm, Lanark, Portage County, Wisconsin USA

(Privately held by Elizabeth Pipe Hansen, Portage County, Amherst, Wisconsin, USA)

Scenery Heights Publications
Neenah, Wisconsin (USA)

Dedication

To my son, Robert John Mittelstaedt, who reintroduced me to the Pipe and Stickland families through his cousins, Marlene Anderson Sannes and Ida Mae Rosin Frizzell, and his aunt, Judy Mittelstaedt Anderson.

and

To my granddaughter, Madeline,
who will know her ancestral roots through those of her
grandfather, Robert Alan Mittelstaedt,
and her great-grandmother,
Helen Anderson Mittelstaedt, daughter of
Oliver and May Elizabeth Pipe Anderson.

Foreword

Susan T. Moore

I was first approached by Joan Steiner to ask if I would be interested in transcribing some family letters concerning a family with connections to Devon and Somerset (England) and jumped at the chance, as I grew up and still live in this rural area and am familiar with the place names, and of course have an interest in the area.

I have been carrying out research into family and local history all my working life as a freelance researcher and have loved every minute. The commissions I have received over the years have varied widely from writing a biography of a Tudor courtier, to modern land disputes where 17th century maps need to be consulted. But what I do mostly is straightforward family history usually in the 16th to 18th centuries, with many requests for finding the 'link across the Atlantic' and the English origins of people who emigrated in the early 17th century from somewhere in England to New England or Virginia.

However, I think my favourite commissions are those where I am asked to transcribe diaries or letters. These give an insight into the characters and lives of the people concerned that cannot be matched anywhere else. I have worked on a number of naval diaries, which give an excellent idea of life aboard ship in the 19th century, the relationships between the crew and the passengers, and the places visited.

However, nothing prepared me for the intimacy and detail to be found in this collection of Pipe family letters. The collection will of course be of great interest to the wider members of the family and there are a great many references to aunts, uncles, brothers, sisters, friends and of course parents and children. But what really interested me, and will interest the wider readership, who are not necessarily related to the Pipe family, are the details of local history.

From these letters we learn of the fire in Oshkosh with a little sketch to show how it took all of Main Street and left just the Court House. Every printing house, every large store and every bank were lost. The sadness the morning after is heartfelt: “I think it the most distressing sight I ever saw with so much property burned.”

Something that not everyone is aware of is just how often people crossed the Atlantic in both directions. Once in America people didn’t stay there all the time. They came back to England to visit family or property. And those in England sailed to America to visit friends and family. The shipping passengers lists that are now readily available online will confirm this constant traffic to and fro.

Something that surprised me when transcribing these letters, which are mostly in the second half of the 19th century is the low level of true literacy. Yes, they could write, but the spelling was phonetic for so many of them. Although spelling was not standard in earlier centuries, by the 19th century there was little variation and there were right and wrong ways of spelling words. So, we have ‘affectionate’ written ‘efexinant’ and ‘window’ written ‘wingo’. Words then can be a little challenging to any transcriber!

Health is something that we generally take for granted today, but in the 19th century it was very fragile and all the letters contain many confirmations that everyone is still healthy or gives details of illnesses. When a letter starts ‘I hope you are well’ which we may think of as a platitude, for them it was serious and a genuine question.

Finally, the details of the way farms were run both in Devon and Wisconsin are absolutely fascinating to those of us with an interest in this way of life. The comparison of weather events, the prices of wheat, the price of land are as interesting as the quantities involved. In Oshkosh we hear of 2000 bushels of wheat and 1000 of oats. Yet in Yarcombe we hear that the price of corn was very low with wheat selling at just £1 per sack. The agricultural information which can be found in these letters deserves some serious study and analysis.

Perhaps the saddest lines in the letters come from Elizabeth Stickland Pipe writing to Mr. William & Mrs. Elizabeth Coleman Jennings on 21st May 1854 concerning the drowning of her husband.

"I had a list of the passengers that was on board of the *City of Glasgow* and I saw his dear name there on the list and the steamer has not arrived which I suppose by the accounts she never will. It is supposed she was encountered ice bergs smashed to atoms and sunk with 373 passengers, 74 officers and crew. Here I am left as everyone thinks a widow with four little children."

I hope that everyone who reads this book will enjoy the details as much as I did when I was transcribing the letters, whether they are family members or those who are interested in life in the past, particularly in the farming areas of Somerset, Devon and Wisconsin.

Contents

The post office in Chard, Somerset County, England, in the later 1800s

Introduction

When did you last receive a handwritten letter? Were you quick to open it? Or did you feel apprehensive and anxious about the information contained inside?

Letter writers in the 1800s found a gentle way to communicate painful news like the loss of a loved one. A black border on the edges of an envelope announced a death. The thicker the black border, the longer the mourning period. Not only did black edging pay respect to the deceased loved one, but it also gave the recipient a forewarning. The letters in this collection include several black-edged envelopes.

Letters are personal. They reveal a writer's private thoughts, feelings, and doubts about themselves and others. Future decisions and plans can be openly discussed in the privacy of a letter to a family member or dear friend. Letters can also be transactional, relating economic, social, and political events of the day. Letters are written records that define the times. Letters also define the people who write them.

This two-volume work includes 105 original letters, many with envelopes, written between 1851 and 1914 and a transcription of each. The Pipe family, including John Valentine's brother, Thomas Pipe, and their relatives and friends wrote these letters. Taken together, the collection grants the reader a much larger view of life at this time in both England and America.

John Valentine and Elizabeth Stickland Pipe were born in southwestern England. They immigrated to America with their two children in 1850. First, they settled in New York. Then, Elizabeth and her four children headed west to Wisconsin. All the while, she and her family wrote to each other, keeping themselves informed of home events and their fast-changing lives on both sides of the Atlantic. The Pipe family letter collection is personal. The letters reveal inner thoughts and family relationships in England and America.

Looking Back

Volume 1 of this work introduced the main letter writers and recipients in the Pipe family letter collection. Both the Pipe and Stickland family roots were detailed. John Valentine and Elizabeth Stickland Pipe, their two children, and John Valentine's brother, Thomas Pipe, immigrated to America and first settled in Monroe County, New York. John Valentine Pipe traveled back to England to settle Elizabeth Stickland Pipe's inherited properties, and on his return trip, traveled the ill-fated *City of Glasgow* and was lost at sea.

Elizabeth Stickland Pipe and her two children moved to Vinland, Winnebago County, Wisconsin, where her brother-in-law, Thomas Pipe, and his mother, Charlotte Jennings Pipe Pillar, lived. They eventually married and moved to the town of Farmington, Waupaca County, Wisconsin, starting their own family. The family moved to the village of Waupaca, where Thomas operated butcher and livery business.

Looking Ahead

Volume 2 begins with letters starting in 1864. Thomas Pipe is feeling the social and economic effects of the Civil War on their everyday lives. The Jennings leave Northay Farm and eventually move to Hursey Farm in Burstock, Beaminster, Dorset.

The English counties of Devon, Somerset, and Dorset are shown in purple, yellow, and magenta, respectively, on the southwest portion of this Phillimore map. The villages and farms mentioned in the letters are mainly located here.

This is the trunk that Thomas and Elizabeth Stickland Pipe took to England in 1875. Their English family (mainly the Jennings) saved letters from the Pipes and returned the letters to the Pipes when they visited. That is the reason we have the letters today. Thomas and Elizabeth also brought back letters from friends and family who wrote to them while they were in England. The trunk transported many of the letters in the collection back to America in 1875. Today it resides in a descendant's home in Amherst, Wisconsin.

In 1874, the Pipes learn from solicitors Dommett & Canning how William Jennings has managed their inherited properties over the last 21 years. The Pipes travel to England in 1875 for a seven-month visit with family and friends. They settle their business regarding the inherited properties. Thomas Pipe dies in 1880. Elizabeth Stickland Pipe lives another 38 years at The Pipe House with her son William's family. Elizabeth dies in January of 1918.

Return Addresses

Like GPS today, return addresses on envelopes and inside addresses on letters document locations of senders and recipients. Pipe family and friends in England wrote letters from primarily three western counties: today's East Devon, Somerset, and Dorset. For the most part, villages and family farms mentioned in the letters are scattered along the borders of these counties.

Locations in England

Elizabeth Stickland Pipe inherited properties from her Uncle John Stickland of Yarcombe, Devon, three years after the family immigrated to America. The properties identified in Uncle John Stickland's will include:

> **Much Hill Farm in the parish of Yarcombe** aforesaid occupied by Joel King, **Combes's Pithayne** and **the allotment in Mannings Common in Yarcombe** aforesaid now in my own occupation **Whithorns otherwise Bardscombe** situate at Membury aforesaid and now in my own occupation and also **Peacross** in Membury aforesaid occupied by John Dening. (See Appendix D.)

Because the Pipes were living in America, Elizabeth's husband, John Valentine Pipe, arranged for his uncle, William Jennings, who lived in Somerset County, to manage the inherited properties on behalf of Elizabeth. Business details regarding farms are frequent topics in the letters.

Birch Oak Farm is another place frequently mentioned in the letters. Both William Jennings and his sister Charlotte Jennings Pipe Pillar, John Valentine Pipe's mother, grew up with their siblings on Birch Oak Farm. William and Charlotte's parents, John and Mary Bond Jennings, first took residence there in 1805. Birch Oak Farm was home of the Jennings family until their brother John Jennings died in 1872. Birch Oak Farm was originally located in Membury Parish, Devon. In 1884, Birch Oak Farm became part of Yarcombe Parish.

Letters reveal that William Jennings, from Birch Oak Farm, and his wife, Elizabeth Coleman Jennings, moved during their married lives. The couple first lived at Northay Farm, Whitestaunton Parish, Somerset County. Letter Number 63, dated July 9, 1870, announced the Jennings move to Forton Village, Chard, Somerset County, on "Lady Day (March 25) last." Letter Number 65, dated August 15, 1872, was written by the couple while living in Hursey Village, Burstock, Beaminster, Dorsetshire. The Jennings remained on Hursey Farm for the rest of their married lives.

Locations in America

The letter collection also documents the lives of the Pipes in America. John Valentine and Elizabeth Stickland Pipe first settled as farmers in Greece Center, Monroe County, New York, near Rochester. Thomas Pipe, brother of John Valentine, first settled in Monroe County as a farm laborer. After a short time, Thomas ventured west to the town of Vinland, Winnebago County, Wisconsin. His mother, Charlotte Jennings Pipe Pillar, also immigrated with her second husband and family to Vinland.

In 1854, John Valentine Pipe died at sea. Thomas Pipe and his mother traveled east to New York. They brought back to Vinland widowed Elizabeth Stickland Pipe and her four children. In 1855, she and Thomas married.

On a 40-acre farm in Vinland, Thomas and Elizabeth Stickland Pipe started their family. After a few years, however, they moved to the town of Farmington, Waupaca County, Wisconsin, near what is known today as the Waupaca Chain O' Lakes.

Thomas Pipe also purchased property in the Village of Waupaca, Wisconsin, and was active in business affairs. In 1875, the Pipes traveled back to England to visit family and friends and to take care of family business involving Elizabeth's properties. Letters from their Wisconsin family and friends are addressed to them in England during their seven-month visit. These letters are packed with local news.

Thomas and Elizabeth Stickland Pipe made one more move. They purchased a farm in the town of Lanark, Portage County, Wisconsin, which is known today as The Pipe House. Three more generations of Pipes would live in The Pipe House.

Overview of Chapters - Volume 2

Chapter 6 includes 11 letters dated 1864 to 1867 during the time the Pipes transitioned their lives a few miles from rural Farmington to the Village of Waupaca where Thomas Pipe had livery and butcher businesses. All 11 letters are between Thomas and Elizabeth Stickland Pipe and William and Elizabeth Jennings. Daughter Mary Ann Jennings also includes a note in one letter to her Pipe cousins. The letters discuss social, economic, political (Civil War), and personal concerns with family and friends in the Waupaca area and in their beloved homeland, "Olde England."

Chapter 7 includes 14 letters dated 1868 to 1874 while the Pipe family is still living in the Village of Waupaca. The Jennings move from Northay Farm in Whitestaunton, Chard, Somerset County to Forton, Chard, Somerset County, and finally to Hursey Farm, Burstock, Beaminster, Dorset County. Ten letters are between Thomas and Elizabeth Stickland Pipe and William and Elizabeth Jennings. Three letters are from Elizabeth Stickland's solicitor in Chard, Mr. Dommett. Thomas Pipe writes one letter to Dommett & Canning. The last of Mr. Dommett's letters, dated December 8, 1874, reveals his understanding of property management, including financial matters, for the last 21 years under the auspices of Uncle William Jennings.

Chapter 8 includes letters dated 1875 to 1880 while Thomas and Elizabeth Stickland Pipe and their children are living in The Pipe House in the town of Lanark, Portage County, Wisconsin. This chapter focuses on Thomas and Elizabeth Stickland Pipe's seven-month trip home to England to visit family and friends and settle family business. Nine letters are written by family and friends in Waupaca, Neenah, and Woodville, Wisconsin, and Chicago, Illinois. These letters highlight local news, including the "biggest of the biggest" fires in Oshkosh, Wisconsin, in April

The Pipe family lived and worked in this house and farm (shown here in the early 1900s) for three generations in the central Wisconsin town of Lanark, Portage County. The Pipe family letter collection was found in the house attic by descendants.

1875. Mary Stickland writes three letters to her sister, Elizabeth Stickland Pipe, while the Pipes are in England. John Stickland's daughter Anna writes to Thomas and Elizabeth Stickland Pipe with family news. Two letters are from William Jennings Pipe, who discusses family and friends in Australia. One letter is from cousins in Dorset after the Pipes return from their trip. Another is from a friend from Norfolk County in England. Five letters involve business matters in England and in Wisconsin. Chapter 8 ends with the death of Thomas Pipe in November 1880.

Chapter 9 includes letters from 1883 to 1914 while Elizabeth Stickland Pipe is living at The Pipe House in the town of Lanark, Portage County, Wisconsin, with her son William Edwin Pipe and his wife Mary Agnes Messer Pipe. One letter is written by William Edwin Pipe to Thomas Messer before William Edwin married his daughter, Mary Agnes Messer. Three letters are about William Edwin and Mary Agnes Messer Pipe's growing family. One letter is from Stevens Point, Wisconsin, where the John Stickland and Elizabeth Johnson Pipe family live. Mary Elizabeth Pipe Woodnorth and her husband Frank Woodnorth write Elizabeth Stickland Pipe to announce their marriage. Mary Elizabeth Pipe Woodnorth also writes to an unknown recipient. One letter is a tribute to William Edwin Pipe in the form of a poem from an attorney in Manitowoc, Wisconsin.

Two letters are to Grandmother Elizabeth Stickland Pipe from her granddaughters, Florence and Ethel McCunn, who are living in Scotland and England, respectively. Both girls ask Grandmother Elizabeth Stickland Pipe where she originated in England. Both express an interest in traveling to their grandmother's homeland to visit any remaining family and friends. Included at the end of this chapter is a hand-written list of deaths in the Jennings/ Bond family from 1837 to 1872. Elizabeth Stickland Pipe died in January 1918 at the age of 91.

Original letters and surviving envelopes are included after each transcription for the reader's ease of comparing transcripts to originals. The Key Ideas include local news, especially in Yarcombe Parish, Devon, England, and in Winnebago, Waupaca, and Portage counties, Wisconsin. Marriages, births, and deaths are noted on both sides of the Atlantic and in Victoria, Australia, where Thomas Pipe's brother, William Jennings Pipe, immigrated.

An Invitation

The 105 letters in this two-volume collection tell the story of a family over 60 years and four generations. We hear from writers in their own words. Their voices at times express joy, astonishment, pain, gratitude, and wonder.

I invite you to take a seat at the dinner table. Listen to Thomas Pipe explain to his Uncle William how farming in Wisconsin differs from farming in England.

Join Elizabeth Stickland Pipe in the parlor and listen to her excitement as she vividly describes the farm that has taken her heart in the town of Lanark, Portage County.

Sit on the front porch with Grandma Pillar and enjoy the impatience of the Pipe children as they wonder when their parents will return from their trip to England.

I invite you to listen to these people. Their voices bring to life their individual personalities while they offer details of their everyday lives on both sides of the Atlantic!

Chapter 6

Village of Waupaca, Waupaca County, Wisconsin
1864 - 1867

Chapter 6 includes 11 letters dated 1864 to 1867 during the time the Pipes transitioned their lives a few miles from rural Farmington to the village of Waupaca, where Thomas Pipe had livery and butcher businesses. All 11 letters are between Thomas and Elizabeth Stickland Pipe and William and Elizabeth Jennings. Daughter Mary Ann Jennings also includes a note in one letter to her Pipe cousins. The letters discuss social, economic, political (Civil War), and personal concerns with family and friends in the Waupaca area and in their beloved homeland, "Olde England."

Letter Number 48

Date: Circa 1864
Writer: Thomas & Elizabeth Stickland Pipe
Recipient: William Jennings
Sent from: Waupaca, Waupaca County, Wisconsin, USA
Sent to: Northay Farm, Whitestaunton, Chard, Somerset County, England

Key Ideas

- Thomas Pipe asks his uncle for his view on the inherited property in England passing only to John Valentine Pipe's children.
- Thomas Pipe describes his stepson, Tom, as a good boy.
- Mary Elizabeth is a nice little girl. She wants to go to a good school and study music.
- John Stickland Pipe has the disposition of his father, John Valentine Pipe, but not the ambition to carry him through.
- Frank is a good-natured boy who is funny and smart. He seems to take after his Uncle John Stickland.
- Thomas Pipe makes clear that he has always viewed and treated all the children as his own.
- Thomas asks his uncle to send him the clause in the will that gives all property to John Valentine Pipe's children.

Dear Uncle [William Jennings] I am fully aware that I am with this business a great bother to you, but I have no other reliable friends to call on, and it is impossible for me to do it myself. And all that being said that you must make your charge and take your pay.

Now, Sir, after reading this my ideas of the matter, I want you to consider the matter, and give me your views on the same, and if those younger children are not entitled to any part of the property are they not entitled to at least a part of the expenses of the bringing up of the older ones. I have treated all and at all times as my own. And there is not half of the community that know the difference. They are good quiet steady children, Tom is a very good boy. Mary Elizabeth is a very nice little girl. She now wants to go to a good school and to learn some kind of music which

she wants in order to be locked in with any kind of respect as it is considered a great part of education in this country. I gave her quite a start last winter, but how can I finish it. John has the disposition of his father, but not the ambition to carry him through. It seems impossible for him to learn, and work. He stands right up and says he should not hurt and he is very careful it should not hurt him. Frank is a good natured, funny fellow, pretty smart and a dear[?] the twin and not unlike his Uncle John Stickland. Now I must close this long wrangle by hoping this will find yourself and family quite well, as it leaves us all at present. Elizabeth joins with me in sending her kindest love to yourself and wife and family

From your affectionate nephew and niece

Thos. and E. [Elizabeth] Pipe

[sideways] Please write as soon as possible and repeat to me the clause in the will that gives the property to John's issue.

Letter Number 48, Page 1

Dear Uncle. I am fooley aware that
I am with this Business a great bother
to you, But I have no other reliable
Friend to call on, and it is impossible
for me to do it my selfe, And all
that I can say that you must make
your charge and take your pay,
Now Sir after reading this my Notice
of the matter, I want you to consider
the matter, And give me your views
on the same, and if those younger
Children ar not intitled to any Part
of the Property, ar they not intitled
to at least a part of the Expences
of the bringen up of the older ons
I have treated all and at all times
as my own, And there is not half
of the community that know the diference
They ar good quiet Study Children
Tom is a very good Boy Mary Elizebeth
is a very nice litte girel She now
wants to go to a good School and to
learn som kind of musick which

Letter Number 48, Page 2

Please prepare as soon as possible and Reply to me the Claims in the
will that gives the property to Johns Spire
The mind in order to be looked
on with any kind of respect as It
is considered a great Part of Education
in this Country, I gave her quite a
Start last winter, But how can I
finish it, John has the disposition
of his Father but not the ambition
to carry him through, It seems impos
-sible for him to learn, and work he
Stands right up and says he shall not
hurt and he is very carefull it shall
not hurt him, Frank is a good natured
funny fellow pretty Smart and a deal
like twin and not unlike his Uncle
John Strickland, Now I must close this
long ramble by hoping this will find
your Self and Family quite well,
As it leaves us all at present
Elizabeth joins with me in sending
her kindest Love to your Self and
Wife and Family
From your Affect Nephew and Niece
Thos & E Pipe

Letter Number 49

Date: Circa March 1864
Writer: Elizabeth Coleman Jennings
Recipient: Thomas Pipe
Sent from: Northay Farm, Whitestaunton, Chard, Somerset County, England
Sent to: Waupaca, Waupaca County, Wisconsin, USA

Key Ideas

- Elizabeth Coleman Jennings thanks the Pipes for the likenesses or photos they sent.
- Mrs. John Jennings, Anna Maria Tucker Jennings, thinks the eldest girl, Mary Elizabeth Pipe, resembles her Uncle John Stickland when he was young.
- Elizabeth Coleman Jennings is sorry that she did not have time to include photos of their children.
- Brother Richard Coleman's wife took the photos to Waterhayn Farm, Devon, to show them to John Stickland who will copy them.
- Old Mrs. John Mathews of Hay Farm, Yarcombe, Devon, is recovering from being very ill.
- Elizabeth Stickland, John Stickland's eldest daughter, is now living with her mother, not her grandmother.
- John Mathews lives at Hay Farm, Yarcombe, Devon, with five children.
- Mrs. Thomasine Spiller of Peterhays Farm, Yarcombe, Devon, died six weeks ago. (Thomasine Spiller was buried in Yarcombe on January 23, 1864. Letter Number 49 was written at the beginning of March 1864.)
- Samuel Eli Wyatt of Newhouse Farm, Buckland St. Mary, Somerset, died in a field working. His wife, Jane Spiller Wyatt, died three months later leaving one child.
- Uncle John Jennings is not well. The eldest Toleman of Watchford Grange, Yarcombe, Devon, has been staying to help for the last four months.

- Mrs. Edwin Jennings has had a seizure. She needs to be carried up and down stairs.
- Frank Jennings lives on a farm in Shepton Beauchamp, Somerset. He is married and has a three-month-old child. Frank Jennings' wife, Emma Wyatt Jennings, is from Bridgwater, Somerset.
- Mr. John Bond died of scarlet fever, leaving a daughter nearly two years old who also died. As a result, Edward, John, and Samuel Jennings each receive a £50 legacy. William did not receive anything.
- John and Harry Bradley, both bachelors, live in Ilton, Somerset. Mrs. Bradley is seriously ill.
- Aunt Betsy (Elizabeth) Coleman lives with her son-in-law William at Crock Street, Ilminister, Somerset.
- Mary Ann Jennings takes after her Aunt Charlotte Jennings Pipe Pillar.
- Ellen (Nelly) was nine years old last December. (Ellen was born December 1854.)
- Bonfield of Pithayne Farm complains about the rent. Mrs. White still lives with them. Harry White use to live at Yarcombe Inn but has taken a farm in Upottery, Devon.

[crosshatched] start not included

I must thank you for the dear children's likenesses [photos]. Mrs. J. [Jennings] at Birch [Oak Farm] says the eldest little girls is like her uncle J. [John] Stickland when a little boy was, sorry Mr. Grant did not bring them out before. We only had them the day before he started. If we had time we should send ours in return. My brother Richard's [Coleman] wife took them at Waterhayn [Farm] to show them to your brother John [Stickland], so he has them to get them copied. Old Mrs. Mathews [Mrs. John Mathews of Hay Farm, Yarcombe, Devon] has been very ill but is now better, but still very feeble. Elizabeth Stickland, John Stickland's eldest daughter, do not live with her grandmother but with her mother now. Her aunt Hannah says she is grown a fine strong girl and has to work very hard. Her mother is expecting an increase to her family soon. I believe they like their farm. You have heard from them since they have been there. It is near Axminster [Somerset]. John Mathews still lives at Hay Farm [Yarcombe, Devon]. They have five children. His wife has been hard up a long time in the Whitely [hospital?], took cold, soon after her confinement. She is a most dressy lady, I can assure you. Do you remember Mrs. [Thomasine] Spiller of Pithayne [Farm] Yarcombe? She died about six weeks since, her eldest daughter [Jane Spiller] married

Mr. Samuel [Eli] Wyatt of Newhouse, Buckland [St. Mary, Somerset] has poor fellow dropped down dead the early part last summer, whilst in the field working with his horses his wife [Jane Spiller Wyatt] died about three months after leaving an orphan daughter and now there is another sister very ill not likely to recover. It must be a great trial for the family, suppose the Miss Spillers must have been young girls when you left. Your uncle J. [John] Jennings was ill all through the fall. The eldest of the young Tolemans of Watchford [Grange, Yarcombe, Devon] has been staying this last four months to superintend a little. If he do not continue

they will get someone else as Mr. Jennings's health is far from good. Mrs. Edwin Jennings has been ill for a long time. She has a seizure in one side, been obliged to carry her up and downstairs. She is now better able to walk alone, and suppose you know Frank Jennings is married and has a daughter three months old, lives in Shepton Beauchamp [Somerset] in a very nice farm. I have not seen his wife [Emma Wyatt Jennings] yet, but I have heard she is a very nice person, one from near Bridgwater [Somerset]. I think I told you of Mr. John Bond's death, he left one child a daughter.

[other way]

She died of scarlet fever about a fortnight since aged one year and eleven months, through the death of the child your uncle Edward, John, and Samuel Jennings will come to a legacy of £50 each left them by

John Bond. My dear William's name was not with them, but we don't care as we do not want it as yet. Old Mrs. Bradley is seriously ill, not expected to be here long.

[other way]

John and Harry Bradley are still living at Ilton [Somerset] both bachelors. It is said they have made a lot of money since they have been there. Your aunt Betsy [Elizabeth] Coleman is still living with her son-in-law Wm. at Crockstreet, Ilminister, Somerset. I paid a visit last fall. She was looking well. She desired to be remembered

[other way]

to Thomas [Pipe]. I suppose your boys are grown up fine lads by this time, is John [Stickland Pipe] at home with you. I can assure you I find my daughter [Mary Ann Jennings] very useful. She is considered like her Aunt Charlotte [Jennings Pipe Pillar], and very much her growth. She will be nineteen next August, my little girl [Ellen (Nellie)] is still at Chard to school. I see her but seldom. She was nine last December, a fine girl for her age,

[other way]

Mr. Bonfield complains of Pithayne [Farm, Yarcombe, Devon] being too dear [expensive] although Wm. has dropped him eight pounds per years that has brought it back to seventy-two pounds per year. John Jennings and Wm. both think it is too dear [expensive] as corn is very low but wheat £1 per sack, the same very careful and industrious people, Old Mrs. White lives with them. Harry White that used to live at the Yarcombe Inn is living at Upottery [Devon] in a farm. I must now bring this long epistle to a close with our united kind love to you all, hoping to hear from you soon.

From your affectionate aunt

E. [Elizabeth] Jennings

Letter Number 49, Page 1

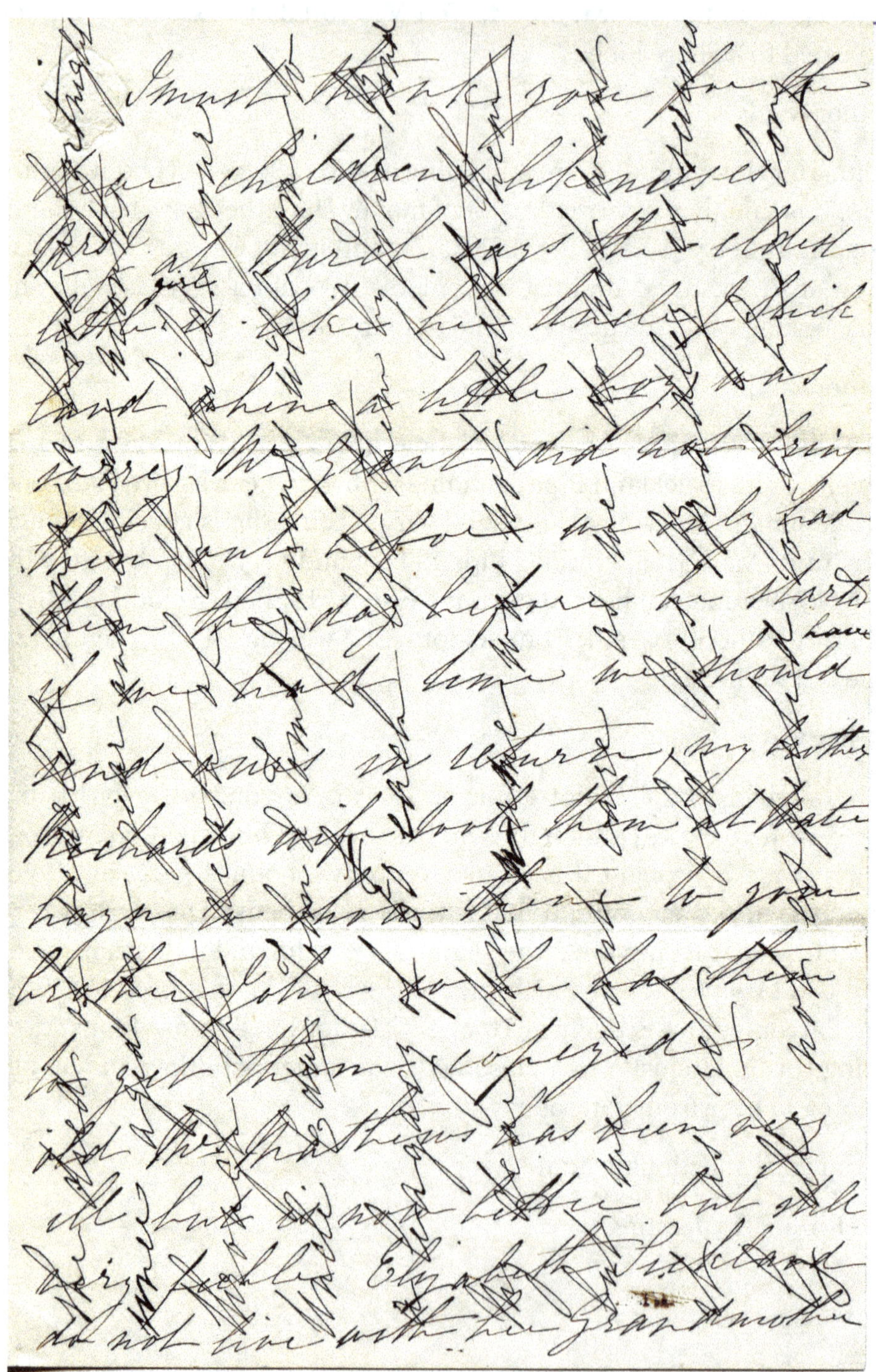

I must thank you for the
four children's likenesses
sent at [illegible] says the eldest
is like his uncle Dick
and when a little boy was
very [illegible] Grant did not bring
them [illegible] before we only had
them the day before he started
if we had time we should have
answered [illegible] my brother
Richard's wife took them to Water
[illegible] to show them to your
brother John so he has them
to get them copied
[illegible] Mathews has been very
ill but is now better but still
very feeble Elizabeth Strickland
do not live with her Grandmother

Letter Number 49, Page 2

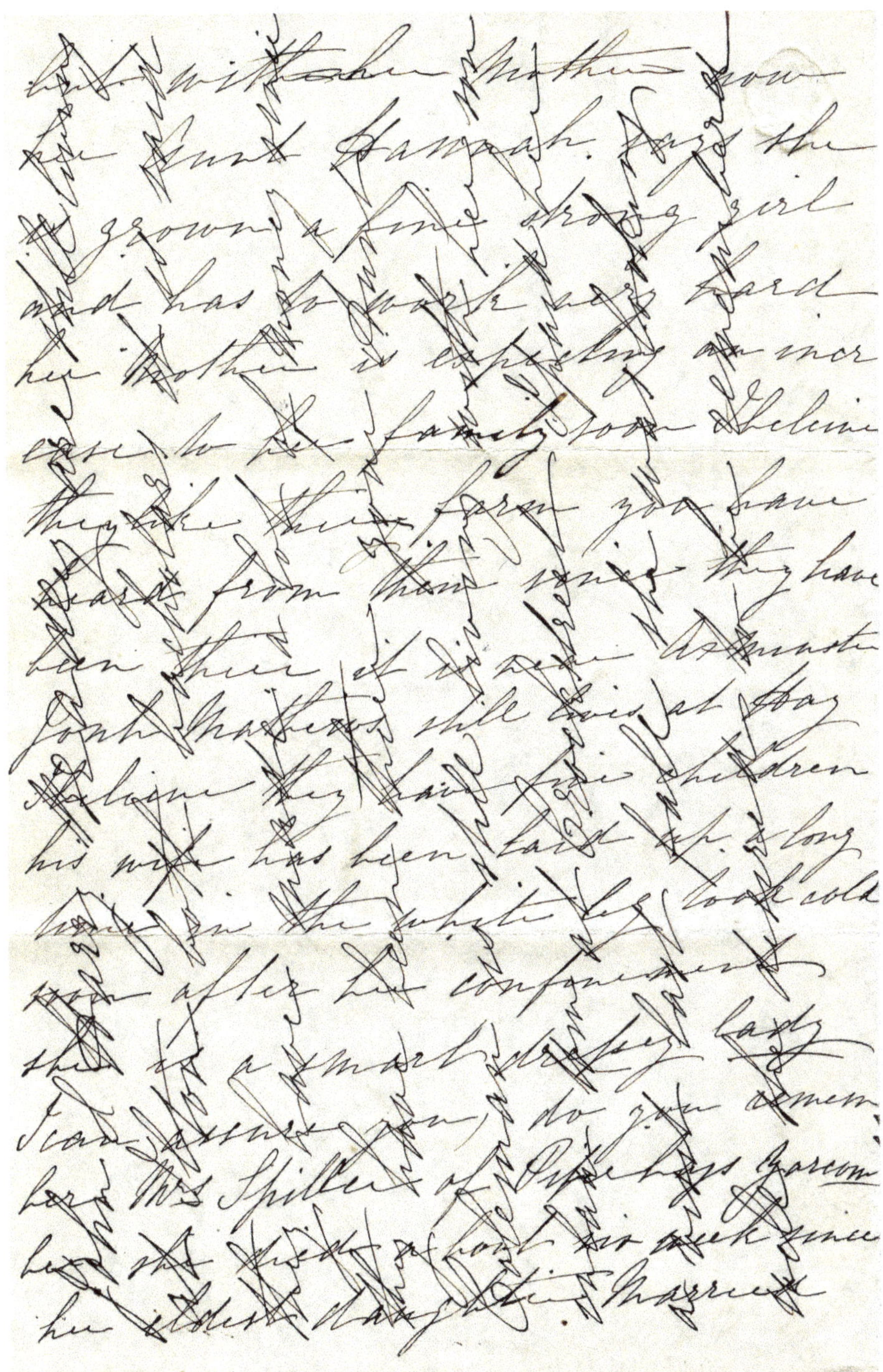

[illegible] with her Mother now
her Aunt Hannah says she
is grown a fine strong girl
and has to work very hard
her Mother is expecting an incr
ease to her family soon [illegible]
they like their farm you have
heard from them since they have
been there it is near Axminster
John Mathews still lives at Hay
[illegible] they have five children
his wife has been laid up a long
time in the white leg took cold
soon after her confinement
she is a smart dressy lady
I can assure you do you remem
ber Mrs Spiller of Pipe Hays Yarcom
be she died about six week since
her eldest daughter married

Letter Number 49, Page 3

Mr Samuel Wyatt of New house Buck land who has poor fellow dropped down dead the early part of last summer whilst in the field working with his horses his wife died about three months after leaving an orphan daughter and now there is a mother [illegible] very ill not likely to recover. It must be a great trial for the family supposing them Miss Spillers must have been young girls when you left. Your Uncle Jennings was ill all through the fall the eldest of the young Colemans of [illegible] has been staying this last [illegible] months to [illegible] a little if he do not continue

Letter Number 49, Page 4

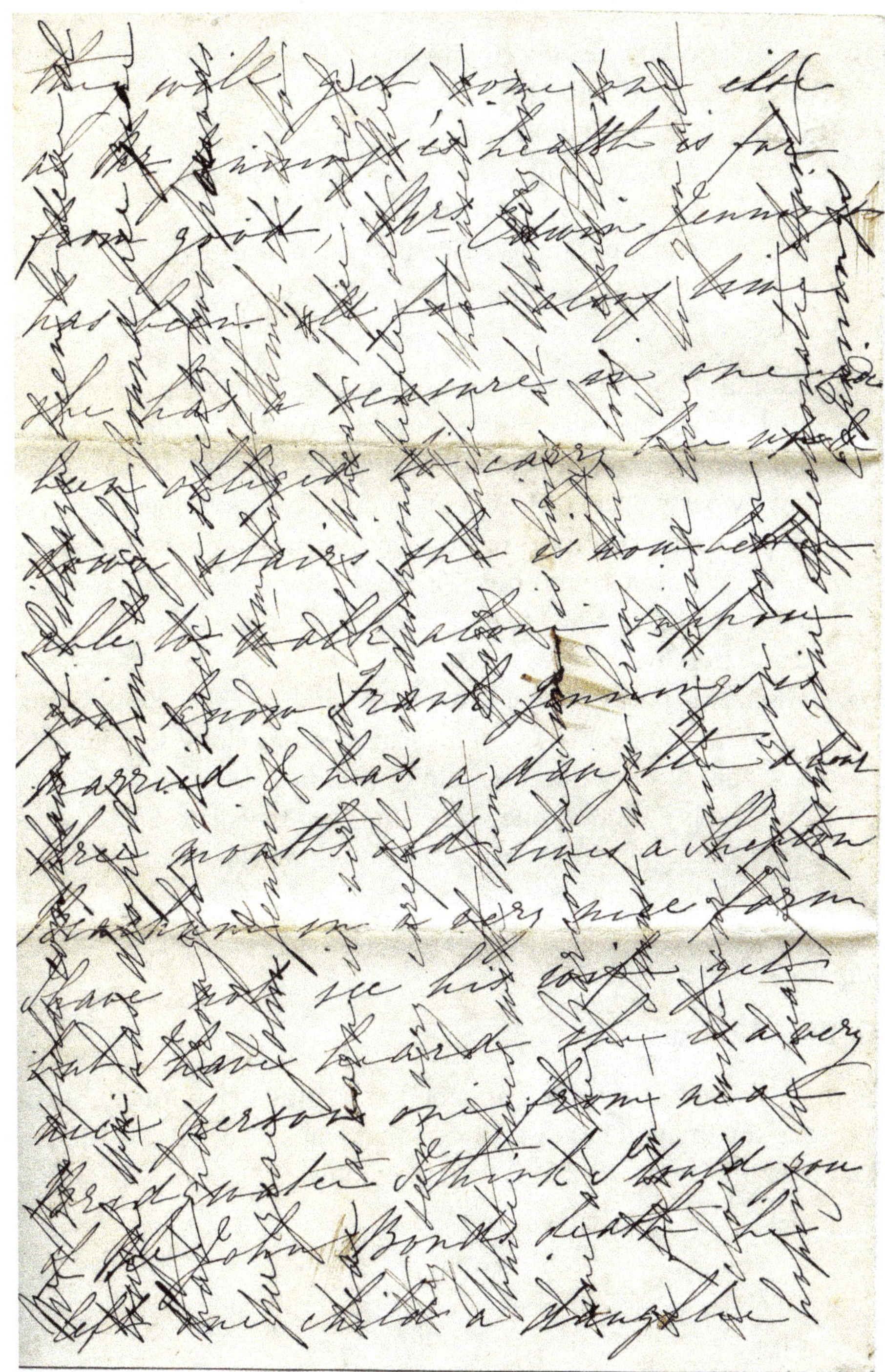

Letter Number 50

Date:	20 March 1865 (Civil War)
Writer:	Thomas Pipe
Recipient:	William Jennings
Sent from:	Waupaca, Waupaca County, Wisconsin, USA
Sent to:	Northay Farm, Whitestaunton, Chard, Somerset County, England

Key Ideas

- Thomas Pipe requests the present year's rent by the first of May.
- He has two reasons for his request: (1) The U.S. is bound to have another draft on the 15th of April. So far, Thomas Pipe has stayed out by paying a tax. President Abraham Lincoln has just made another call for 2,000 more men on that date which makes 1 million men in six months. Thomas states that they do not have another man in town to enlist. (2) $300 will save him from going to the Civil War.
- Thomas is perfectly disgusted with what he calls "Yankee talk" about whipping the whole of Europe, especially England. He says that he does not intend to help them.
- Thomas is sure that one half of the county will go uncultivated this summer. He includes a small news article.

Waupaca March 20th/1864

Dear Uncle [William]

I suppose that you will think I am good at writing when it is to my interest so to do. But still I am well aware that you know that it is what we are all after, our interest, that is when we know it.

Therefore, I will leave all ceremonies aside and come to the point, I am about to ask you if it is possible for you so do to, to send me the present year's rent by the first of May. As the prospect is that I shall be greatly in need of it at that time. I am willing to pay you a good liberal remuneration if it should discommode you. I should not trouble you now if I had not two good reasons for it. One is we are bound to have a draft for Solzero [soldiers] on the 15th of April next.

We have kept of two drafts in the last two months by taxing ourselves to Lng Volunteers which I believe is now paid out. As the President [Abraham Lincoln] has just made another call for two hundred thousand more men on that date makes one million men in six months. I am well aware that this time we shall have to stand the draft as I believe that we have not another man to enlist in our town. As to my going, I am sure that shall not, at least whilst three hundred dollars, will save me. I am perfectly disgusted with this Yankee Greagor [Galvanized Yankees?] they are too fond of talking of whipping the whole of Europe and especially England. But I do not intend to help them. I do hope this war will soon end. We are gotten very destitute of men and money at the West. I am sure that at least one third of this county will go uncultivated this summer.

I will enclose to you a small piece cut from a newspaper which will give you a slight insight to how matters are on this side of the Atlantic. I hope this will find you all well as I am happy to say that it leave us all quite well at present except Elizabeth [Stickland Pipe] who is troubled with a boil on the arm.

As I think of nothing more of interest to write I will close by saying that E. [Elizabeth Stickland Pipe] joins with me in sending our kindest respects to all inquirer friends. Not forgetting yourselves and family.

From your affectionate nephew

Thos. Pipe

Letter Number 50, Page 1

Vanpeer March 20th/1864

Dear Uncle,

I Sopose that you will think Send good at wrighten when it is to my Intrest so to do But Stil I am well aware that you know thatt that is what we ar all after our Intrest that is when we know it, Therefore I will leave all cerimonies a side and com to the point I am about to ask you if it is possible for you so to do, to send me the present years rent by the First of May. As the prospect is that I shall be greatly in neede of it at that time, I am willin to Pay you a good liberal Renumeration if it should discommode you, I should not trouble you if I had not two or three good reasons for it one is we ar abound to have a Draft for Solgers on the 15th of Aprill next

Letter Number 50, Page 2

We have kept of two Drafts in the last two Months by Taken ous Selves to buy Valentears which I believe is now played out, As the President has just Made a nother Call for two hundred thousand More Men on that date that Makes one Million Men in in Six Months, I am well a ware that this time we Shall have to Stand the Draft as I believe that we have not a nother Men to inlist, in our town As to My goin I am Shore that I Shall not at least whilest three hundred Dollars will Save Me,
I am perfietty disgusted with this Yankey Swagor, they or two fond of talken of whippen the Whole of Europe and espicialy England.
But I do not intend to help them,
I do hope this War will soon end We or getten very destitute of Men and Money at the West, I am Shore that at least one third of this County will go uncultivated this Summer

Letter Number 50, Page 3

I will inclose to you a Small piece
Cut from a Newspaper which will
give you a Slite incite to how Matters
ar on this Side of the Attlantic
I hope this will fiend you all
Well as I am happy to Say that it
leaves us all quit well at Present
except Elizebeth who is troubled with
a boil on the arm,
As I think of nothing of nothing more
of Intrest to Wright I will close by
Sayen that E. joins with me in
Sending our kindest respects to
all inquirer Friends Not forgetan
your Self & Family
From your Afft Nephew
Thos Pipe

Letter Number 51

Date: 29 January 1865
Writer: Elizabeth Stickland Pipe
Recipient: William & Elizabeth Coleman Jennings
Sent from: Waupaca, Waupaca County, Wisconsin, USA
Sent to: Northay Farm, Whitestaunton, Chard, Somerset County, England

Key Ideas

- Elizabeth Stickland Pipe received a letter from her brother John Stickland saying that William and Elizabeth Coleman Jennings are quite ill.
- John Stickland also stated his mother, Elizabeth Wall Stickland Bartlett, had visited them for two months.
- Mary Stickland gave up her business and is now a salesperson.
- John Stickland told Elizabeth Stickland Pipe that he feels it is her duty to pay him £5 a year for their mother's care. He requests Elizabeth Stickland Pipe pay twice yearly.
- Elizabeth Stickland Pipe tells William Jennings that she cannot afford the money.
- Elizabeth Stickland Pipe says the president called for 300,000 more men. The previous call was for 500,00 men last September. She is worried Thomas Pipe may be called to war.
- Elizabeth Stickland Pipe asks whether William Jennings ever hears from William Jennings Pipe. He visited John Stickland when he was home.
- Elizabeth Stickland Pipe tells William Jennings to pay £2 10s every half year if William feels Elizabeth Wall Stickland Bartlett needs it for her care.
- Elizabeth Stickland Pipe details prices in America.

Butcher shop at Waupaca [Written later by a descendant.]

Waupaca, Jan 29th 1865

Dear Uncle [William Jennings] & Aunt [Elizabeth Coleman Jennings]

I thought I would write to you as Thomas has written and left for me to finish up which I have neglected to do, therefore I will write now in full. I hope you are much better than when I heard last. I received a letter to my surprise from John Stickland saying that you are quite sick, but I hope you are now better. And likewise stating that Mother [Elizabeth Wall Stickland Bartlett] had been down to make a visit about 2 months and likewise that Mary [Stickland] had given up business and was now as saleswoman, and he also said that Mother was getting old and needy and he thought it was my duty to allow her something to live on which he gave her £5 a year and wanted it allowed half yearly. I should like to very much but everything is so <u>dear</u> at the present that it is as much as a person can do to live with

such a family as we have and likewise such heavy taxes on account of this war. We have first received another call from the President for 300,000 more men, only last September the call for 500,000. This town filled her quota and now they have the same thing again. They have voted a tax 4,000 dollar. The quota for this town 25 or 30 men but the question is where are they to be got. They are about all cleaned out. I am afraid Thomas will have to go but I hope not, what should I do. You cannot do a thing but you have to pay tax. You can't kill a beef but there is a tax on it. It was over 10 per cent on the assessor's valuation for the past year. Thomas paid 32 dollar tax on what cattle he has killed for the last 2 months. He has packed 100 barrels of beef and 100 barrels of pork. I have tried out 100 lbs. of lard and have about 3 or 4 hundred more. It will be quite a relief for me to say I have finished for this season. I should like to know if you have ever heard from Wm. [Jennings] Pipe since he left England. John [Stickland] says he was there and made them a visit before he left, but has never heard anything of him since. Thomas [Pipe] is thinking of going down to see his mother in about a week. They were all well when he last heard from them. Frank [Pipe] our third boy is now with them, went last spring but has not been home since. Thomas [Pipe] has seen him 2 or 3 times this summer but he seems contented and not say a word about coming home. If you think Mother [Elizabeth Wall Stickland Bartlett] needs anything to help support her and if it is my duty you have to allow her £2 10 0s every half year. I have to say a little about the prices of goods, prints 45 cents per yard, cotton cloth fit for sheets 62 cents per yard and that is the very lowest price, for boys pants 12d per yard, all cotton boots for the boys 6 dollars the lowest black tea 2 dollars per lb. the lowest brown sugar 30 cents per lb., flour 10 dollars for 196 lbs. you can't get a reel of cotton less than 20 cents a real. These are all American prices. I must now conclude and hope this will find you in better health and the family well. Our family are in good health at the present. I should like to hear from you all soon.

From

Your affectionate niece

E. [Elizabeth] Pipe

P.S. The crops raise in this yard last year were very poor. At least you might as well say there was not anything. There was many a farmer of this crop if they would harvest it for him to anyone if they would let him have so much grain as he put in seed.

Letter Number 51, Page 1

Butcher shop at Waupaca

Waupaca Jany 29th 65

Dear Uncle & Aunt,

I thought I would write to you as Thomas has writen and left for me to finish up which I have neglected to do therefore I will have to write now in full, I hope you are much better than when I herd last, I received a letter to my suprise from John Strickland saying that you are quite sick but hope you are now better, And likewise stating that Mother had been down to make a visit a bout 2 months and likewise that Mary had given up Buisness and was now as saleswoman and he also say that Mother was getting old and needy and he thought it was my duty to alow her something to live on which he gave her £5 a year and wanted it alowed half yearly I should like to very much but every thing is so dear at the present that it is as much as a person can do to live with

Letter Number 51, Page 2

such a family as we have and
likewise such heavy taxes on a count
of this war, We have just received
a nother call from the Presedant for
300000 more men only last September
the call for 500000 this town filled
her quota and now they have to the
same thing over a gain they have
voted a tax 4000 Dollar the quota for
this town 25 or 30 men but the question
is where or they to be got they or about
all cleaned out I am a fraid Thomas will
have to go but I hope not what should
I do you cannot do a thing but you
have to pay tax you cant kill a beef
but their is a tax on it it was over
10 pr cent on the asses valuation for the
past year Thomas payed 32 Dollar tax
on what cattle he has killed for the
last 2 month's he has packed 110 Bls
of Beef and 100 Barrels of Pork
I have tried out 1000 lbs of Lard and
have a bout 3 or 4 hundred more it

Letter Number 51, Page 3

will be quite a relife for me to say
I have finished for this season
I should like to know if you have
ever herd from Wm Pipe since he
left England John says he was their
and made them a visit before he
left but has never herd any thing
of him since. Thomas is think
of going down to see his Mother
in a bout a week they were all
well when we last herd from
them Frank our third Boy is
now with them went last Spring
but has not been home since
Thomas has seen him 2 or 3
times this summer but he seams
contented and dont say a word
about coming home. If you
think Mother needs any thing to
help support her and if it is my
duty you can a low her £2.10.0 every
half year I have to say a little about
the prises of Goods Prints 45 cents pr yd.

Letter Number 51, Page 4

cotton Cloth fit for Sheets 62 cent pr yd and that is the very lowest price for Boys pants 12s pr yd all cotton Boots for the Boys 6 Dollars the lowest Black Tea 2 Dollars pr lb the lowest Brown Sugar 30 cents pr lb Flower 10 Dollars for 196 lbs you cant get a reel of Cotton less than 20 cents a reel these or all American prises I must now conclude and hope this will find you in better health and the family well our family or in good health at the present I should like to here from you all soon

from Your affectionate Niece
E Pipe

PS The crops raise in this part last year were very poor at least you might as well say their was not any thing their was many a Farmer offer his crop if they would harvest it for him to any one if they would let him have so much grain has he put in seed

Letter Number 52

Date: 12 May 1865
Writer: William & Elizabeth Coleman Jennings
Recipient: Thomas Pipe
Sent from: Northay Farm, Whitestaunton, Chard, Somerset County, England
Sent to: Waupaca, Waupaca County, Wisconsin, USA

Key Ideas

- William Jennings tells Thomas Pipe that he cannot send the money he requested. The office will not ensure lines for America. Without insurance there is no security.
- William Jennings says the inherited property is titled to Elizabeth Stickland Pipe. According to John Stickland's Will, proved 30th July 1850, the estates are called: "Much Hill Farm, Combes's Pithayne Farm, with the allotment on Mannings Commons, Whitehorns, otherwise Bardscombe, and Peacross Farm." (See Appendix D.)
- William Jennings explains that the property goes to John Valentine Pipe's children, John Stickland, Tom, Frank , and Mary Elizabeth, after Elizabeth Stickland Pipe dies.
- William Jennings states that there is no chance for Thomas Pipe to mortgage any of the property. (John Valentine Pipe of America, who died at sea in 1854, is listed as property owner in the *1873 Land Returns*, not Elizabeth Stickland Pipe.)
- William Jennings claims to have gotten Mr. Dommett's (Dommett & Canning) legal opinion on the property title.
- William Jennings says that times are difficult in Devon, as well. His sheep and cattle are dying.
- Elizabeth Wall Stickland Bartlett, Elizabeth Stickland Pipe's mother, was at the drunk at Yarcombe. She was not looking well.
- Mr. Bonfield's lease has expired, and he wants another for less rent.

Elizabeth Coleman Jennings finishes:

- Elizabeth Coleman Jennings tells Thomas Pipe that she is better from a spinal infection. She says that she has suffered dreadfully the last three years.
- Elizabeth Coleman Jennings includes a list of accounts.
- William Jennings Pipe wrote a few months ago. He is well. He does not speak highly of Australia.
- Carrie Coleman is to be married next Tuesday the 16th to Mr. Wheadon near Ilminister, Somerset.
- Elizabeth Coleman Jenning' little girl Ellen (Nelly) is at Broadwindsor, Dorset, with Aunt Mary Ann Jennings Dommett. She has not been in school this half.
- Elizabeth Coleman Jennings comments on the poor quality of servants.

[crosshatched]

Whitestaunton
May 12th, 1865

Dear Tho.

I am sorry to tell you that I cannot send you the cash you sent for as the office will not insure lines for America and unless that is done there is no security for the money. As the property is titled thus after Elizabeth [Stickland Pipe] it comes to John [Valentine] Pipe's children share and share alike and no one else so you see there is no chance of mortgaging the aforesaid.

I have had Mr. Dommett's [Dommett & Canning] advice on it. I should have very glad to have sent you the money if could be done with safety but it was impossible to have sent it by the time you required it. I can assure you that times here are very hard. We have had a hard long winter and owing to the root crop failing there. Has been a lot of sheep and cattle die. Some have lost as many as 200 sheep. I have lost more than I have for ten years past.

You ask my opinion on Mrs. [Elizabeth Wall Stickland] Bartlett whether she was in want of any assistance. I can only tell you that I saw her at the drunk at Yarcombe. She was not looking remarkable, well and dressed very hardly. I have not paid anything this time so you can please yourselves for the time to come. Mr. Bonfield's lease is expired and he is wanting a fresh agreement and less rent. I don't tell him so heed it is very dear [expensive]. It ought not to cost more than sixty pounds a year, but I will do my best.

With our fond love to all from your affectionate

Uncle [William] Jennings

My dear Mrs. Pipe

As your uncle is in a hurry I thought I would finish this, am glad to tell you I am much better than I have been for a long time, mine is a spinal affection, I have suffered dreadfully at times this last three years. I hope this will find you all well. I will now put down your account as you may see

1864	
Overpaid the last account	£ 5s 4d
Oct. 17 Mr. [John] Stickland's	£12 0s 1d
Income tax	2s 7d
	£14 8s 0d

1865	
May 1st	
Paid Mr. [John] Stickland	£12 0s 0d
Thatcher's bill	2s 7d
Glaziers	8s 0d
Income tax 3 quarters	17s 6d
Fire insurance	£1 15s 6d
	£15 3s 7d

[note written sideways]

Rent £31 0s 0d

£29 11s 7d

£51 8s 5d

[crosshatched]

Your brother [John Stickland] was here about a fortnight ago, he was looking very well, we last heard from Wm. [Jennings] Pipe about two months since. He was very well, He don't speak very highly of the country [Australia]. He has written home. He has never said what he was doing. We shall write to him by the next mail. When you see Mrs. [Charlotte Jennings Pipe] Pillar give my love to her. I hope to write her soon. My youngest sister Carrie [Coleman] is to be married next Tuesday the 16th to a Mr. Wheadon near Ilminster [Somerset], a farmer in business, a good match for her, then all will be married, but my youngest brother. He is always sickly, has been for several years. My little girl is at Broadwindsor [Dorset] to

[other way]

her Aunt [Mary Ann Jennings] Dommett's. She has not been to school this last half. She was not well. Pollie [Dommett] is a very industrious. We have no servant. She does nearly all the indoor work Servants are very scarce, and when you have them they are worthless, so very fond of dress, not as they used to be and wages about as high again, now I must conclude with fondest love.

From your affectionate

Aunt [Elizabeth] Jennings

Letter Number 52, Page 1

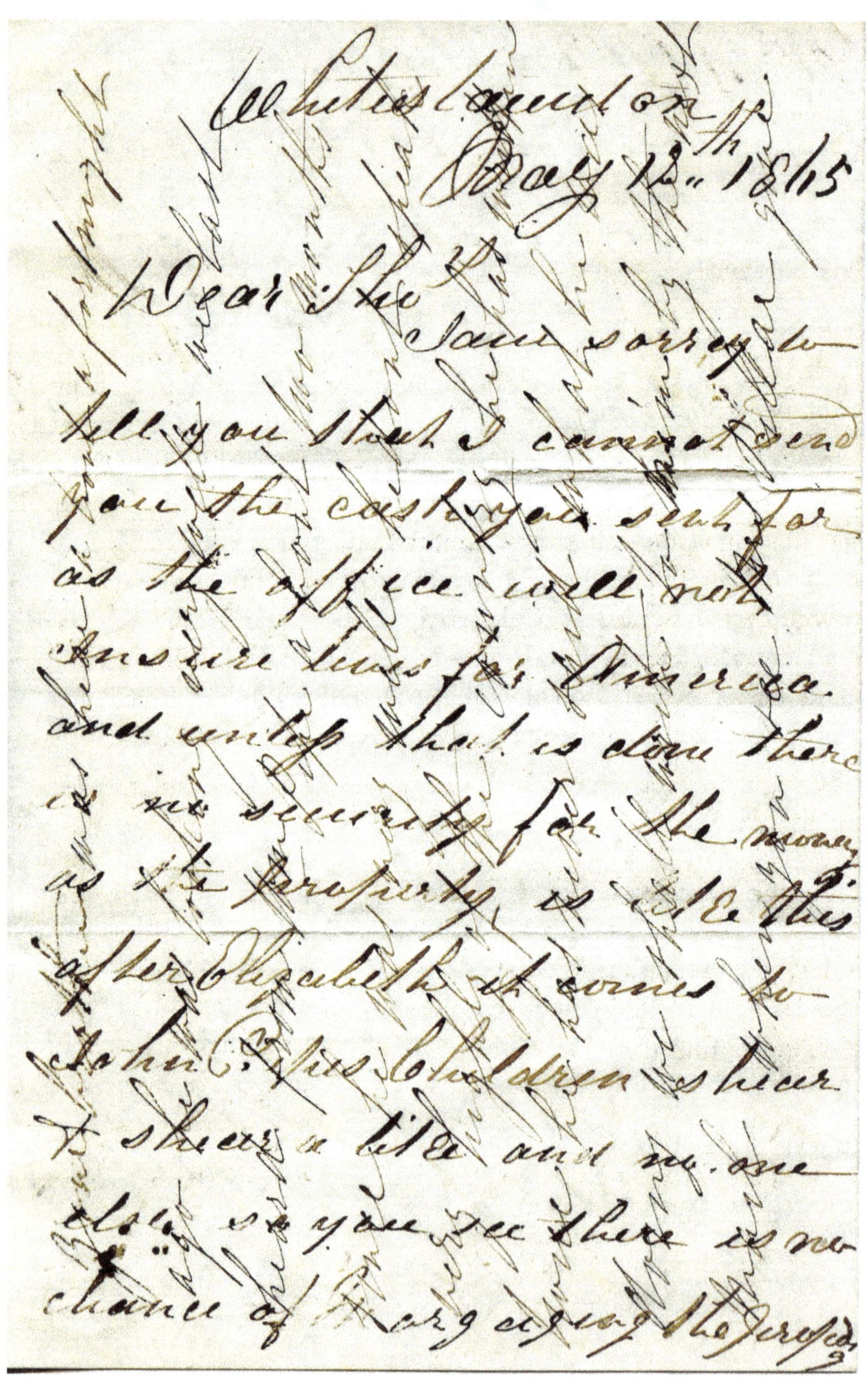

[illegible]
May 12th 1845

Dear Sir
I am sorry to
tell you that I cannot send
you the cash you sent for
as the office will not
Ansure lives for America
and untill that is done there
is no security for the money
as the property is tied thus
after Elizabeth it comes to
John & his children share
& share alike and no one
else so you see there is no
chance of [illegible] the prope[illegible]

Letter Number 52, Page 2

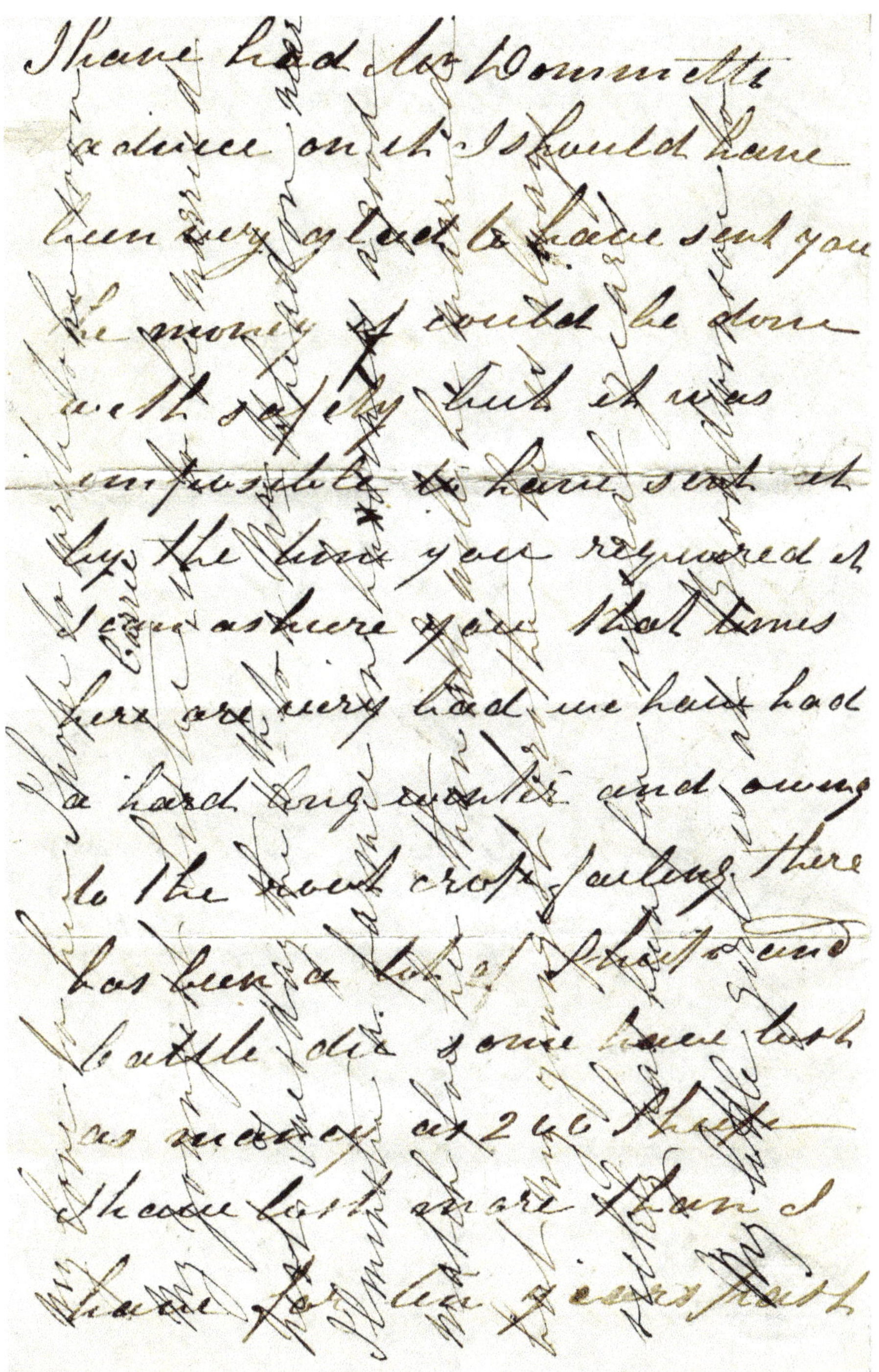

I have had Mr Dommett's
advice on it I should have
been very glad to have sent you
the money if could be done
with safety but it was
impossible to have sent it
by the time you required it
I can assure you that times
here are very bad we have had
a hard long winter and owing
to the root crop failing there
has been a lot of sheep and
cattle die some have lost
as many as 200 sheep
I have lost more than I
have for ten years past

Letter Number 52, Page 3

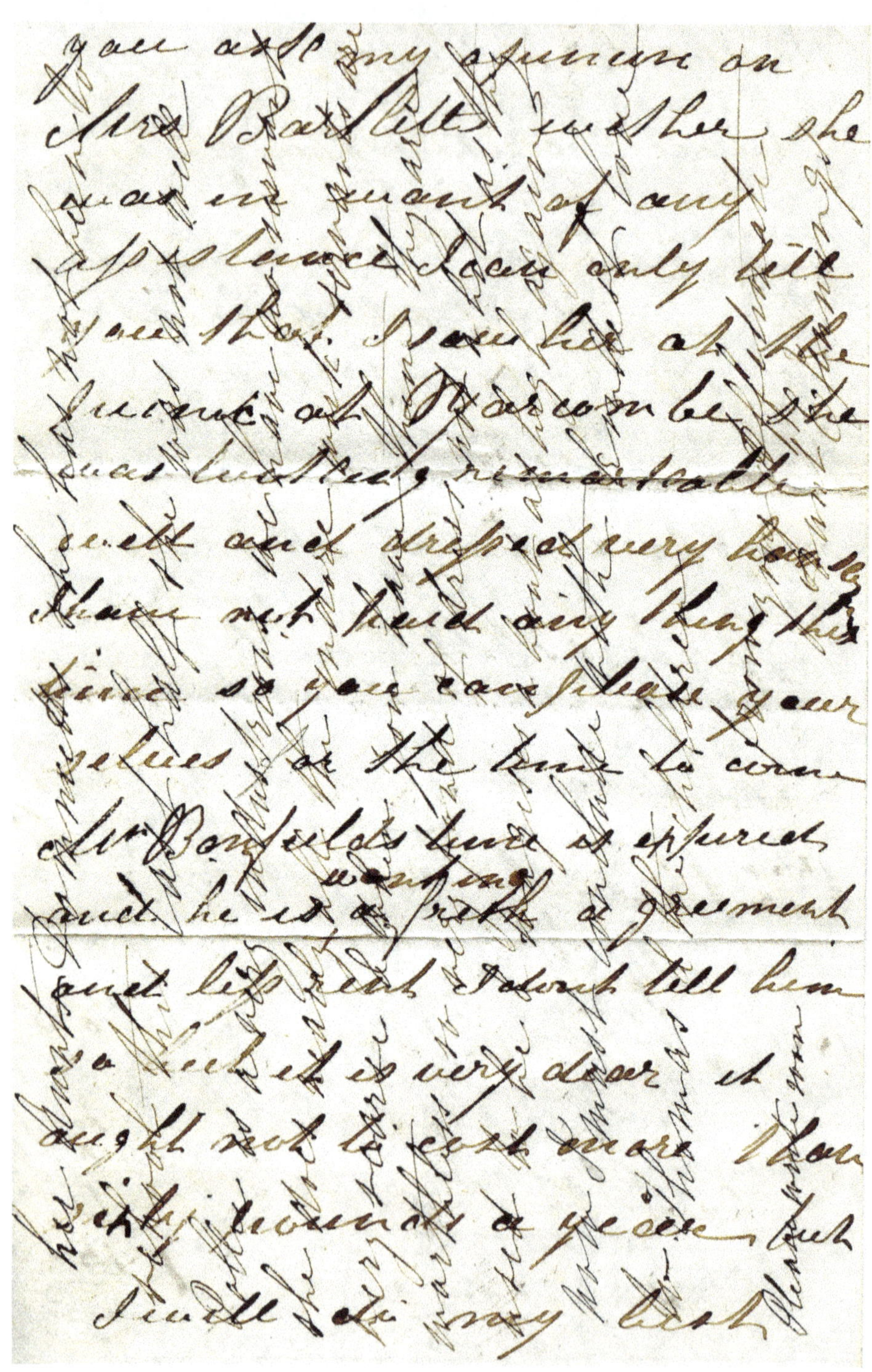

you ask my opinion on
Mrs Bartletts wether she
was in want of any
assistance I can only tell
you that I saw her at the
funeral at Barcombe she
was looking remarkable
well and dressed very hands
I have not heard any thing the
time so you can please your
selves as the time to come
Mr Bonfields time is expired
and he is a [working] agreement
and lets reach I don't tell him
so ... it is very dear it
ought not to cost more than
sixty pounds a year but
I will do my best

Letter Number 52, Page 4

with our kind love to all
from your affectionate
Uncle W. Jennings

My dear Mrs Pipe As your uncle is in a hurry I thought I would finish this I am glad to tell you I am much better than I have been for a long time mine is a spinal affection I have suffered dreadfully at times this last three years I hope this will find you all well I will now put down your account as you may see

		£ s d
1864 Dec	paid the last account	2..5..4½
Octr 17	Mr Strickland	12..0..0
	Income tax	2..7½
		14 8..0
1865 May 1st	Pd Mr Strickland	12..0..0
	Thatchers Bill	2..7
	Glaziers	8..0
	Income Tax 3 quarters	17..6
	Fire Insurance	1..15..6
		15..3..7

Letter Number 52, Envelope Front

Letter Number 52, Envelope Back

Letter Number 53

Date: 1 July 1865
Writer: Thomas Pipe
Recipient: William Jennings
Sent from: Waupaca, Waupaca County, Wisconsin, USA
Sent to: Northay Farm, Whitestaunton, Chard, Somerset County, England

Key Ideas

- On the first page of this letter, "*Farmington July 1st 1865*" is written. Thomas Pipe may have written the letter while he was at his former home in Farmington. In Letter Number 37 dated December 2, 1860, Thomas Pipe states that he was living in Waupaca and renting property in Farmington, except for 10 acres.
- Thomas Pipe acknowledges the receipt of a letter and a draft of money.
- Thomas Pipe says he paid last year's bounty tax.
- Thomas Pipe tells William Jennings that he was aware that the inherited property goes to John Valentine Pipe's children after Elizabeth's death. What seems unreasonable to Thomas is the property goes to John Valentine Pipe's children, not Elizabeth Stickland Pipe's children.
- Thomas Pipe asks his uncle a question: What if Elizabeth had died and John Valentine had remarried and had more children. Would the same apply?
- Thomas Pipe continues to build a case for his younger children: William Edwin, Florence, Effie, and Charlotte.
- Thomas Pipe states that Elizabeth Stickland Pipe was 27 years old when she lost her husband, John Valentine Pipe. She was a widow with four children, the oldest under 7 years old. She had a total of £20 with a debt of £205 by the time it could be paid.

Farmington July 1st 1865

Dear Uncle [William Jennings]

Yours of May 12th is at hand with the draft for £51 8s 5d. It sold in New York for 335 dollars which is 35 per cent premium which is quite a drop in the last two months, but entirely satisfactory to me, as the peace prospects are so favourable. That is near the amount that I paid the last year Bounty Tax.

Dear Uncle [William Jennings] I was not at all disappointed in your not sending me the money which I sent for [requested], as I supposed it was difficult to give the security required without a life insurance. As I was aware, the property belongs to the children after Elizabeth's death. But I must say that I am disappointed in one thing, as it seems to me so unreasonable. That is

that the property should belong to John Pipe's children and not to Elizabeth Pipe's children.

Here I want to ask a few questions. Suppose that Elizabeth had died in the stead of John and he had the second family. What would become of the property? As you say that it is to come to John's children and to no one else. You have no limit to whether it is one or three families. It strikes me that Elizabeth's privileges so very much limited under the circumstances. Especially if she has to bring up and educate those children, which must be to the expense of any other family that she might have, to a certain extent. Now you see she was left at the age of 27 years with four children the oldest under 7 years old, with not more than £20 all told and £170 in debt with interest on the same which amount to about £205 by the time it could be paid, which was done quicker than it could have probably been done, had she been thrown entirely on her own resources.

Now it would be as much as could have been done to have kept those four children on the whole rent for the first five years, and I am sure they have not been kept on a less expense to me for the balance of the time for less than £75 to £80 per year, at the very least calculation it takes £50 per year to clothe them. I paid last fall for the two oldest boys to fit them for the winter and school. That is their clothing £18. And now they are all expecting to be sent to school this winter. Now Sir how am I to do it without doing it to the expense of the other children. Supposing that I should lose my wife in the course of

a few years. They can step out and say we have been brought up and schooled and now we take the property, under the circumstances that would be a robbery on those younger children and it is not them or me that can prevent it. You might say or not those boys of some benefit to you. It is true they might be was you a good farmer, but how am I to get the farm under the present prospect. It took me at the least calculation last year to keep my family and pay my taxes that is bounty and civil 1400 dollars. Now you see I have to be doing in order to live through these war times. Now Sir I do not write you this letter to have you think that I consider you to blame in the least. I only write to explain my ideas of the facts. As of course I know it was not your will but that of another man [Uncle John Stickland?].

Letter Number 53, Page 1

Farmington July 1st/1865

Dear Uncle,

Yours of May 12th is at
hand with the Draft for £51. 8. 5
it sold in New York for 335 Dollars
Which is 35 Per ct Preimum, Which
is quit a drop in the last two months
But intirely Satisfactory to me, as the
Peace prospects ar so faverabell,
that is near the amt that I paid the
last year Bounty Tax,

Dear Uncle I was not at all disapo
-inted in your not Sendin me the
Money which I sent for, as I
sopposed it ould dificult to give
the Security requiried, with out
a Life Insurance, As I was aware
the Property belong to the Children
after Elizabeth's death,

But I must Say that I am disa
-pointed in one thing, As it seems,
to me so unreasonabell, that is

Letter Number 53, Page 2

that the Property should belong to
John Pipe Children and not to
Elizebeth Pipe Children
Hear I want to ask a few questions
sopoos that Eliz had died in the
Stead of John and he had the second
Family, what ould becom of the
Property, As you say that it is
to com to John Children and to
no one else. You have no limit
to wither it is one or three Family
It strike me that Eliz priviledges
are very Mutch limited under the
Circumstances, Especially if she is
has to bring up ~~those~~ and Educate
those Children, Which must be
to the expence of any other Family
that she might have, To a certen
extent, Now you see she was
left at the age of 27 years, with
four Children the eldest under Seven
years old, With not more than £20
all told, and £170 in debt with
Intrest on the Sam

Letter Number 53, Page 3

which amount to about £ 205
by the time it cold be paid,
which was don quicker then it cold
have probably been don, had she been thron
intierly on her one resoroes,
Now it onlel be as mutch as cold
have been don to have kept those
four Childeren on the whole Rent
for the first five years, and I
am Shore they have not been kept
on a les expence to me for the balance
of the time for les than from £75
to £80 Per year, at the very least
calculation it takes £40 Per year to
Cloth them, I paid last Fall for
the two oldest Boys to fit them
for the winter and School, that is
there Clothing £18, And now they
ar all expectin to be sent to School
this winter, Now Sir how am I to
do it without doin it to the expence
of the other Childeren, Supoosin that
I Shold lose my wife in the corse of

Letter Number 53, Page 4

a few years, they can step out and say
we have been brought up and Schooled
and now we take the Property
under the circumstances that would be
a robery on those younger Children
and it is not them or me that
can prevent it you might say
ar nat those Boys of som benifit
to you, It is true they might be
was I on a good Farm, But how
am I to get the Farm under the
present prospect, It took me at
the least calculation last year to
keep my Family and Pay my Taxes
that is Bounty and civil 1400 Dollars
Now you see I have to be doin in order
to live through these war times,
Now Sir I do not wright you this
letter to have you think that I
consider you to blame in the least
I onley wright to explain my Ideas
of the Facts, As of corse I know it
was not your will but that of a nother
man

Letter Number 54

Date: 12 June 1866
Writer: William & Elizabeth Coleman Jennings
Recipient: Thomas Pipe
Sent from: Northay Farm, Whitestaunton, Chard, Somerset County, England
Sent to: Waupaca, Waupaca County, Wisconsin, USA

Key Ideas

- William Jennings sent money to Thomas Pipe.
- The cattle ague is in Buckland St. Mary, Somerset, and Martock, Somerset. Uncle Edwin Jennings says it is too close for comfort.
- Fairs and markets are canceled.
- Thomas Pipe's uncles are all well.
- William Jennings reports that William Jennings Pipe got wounded.

Elizabeth Coleman Jennings continues

- Elizabeth Coleman Jennings is feeling better this spring.
- Mary Ann Jennings Davy has been to London to visit her (?)
- John Bradford is a cousin of William Coleman's wife. John Bradford was home for three years. He married Miss Garland. A few days after they married, they returned to America.
- Aunt Betsey (Elizabeth) Coleman is still living.
- Elizabeth Coleman Jennings asks Charlotte Jennings Pipe Piller to send a picture of herself.

[crosshatched]

Whitestaunton
June 12th 66

Dear Thomas

I have been expecting to hear from you for some time & must I suppose you are at the same place as you were when we last heard. I have sent you the rent £52 9s 3d due Lady Day [25 March] last which I hope you will receive safe. I hope this money you are saving for a future day. I am sorry to tell you the cattle ague is in this

country, great many bullocks [male cattle raised for meat] has been lost but I am glad to say not very near. It has been to Buckland [St. Mary, Somerset] and Martock [Somerset]. Your Uncle Edwin [Jennings] says it is too near to be comfortable. There are no fairs nor markets for beasts, great bore [difficulty] to sell them. Your uncles are all well when I last saw them. How is your mother [Charlotte Jennings Pipe Pillar] and how are they getting along. We heard from W. [Jennings] Pipe not

long since he is a wounded invalid. I don't think he like it very well. He ought not to have left home. He might have done very well here.

With kind love to all

From your affectionate

Uncle

Wm. Jennings

[other way]

My dear Mrs. Pipe

Just a word or two with Wm. We have not heard anything of your mother [Elizabeth Wall Stickland Bartlett] or sister [Mary Stickland] since we last wrote. No doubt but you have. I have been better this spring than I have this last 4 years. Mary A. [Jennings Davy] has been to London to visit her [?], been home a week. I have been well enough in her absence to attend to all my house duties with the help of a little [servant??] and now I have a very violent cold which I hope will soon pass away.

[other way]

Mr. John Bradford has left England again for America. He has been home about three years, married and went off in a day or two after. He is a cousin of my brother William's [Coleman] wife [Elizabeth Bradford] gone Nebraska to them. He married a Miss Garland, also a cousin of Mrs. Colin and he stopped with them when last in America. Your Aunt Betsey Coleman is still living. How is dear Mrs. Pillar, give our very kind love to her and ask her to send me her likeness.

[other way]

With our united kind love to all kindness this may find you all well and happy

From your affectionate

Aunt [Elizabeth] Jennings

Thanks for the newspaper. I have sent one with this letter, please write soon.

Letter Number 54, Page 1

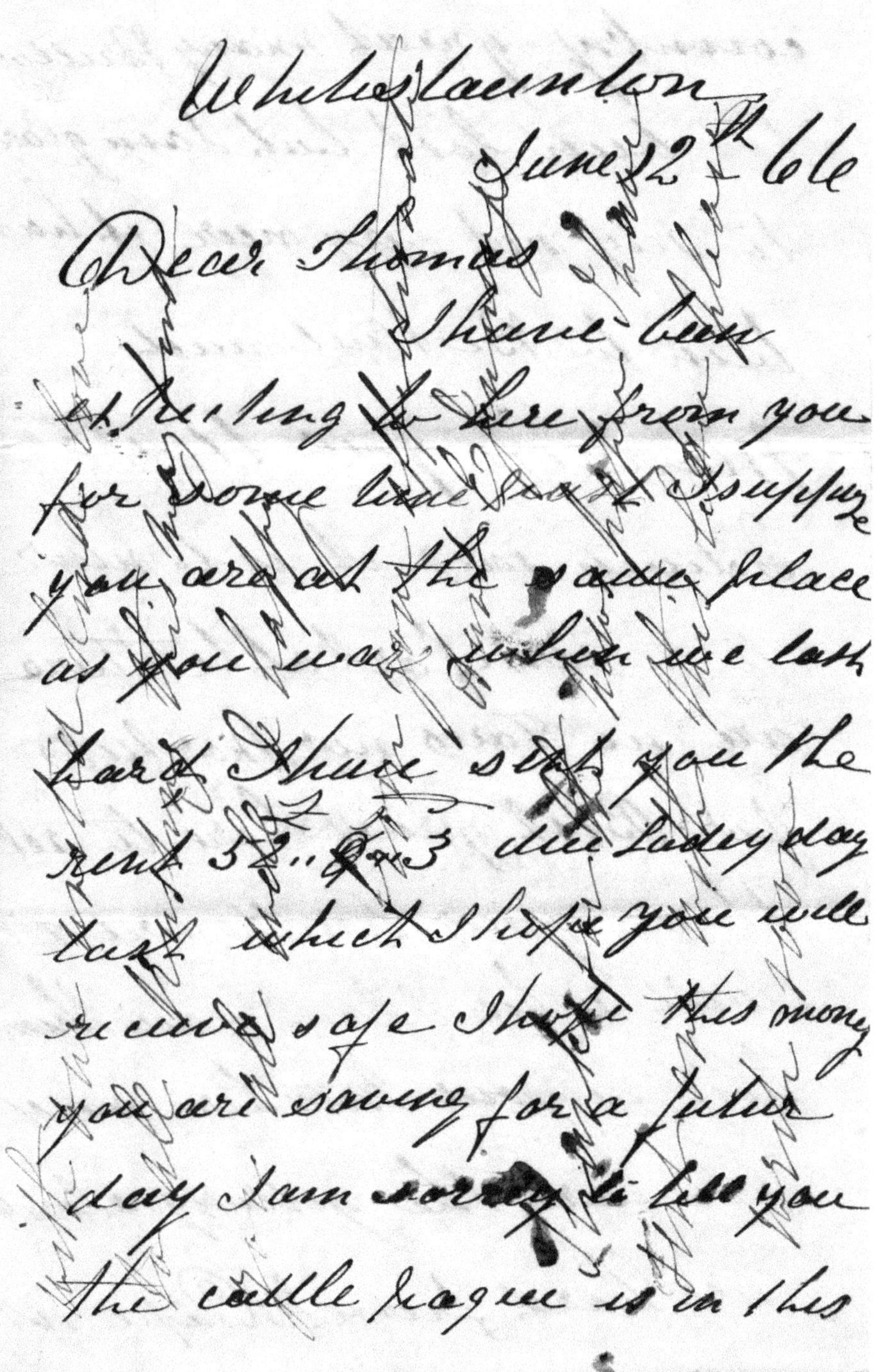

Whitestaunton
June 12th 66

Dear Thomas
I have been
expecting to here from you
for some time past I suppose
you are at the same place
as you was when we last
hard I have sent you the
rent 52..0..3 due lady day
last which I hope you will
receive safe I hope this money
you are saving for a future
day I am sorry to tell you
the cattle plague is in this

Letter Number 54, Page 2

country great many Bullocks
has been lost but I am glad
to say not very near it has
been to Bethnel and
Martock your Uncle
Edwin says it is to near
to be comfortable there
are no Fares nor Markets
for Best great bore to sell
them your Uncles are all
well when I last saw them
how is your Mother and
how are the getting along
we hard from W. Pepe not

Letter Number 54, Page 3

long since he is a
mounted police I doubt they,
he likes it very well he
aught not to have left
home he might have
done very well here
with kind love to all
from your affectionate
Uncle Wm Jennings

Letter Number 54, Page 4

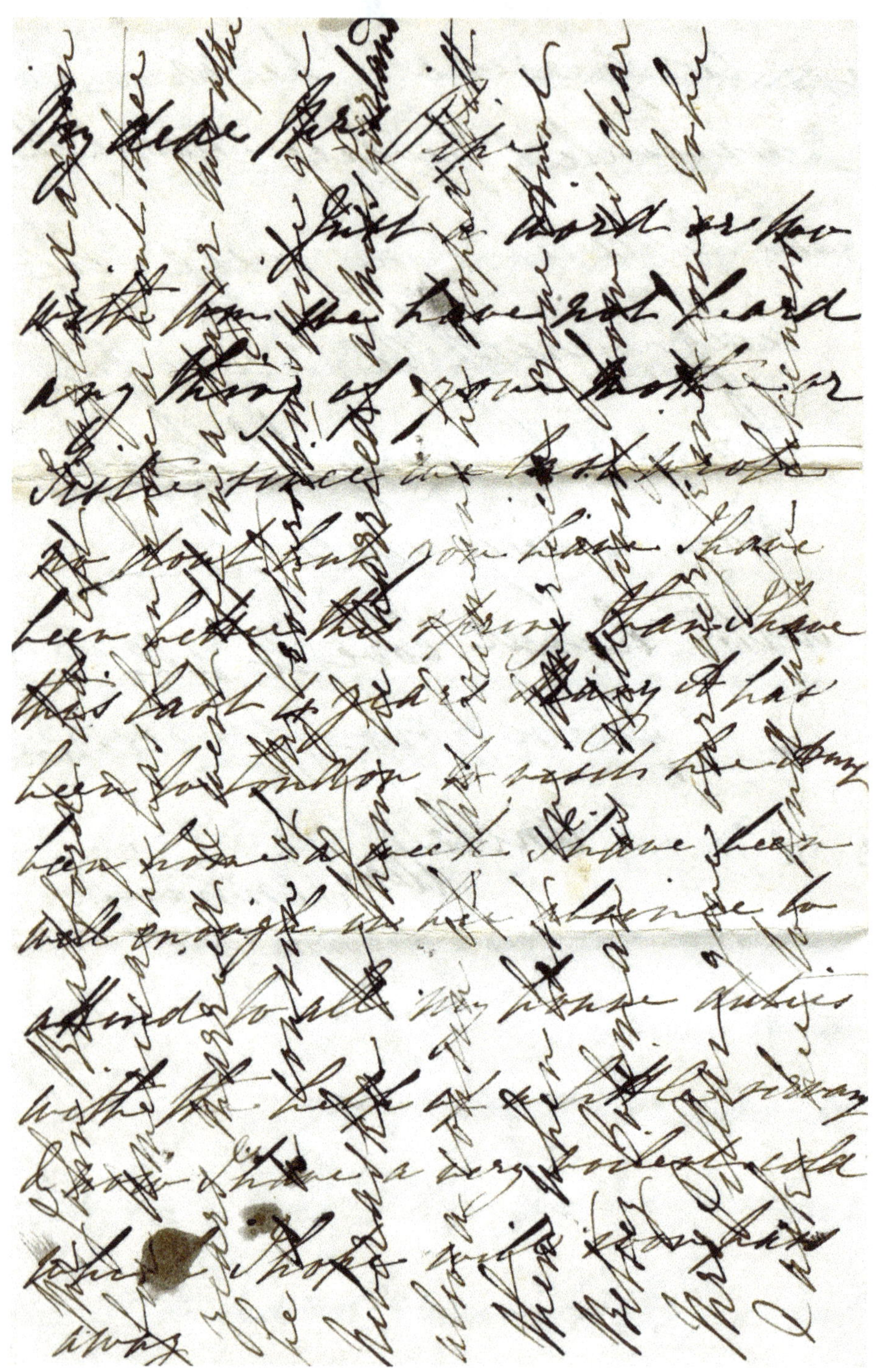

My dear [illegible]

Just a word or two
with them we have not heard
any thing of your Mother or
Sister since we last wrote
no doubt but you have. I have
been better this spring than I have
this last 4 years. [illegible] has
been to London 2 weeks she only
been home a week. I have been
well enough as we [illegible] to
attend to all my house duties
with the help of a little [illegible]
& now I have a very [illegible]
[illegible] I hope will [illegible]
always

Letter Number 54, Envelope Front

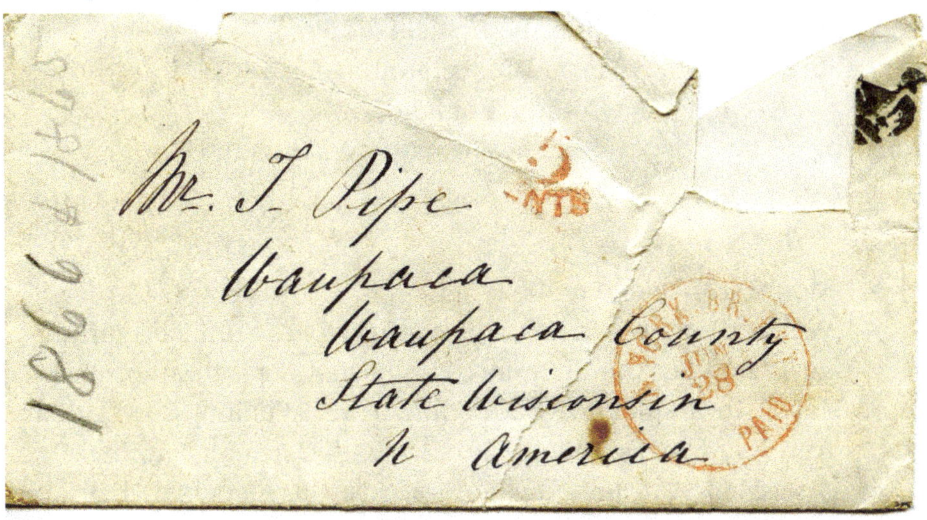

Letter Number 54, Envelope Back

Letter Number 55

Date: 24 September 1866
Writer: Elizabeth Coleman Jennings & Mary Ann Jennings
Recipient: Thomas & Elizabeth Stickland Pipe
Sent from: Northay Farm, Whitestaunton, Chard, Somerset County, England
Sent to: Waupaca, Waupaca County, Wisconsin, USA

Key Ideas

- Money is included in the letter.
- William Jennings is not happy with George Bonfield's farming.
- Last Tuesday the Jennings family had a party at Birch Oak Farm. In attendance were John, Tom, William, Edwin, Mary Ann Jennings Dommett, and Elizabeth Coleman Jennings.
- Aunt Mary Ann Jennings Dommett is still a person with disabilities.
- Elizabeth Coleman and William Jennings never see anything of Mary Stickland or her mother, Elizabeth Wall Stickland Bartlett.
- Elizabeth Coleman Jennings' brother, Frank Coleman, rents Elizabeth Wall Stickland Bartlett's land. Frank Coleman lives at New Barn, Yarcombe, Devon.
- Richard Coleman, Elizabeth Coleman Jennings' brother, has taken on her father's, Richard Coleman, Sr., farm since his retirement.
- Elizabeth Coleman Jennings mentions two deaths: Miss Ann Toleman and Samuel Eli Wyatt who married Jane Spiller of Yarcombe. They have one child.
- Cousin William (Jennings?) will visit the day before the Club (social gathering in Yarcombe, Devon). He is staying at Birch Oak Farm, Yarcombe, Devon.
- Ellen (Nellie), aged 9, goes to school in Chard, Somerset.

Mary Ann Jennings continues.

- Pollie Dommett's intended husband, William Wyatt of Beaminster, Dorset, is a large farmer near her Uncle William Dommett.
- Frank Jennings is on a farm at Kingsbery (Kingsbury Episcopi) near Martock, Somerset, since Lady Day (25 March).
- Mary Ann Jennings says Ellen (Nelly) is nearly 9 years old.

Whitestaunton

Sep 24th 1866

My dear Mr. & Mrs. Pipe

The enclosed cheque or draft £54 16s I hope you will receive all right. Please write to acknowledge the same. Wm. Is not very pleased with the tenant Mr. G. Bonfield. He is not up to the mark as a farmer, was it not for his wife and her mother [Mrs. White] who is still living with them and their large

family of children. He would like to change. Mrs. Bonfield is a very active and industrious little woman and wishes to remain there in hope it will be better soon as her boys are growing up to assist them. It is almost as bad here with labourers and servants as it is in America, so very independent. And wages very much higher than when you left the old country. We had quite a family party

at Birch [Oak Farm, Membury, Devon] last Tuesday, all your uncle John's brothers [Tom, William, and Edwin Jennings], his sister [Mary Ann Jennings Dommett], and myself dined together. Your aunt [Mary Ann Jennings] Dommett is still an invalid. We none of us think she will ever be able to use her hands again. It is very sad for her, but she has many blessings to be thankful for, everything done to make her comfortable. I am glad to say she seems very happy and cheerful under her afflictions. I never see anything of your sister Miss [Mary] Stickland or her mother [Elizabeth Wall Stickland Bartlett]. My brother Frank [Coleman] rents her [Elizabeth Wall Stickland Bartlett] land. He is living at New Barn [Yarcombe, Devon]. Richard [Coleman] has taken on my father's [Richard Coleman, Sr.] farm who is now retired from business.

We have not heard from your brother Wm. [Jennings Pipe] for some time He was about making a change when he last wrote which I believe was in January last. How is your dear Mother [Charlotte Jennings Pipe Pillar]. I hope she is more happy now. Please give our kind love to her. Any of us should be very glad to get a letter from her. Mrs. Dommett has been expecting one for some time past, so Elizabeth [Dommett or Stickland] is married.

[crosshatched]

They seem to be very happy and comfortable and like it very much indeed. It was their club a few weeks since but unfortunately it was wet and our account of two deaths was also a gloom case on it, and now the eldest of the Miss [Ann] Tolemans. She died after three days illness and she there was a Mr. Samuel [Eli] Wyatt of Buckland [St. Mary, Somerset] who married one of the Miss [Jane] Spillers of Yarcombe, he died suddenly in a field. It was a dreadful thing was it not, they have only one child.

[other way]

I hope happy and comfortable, she has taken the start of all her English cousins, suppose we shall lose Pollie [Dommett] soon perhaps before Christmas if so her intended is a large Farmer [William Wyatt of Beaminster, Dorset] near her uncle [William] Dommett's, the only child will miss her very much. Nellie [Ellen Jennings] is still at Taunton [Somerset] to school. It will be some time before her education will

[other way]

be finished. We have had a very dry and hot summer here, scarcely any roots but corn good Sheep are now selling lower than they have for years past. Your cousin Frank Jennings is in a beautiful farm at Kingsbery [Kingsbury Episcopi] near Martock [Somerset]. He made a change last Lady Day [25 March]. He has hitherto been very fortunate. We paid him a visit

[other way]

the early part of this month. He has a very nice wife and three children. The house and garden are beautiful. They keep two women servants, no dairy. He lets [rents] his dairy 45 cows.

When you write give us a good long letter. Your uncle and Pollie [Dommett] join with me in kindest love to all.

From your affectionate

Aunt E. [Elizabeth] Jennings

[other way]

[Beginning of letter from Mary Ann Jennings]

Cousin William [Dommett] came down the day before the Club, but it was so wet we did not enjoy it much. He is now at Birch [Oak Farm, Membury, Devon] coming here tomorrow morning and we are going to ride to Membury [Devon] together. I like riding on horseback very much indeed. I was at Broadwindsor [Somerset] at Aunt Mary Ann's [Jennings Dommett] not long since. I often go there. My cousins are the only companions I have. They are both grown up and have finished their education. Willie [Dommett?] goes to Taunton [Somerset] to school, he is going to stay home for a time now. My little sister [Ellen (Nelly)] is home for her holidays. She goes to Chard [Somerset] to school. She is now nearly nine years old. We are a short family are we not, only two. I see father has told you dear mother has been ill. I assure you it has made me look about a bit. We have not much dairy work, to do that is one thing I make about eighteen pounds

[other way]

butter a week. She is quite disabled not able to do a thing on account of the rheumatism in her back. I do hope she will soon get better. She has been ill nine months. I hope all your family are quite well. I do not know how many it is now. Dear cousin I must say goodbye as it is past time dear. Please give our trusted kind love to Cousin John [Stickland Pipe] and each one of your family and a large share for your own dear self.

From you loving Cousin Mary Ann Jennings

Father desired me to say he wishes you to write as soon as you receive this as he is always anxious until he has heard from you. You have sent it before, but it was not paid.

Goodbye once more.

Letter Number 55, Page 1

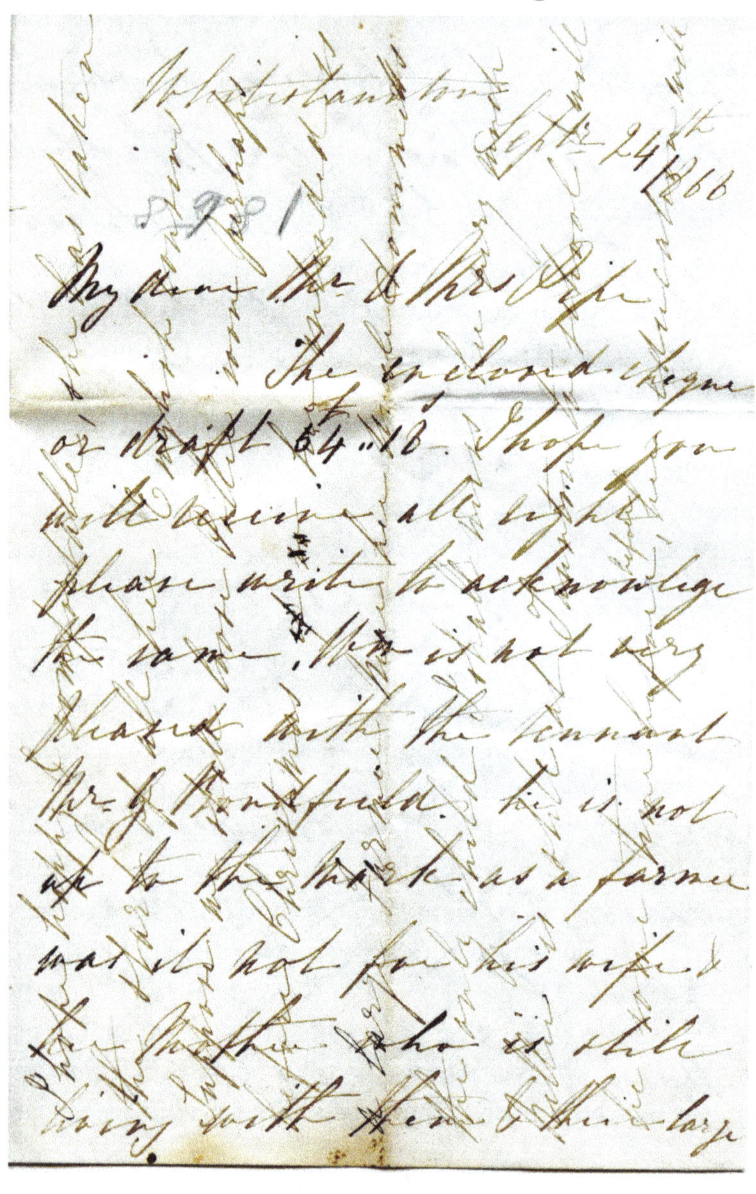

[illegible]

Sept 24th 1866

My dear Mr & Mrs [illegible]

The enclosed cheque or draft 54..18. I hope you will receive all right please write to acknowlege the same. [illegible] is not very pleased with the tennant Mr [illegible]. he is not up to the work as a farmer was it not for his wife & her Mother who is still living with them & their large

Letter Number 55, Page 2

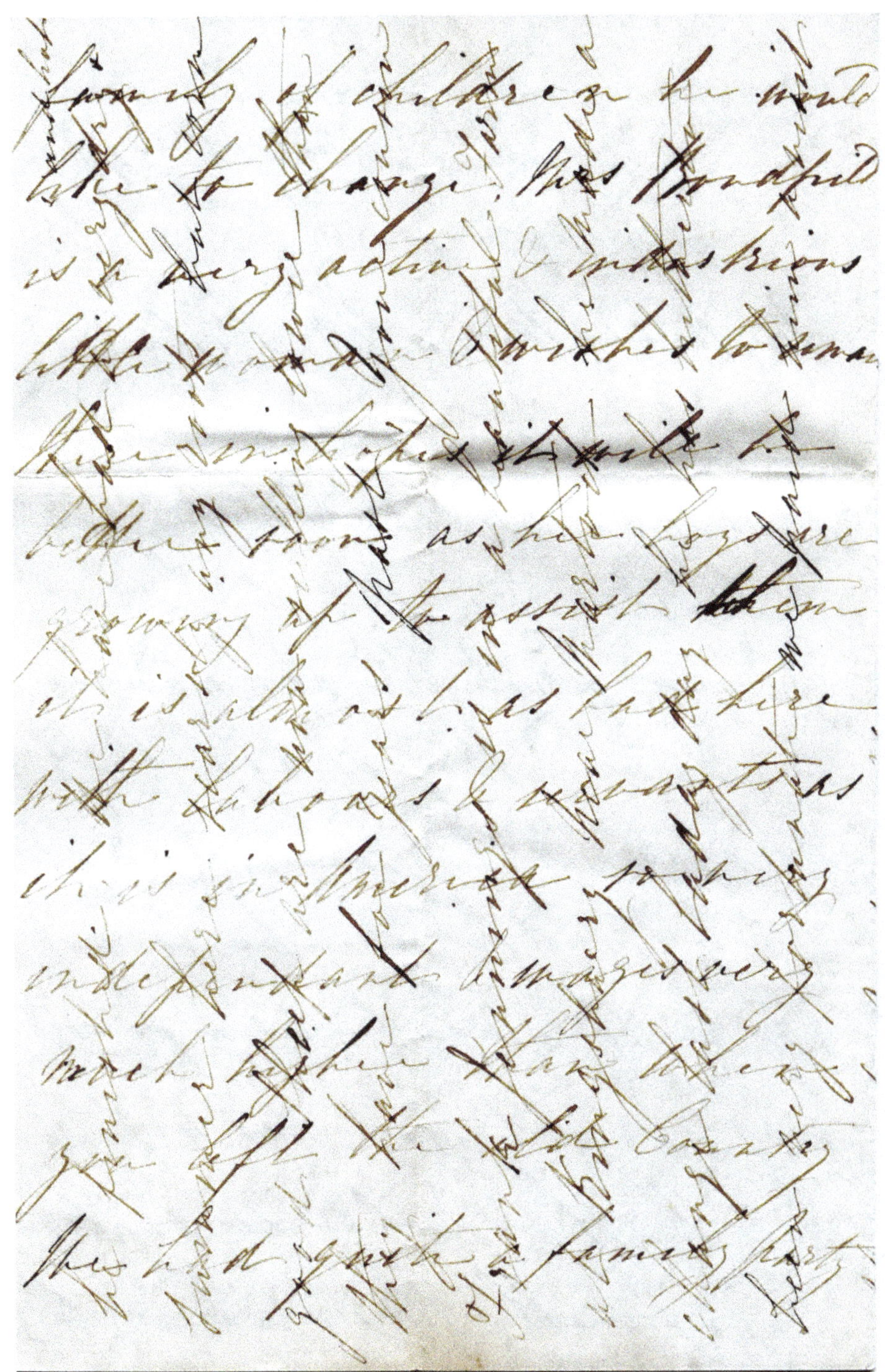

family of children he would
like to change. Mrs Bondfield
is a very active & industrious
little woman & wishes to [illegible]
[illegible] it would be
better soon as her boys are
growing up to assist them
it is almost as bad here
with [illegible]
[illegible]
independant & wages very
much higher than [illegible]
you [illegible]
[illegible] quite a family [illegible]

Letter Number 55, Page 3

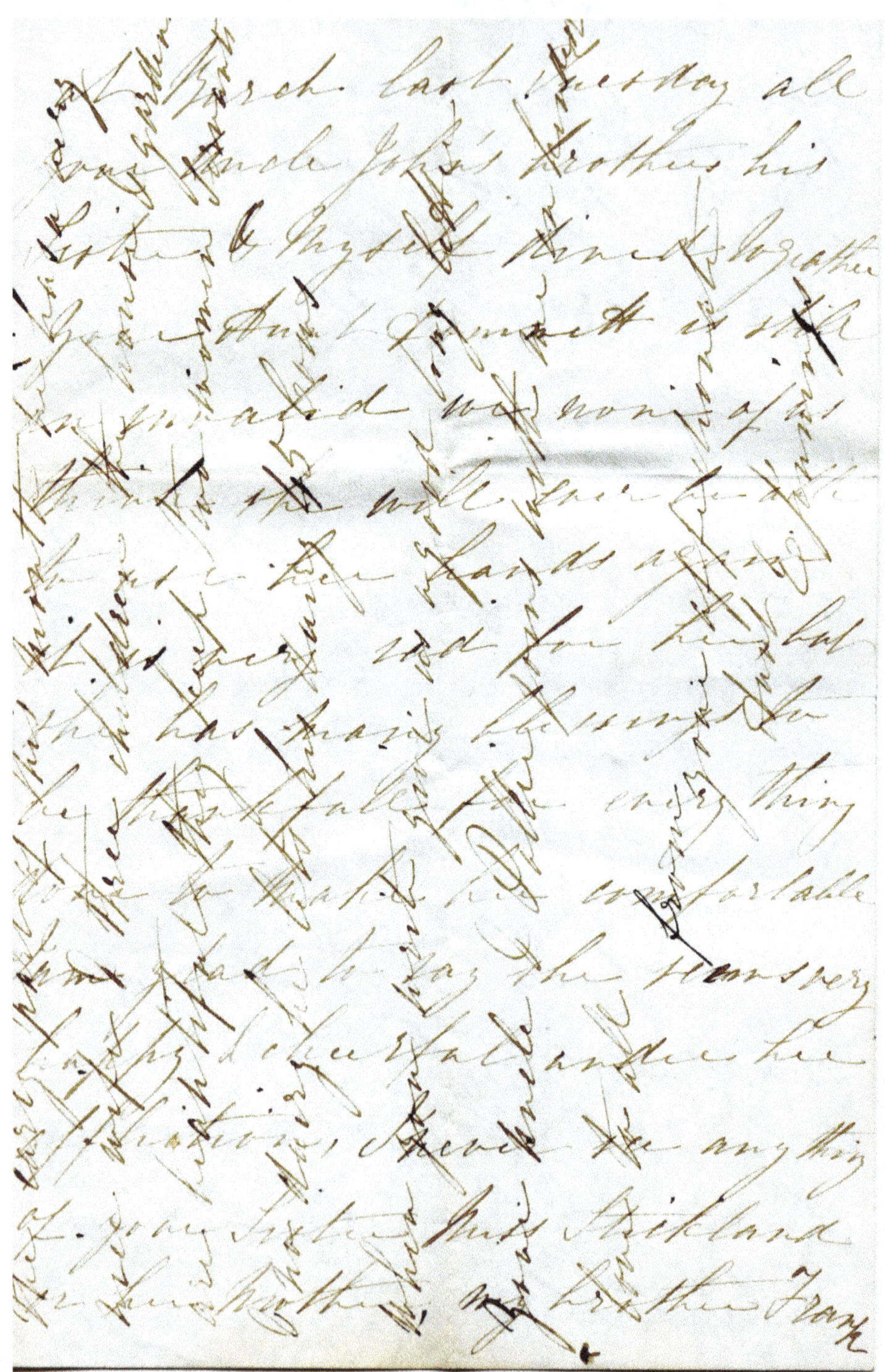

March last Tuesday all
your Uncle John's brothers his
sisters & myself dined together
your Aunt Emmett is still
an invalid [illegible]
[illegible] will [illegible]
[illegible] hands [illegible]
[illegible]
[illegible]
[illegible] every thing
done to make her comfortable
and glad to say she [illegible] very
happy & cheerful under her
afflictions I never [illegible] any thing
of your sister Miss Strickland
[illegible] mother [illegible] brother Frank

Letter Number 55, Page 4

rents her land he is living at
New Barn Richard has taken
on My Fathers farm who is now
retired from bussiness,
We have not heard from your
brother Wm for some time
he was about making a change
when he last wrote which
I believe was in January last,
How is your dear Mother I hope
she is more happy now, please
give our kind love to her any
of us should be very glad to
get a letter from her Mrs -
Donnett has been expecting one
for some time past, so
Elizabeth is married -

Letter Number 55, Page 5

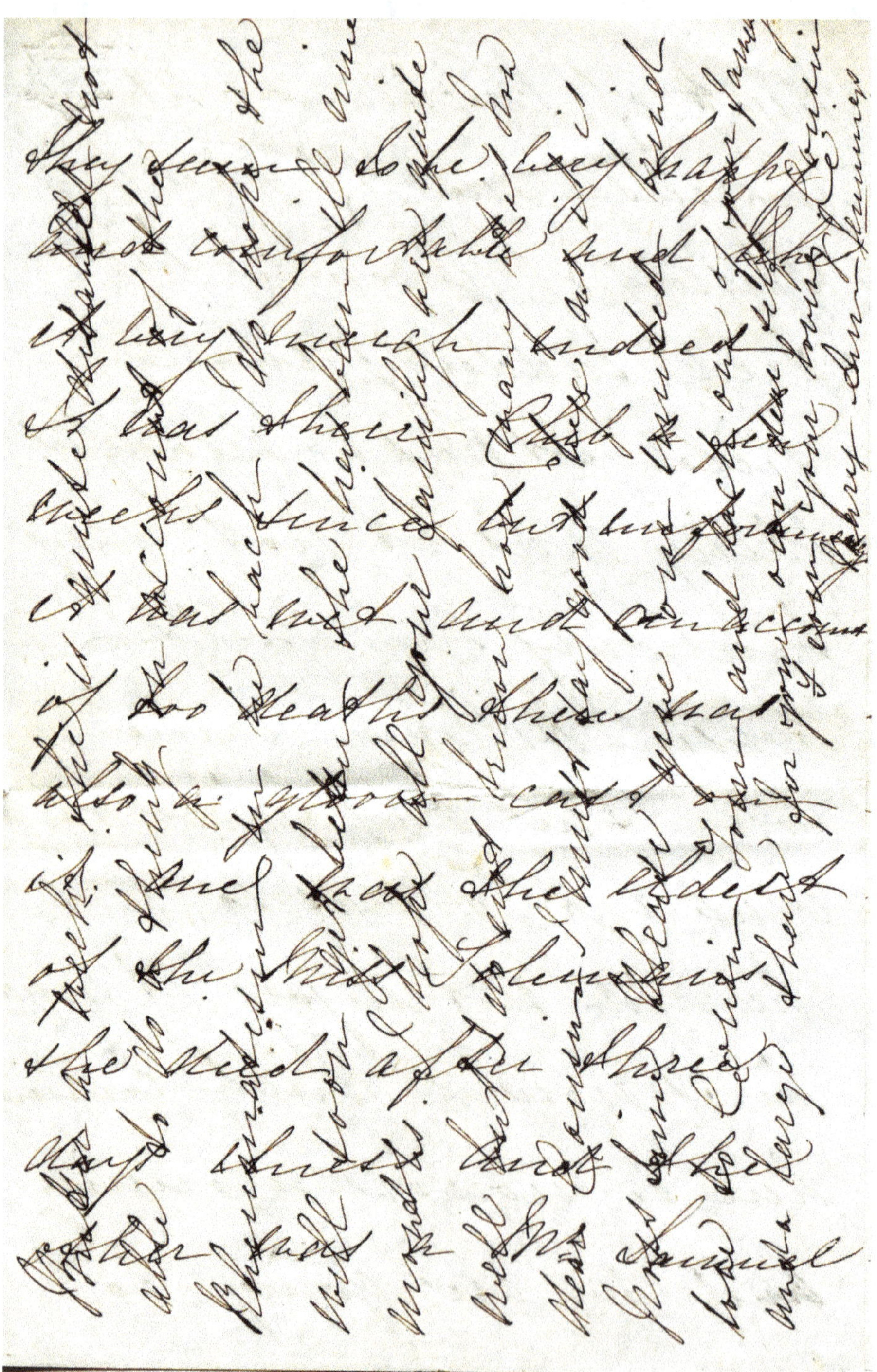

They seem to be very happy
and comfortable and like
it very much indeed
I was there [illegible] & see
weeks since but unfortunately
it was wet and on account
of two deaths there was
also a [illegible] case on
it. And that the oldest
of the [illegible]
the [illegible] after three
days [illegible] and the
other was Mr Samuel

Letter Number 55, Page 6

Hyatt of Buckland who
married one of the Miss
Spillers of Yarcombe he
died suddenly in a
field It was a dreadful
thing was it not? they
have only one Child
Cousin William came
down the day before the
Club but it was so wet
he did not enjoy it much
he is now & Birch coming
here to morrow morning
and we are going to

Letter Number 55, Page 7

ride to Membury together
I like riding on horse
back very much indeed
I was at Broadwinsor at
Aunt Mary Ann's not long
since I often go there
my cousins are the
only companions I have
they are both grown up
and have finished their
education Willie goes
to Taunton to school
he is going to stay
home for a time now.

Letter Number 55, Page 8

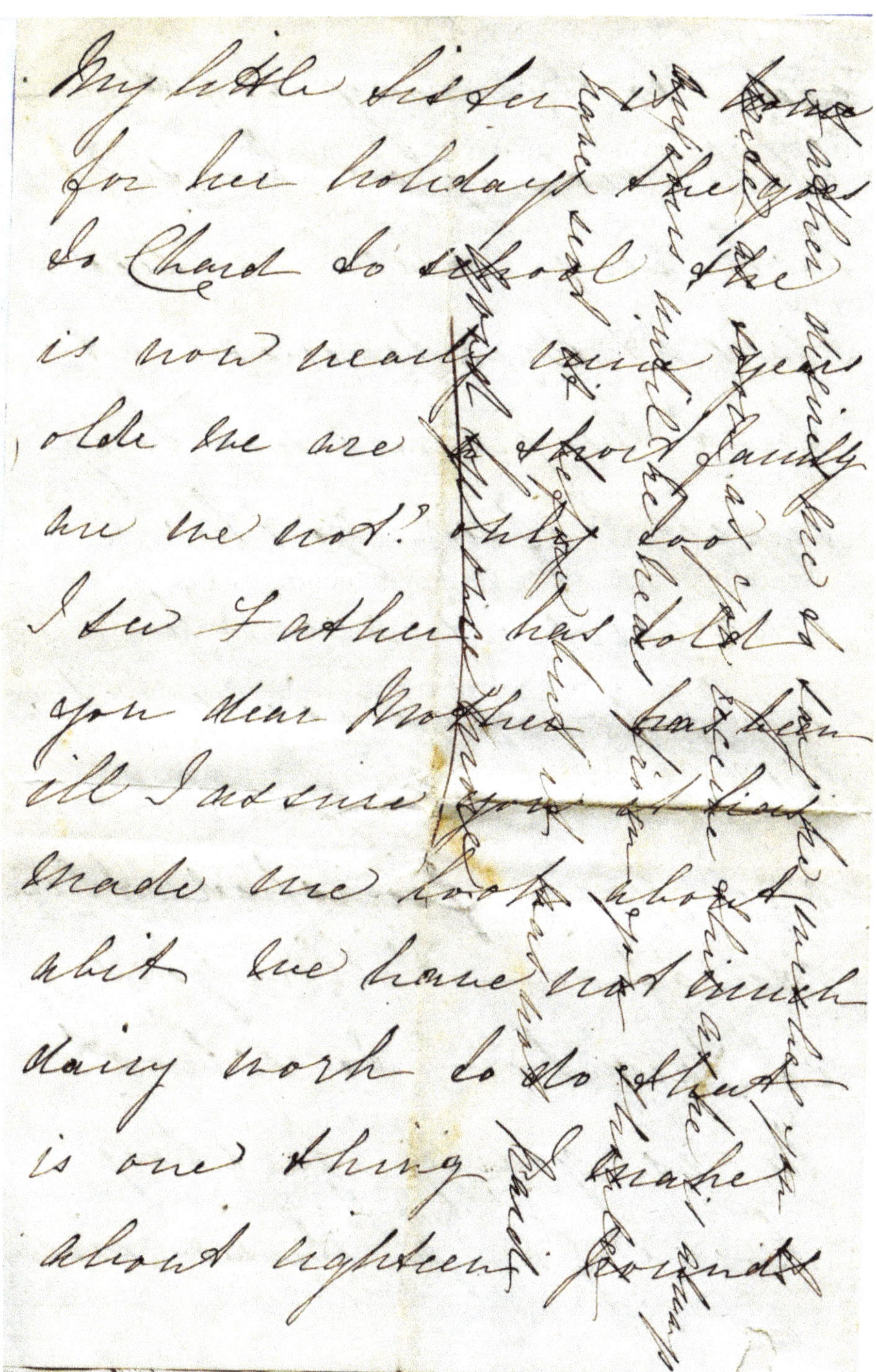
My little sister is home
for her holidays she goes
to Chard to school she
is now nearly nine years
olde we are a short family
are we not? only two
I see Father has told
you dear Mother has been
ill I assure you it first
made me look about
abit we have not much
dairy work to do there
is one thing I make
about eighteen pounds

Letter Number 56

Date: 7 November 1866
Writer: William Jennings
Recipient: Thomas & Elizabeth Stickland Pipe
Sent from: Northay Farm, Whitestaunton, Chard, Somerset County, England
Sent to: Waupaca, Waupaca County, Wisconsin, USA

Key Ideas

- William Jennings collected rent from Mr. Bonfield

[Receipt] Nov. 7th, 1866

Received of Mr. G. Bonfield the sum of twelve pounds for half year's annuity due on Pithayne [Farm] and Whitehorns estates

Letter Number 56, Page 1

Novr 7th 1866.

Received of Mr. G. Bonfield the sum of Twelve pounds for ½ years annuity due on Pitthayne & Whitehorns Estates —

Nov 7 1866

Stickland

ONE PENNY

Letter Number 57

Date: 26 May 1867
Writer: Thomas Pipe
Recipient: William Jennings
Sent from: Waupaca, Waupaca County, Wisconsin, USA
Sent to: Northay Farm, Whitestaunton, Chard, Somerset County, England

Key Ideas

- Thomas Pipe tells William Jennings that he has heard from Francis Gillingham. He has safely returned from England.
- Charlotte Jennings Pipe Pillar has been staying with Thomas Pipe the last two months.
- Charlotte Jennings Pipe Pillar has sued James Pillar for a divorce. She will receive a very good settlement, according to Thomas.

Waupaca 1867 [Written later by a descendant.]

Waupaca, May 26th, 1867

Dear Uncle [William Jennings]

I have just received a letter from my friend Mr. Gillingham informing me of his safe return from England and that he had a very pleasant trip and found all well on his return. He says that you are anxious to hear from me as you have not heard from me since my receipt of the last year's rent and that you could not send any more until I had acknowledged the same. That I do not blame you for in the least, as I know it was my duty to have done so immediately. But I must say that I have been detained from writing to you for the reason that I could not write you the full particulars of the family. But I will return

to tell you now as far as I can at the present, as I do say that you had a hint from my friend Gillingham. The facts are these. There is great trouble with mother [Charlotte Jennings Pipe Pillar] and her husband

[James Pillar]. Mother [Charlotte Jennings Pipe Pillar] is now with me and has been for the last two months, also her girl Elizabeth [Pillar], Mother [Charlotte Jennings Pipe Pillar] has sued [James] Pillar for a divorce and it should have been settled this last spring's court but for some reason it is put over till the fall term of court when I hope it will be settled. [James] Pillar turned them out dollar-less and Mother [Charlotte Jennings Pipe Pillar] indecently clothed. The facts are that [James] Pillar is a disrespectful, inhuman brute. He thinks that a wife has no rights, but I hope to learn [teach] him this fall that there are here [rights], especially in America. I calculate that he will have to fork over full one third of his property to Mother, for her support. It is costing a good deal of money and will before it is through with

when you write if you have anything to say on the subject please write it on a different slip of paper as I know it will trouble her to think that you know anything of it until it is settled. She has kept her troubles from me as much as possible until the last year and now she wishes to keep it from her English friends until after it is settled. I hope to write you full particulars this fall.

I here wish to acknowledge the receipt of the last year's draft for the rent of 65 and 66 as I might say the rent due up to Lady Day [March 25] 1866.

I will here say that it will be an accommodation to me to get this year's rent as soon as you are able, as I have bought a lot of pine land with the intention to go lumbering next winter. The lumber business is one of the greatest businesses of this country and most profitable for the last few years.

Please to give my kindest respects to all enquiring friends and tell them that we are all well and I hope this will find yourself and family the same. I will now close this by sending my kindest love to yourself and family.

From your affectionate nephew

Thos. Pipe

Letter Number 57, Page 1

Tanpaca May 26th/1867

Dear Uncle

I have just Recd a Letter from my Friend Mr Gillingham informing me of his safe return from England and that he had a very pleasant trip and found all well on his return, He sais that you ar anxious to hear from me as you have not herd from me since my receipt of the Last years Rent and that you ould not send any more untel I had acknolidged the same, that I do not blame you for in the least, as I know it was my duty [illegible] to have don so imed-iatley, But I must say that I have been detained from wrightin to you for the reason that I cold not wright you the full partiulers of the Family, But I will ventur

Letter Number 57, Page 2

to tell you now as far as I am at the
present as I [illegible] say that you had
a hent from my Friend Gillingham
The facts ar these there is great
troubele with Mother and her Husband
Mother is now with me and has been
for the last two Months also her Girl
Elizebeth Mother has Sued Piller
for a Divorce and it Shold have been
Settled this last Spring's Cort but
for som reason it is put over untill
the Fall term of Cort when I hope
it will be Settled Piller turned them
out Doorsless and Mother indecently
Clothed, the facts ar that Piller is
a disrespectful inhuman brute he
thinks that a wife has no rightes
but I hope to learn him this Fall
that they have especially in America
I calculate that he will have to fork
over full one third of his property
to Mother, for her Suport, It is costin
me a good deal of Money and will before it is
through with

Letter Number 57, Page 3

then you wright if you have any thing
to say on the Subject pleas wright it
on a diferent slip of paper as I know
it will trouble her to think that you
know any thing of it untel it is sittled
She has kept her troubeles from me
as much as possabell untele the last
year and now shee wishes to keep it
from her English Friends untel after
it is setttled, I hope to wright you
full partienlars this Faule
I hear wish to acknolidge the receipt
of the last years draft for the Rent
of Sixty Five and Six, as I might say the
Rent due up to Lady day 1866
I will hear say that it will be a
commodation to me to get this years Rent as soon
as possible as I have just bin buyen
a lot of Pine Land with the intention
to go Lumbering next winter,
the Lumber Business is one of the greatest
Business of this Country and the
most Profitabile for the last few years

Letter Number 57, Page 4

Pleas to give my kindest Respects
to all inquirien Friends and tell them
that wea all well and I hope this
will find your Self and Family
the Same, I will now Close this
by Sending my kindest love to your
Self and Family
From your Aff't Nephew
John Pipe

Letter Number 58

Date: 12 August 1867
Writer: Elizabeth Coleman Jennings
Recipient: Thomas & Elizabeth Stickland Pipe
Sent from: Northay Farm, Whitestaunton, Chard, Somerset County, England
Sent to: Waupaca, Waupaca County, Wisconsin, USA

Key Ideas

- George Bonfield's father was buried on August 11, 1867, at the age of 81.
- Mary Ann Jennings Dommett is quite disabled with chronic rheumatic gout. She has been in Bath, Somerset, for five weeks.
- Uncle John Jennings received a letter from Thomas Pipe's brother, William Jennings Pipe, last month. He was well but not yet feeling settled. He said he wanted to "pick up some old widow with a good income."
- Nellie (Ellen) Jennings was at school in Taunton, Somerset, but now she is in poor health and at home.

Whitestaunton
August 12, 1867

Dear Mr. & Mrs. Pipe

Mr. Jennings has at last got the rent. Mr. Bonfield has a very large family which makes it rather hard for him, and it is hard times for small farmers as wages out are so very high. He hopes to be more punctual in the future. His father was buried yesterday aged 81. He managed his business till within a week of his death. Your aunt Mrs. [Mary Ann Jennings] Dommett am sorry to say is quite a cripple

not able to do anything even for herself, she has no use of her hands not to cut her meat on her plate. Herself, husband and her Pollie [Dommett] has been down spent last week at Birch [Oak Farm]. She has been at Bath [Somerset] to try the waters for five weeks, but found no good there. It is chronic rheumatic gout. Her hands, feet and legs are wooden. It is a very great blessing for her, she has such a very kind attentive husband [William Dommett] and children [William and Polly]. He has bought a very nice carriage to take her out in. He never tires of

waiting on her, nor begrudge expense. I think there is a doubt of her ever being well again, your Uncle John [Jennings] had a letter from your brother Wm. [Jennings Pipe] last month. He was well but don't write very cheerful. He is not feeling settled yet. He says he want to pick up with some old widow with a good income, should not be surprised to see him home again. It is lovely weather now. We have had it very stormy for the late hay. We finished ours before the wet came, had a very good crop. Today we began

to reap. Wheat is rather high, from 8 to 9 shillings per bushel. The early potatoes are quite a failure. We were glad to hear of Mr. [Francis] Gillingham's [Neenah, Wisconsin] safe arrival home. My youngest daughter Nellie [Ellen] is very poorly. She has been at Taunton [Somerset] to school the last half but now too poorly to go. All the rest are pretty well. I trust this may find you all well. When you see your dear mother [Charlotte Jennings Pipe Pillar] give our kindest love to her. Thank her for her likeness [photo] she kindly sent us with kind regards to you all.

From Your affectionate

Aunt [Elizabeth] Jennings

[sideways]

Mr. [John] Stickland	
Annuity	£24 0s 0d
Fire insurance	£1 10s 3d
Income tax	33s 8d
	£26 1s 11d
Rent	
	£81 0s 0d
	£26 1s 11d
	£54 18s 1d

Pd. Please to acknowledge the receipt of the same soon, should be glad to hear how you are getting on.

Letter Number 58, Page 1

1867 Whitestaunton Augt 12th
1867

Dear Mr & Mrs Pipe

Mr Jennings has at
last got the rent. Mr Bond
field has a very large family which makes it rather
hard times for him, & it
is hard times for small
farmers as wages & out are
so very high, he hopes to
be more punctual for the future,
his Father was buried yesterday
aged 81 he managed his business
till within a week of his death.
Your Aunt Mrs Dommett am
sorry to say is quite a cripple

Letter Number 58, Page 2

not able to do any thing even
for herself she has not use of
her hands not to cut her
meat on her plate, her self
husband & her daughter Pollie
has been down spent last
week with us & at Birch she
has been at Bath to try the
waters for five weeks but found
no good from them, it is
Cronic rehumatic gout her
hands feet & legs are swolen
it is a very great blessing
for her she has such a very
kind attention husband &
children he has bought a
very nice carrage to take
her out in he never tires of

Letter Number 58, Page 3

waiting on her nor begrudge
expence, I think there is a
doubt of her ever being well
again, your Uncle John had
a letter from your brother Wm
last Month he was well
but dont write very cheerfull
& he is not feeling settled yet
he says he wants to pick up
with some old widow with a
good income, should not
be suprised to see him home
again, It is lovely weather now
we have had it very stormy for
some time very troublesome for
the late hay we finished ours
before the wet came had a very
good crop to day we began

Letter Number 58, Page 4

to reap wheat is rather high
from 8 to 9 shillings per Bsl. the
early potatoes are quite a fil-
ure we were glad to hear of
Mr Gillinham's safe arrival home
My youngest daughter Nellie is
very poorly she has been at
Taunton to school the last
half but now to poorly to go
all the rest are pretty well
I trust this may find you all
well when you see your dr Mother
give our kindest love to her thank
her for her likeness she kindly
sent us with kind regards to
you all from your affectionate
Aunt E Jennings

Mr Stickland
Annuity 24..0..0
Insurance 1..10..9
Income tax 11..2
26..1..11

Rent £81..0..0
26..1..11
£54..18..1

PS Please to acknowledge the receipt of the same from you should be glad to hear how you are getting on

Chapter 7

Village of Waupaca, Waupaca County, Wisconsin
1868 - 1874

Chapter 7 includes 14 letters dated 1868 to 1874 while the Pipe family is still living in the village of Waupaca. The Jennings move from Northay Farm in Whitestaunton, Chard, Somerset County to Forton, Chard, Somerset County, and finally to Hursey Farm, Burstock, Beaminster, Dorset County. Ten letters are between Thomas and Elizabeth Stickland Pipe and William and Elizabeth Jennings. Three letters are from Elizabeth Stickland's solicitor in Chard, Mr. Dommett. Thomas writes one letter to Dommett & Canning. The last of Mr. Dommett's letters, dated December 8, 1874, reveals his understanding of property management, including financial matters, for the last 21 years under the auspices of Uncle William Jennings.

Letter Number 59

Date: 14 February 1868
Writer: Thomas Pipe & Elizabeth Stickland Pipe
Recipient: William Jennings
Sent from: Waupaca, Waupaca County, Wisconsin, USA
Sent to: Northay Farm, Whitestaunton, Chard, Somerset County, England

Key Ideas

- Thomas Pipe thanks his uncle for the rent through March 25, 1868. He is sorry that George Bonfield is not happy.
- Thomas will return to the woods this winter until spring. He will take twelve men and four teams. He intends to put 1,000,000 to 1,200,000 feet of logs in the river before the snow leaves.

Elizabeth Stickland Pipe continues:

- Miss Pollie Dommett was married at Christmas. Letter Number 63 states she married William Wyatt near Winsham, Somerset. Elizabeth Stickland Pipe wishes them well.
- Elizabeth Stickland Pipe describes the weather as mild with big snowstorms.
- Thomas Pipe's mother, Charlotte Jennings Pipe Pillar, is living with her daughter Elizabeth Pillar Bowron who got married last November and has a son (named James after his grandfather) who is 3 months old.
- Elizabeth Stickland Pipe says she hears that James Pillar is married to a young girl (Eliza Morgan) after the divorce from Charlotte Jennings Pillar Pipe in 1867.
- She says the judge granted Charlotte Jennings Pipe Pillar $2,000.
- James Pillar went to a higher court and lost. He had to pay more expenses. He has a very "long face."

- Elizabeth Stickland Pipe says that Charlotte Jennings Pipe Pillar kept house for her last winter when she went to the woods to cook for twelve in Thomas Pipe's lumber camp. Tom, her second son, is cooking this winter.
- Mary Elizabeth Pipe, daughter of Elizabeth Stickland and John Valentine Pipe, received a letter from Mary Stickland who said that John Stickland's son is sick.
- Elizabeth Stickland Pipe asks whether John Mathews still lives at Hay Farm, Yarcombe, Devon.

Waupaca, Feb 14th,1868

My dear Uncle and Aunt [William and Elizabeth Coleman Jennings]

I am happy to inform you that yours of Sep 24th has been duly received with the draft for £54 19s 0d for the rent due up to March 25th, 1868, for which I give you a thousand thanks for the present. I am sorry to hear that Mr. G. Bonfield does not give you better satisfaction as a tenant. I hope to hear of his improvement by the next spring.

Now as winter is coming. I am about to return to the woods [northern Wisconsin] where I shall remain until the spring. I take with me 12 men and 4 teams. I intend to put in the river from 1,000,000 to 1,200,000 feet of logs before the snow leaves in the spring, so I am very busy. I must leave this letter for my wife to finish.

[This letter is very faded, possibly written in pencil.]

Dear Mrs. Jennings [Elizabeth Coleman Jennings]

As Thomas has left this for me to finish which has been some little time since he wrote his. He has been home since for more men and another team of horses. He has about 16 or 18 men and 5 teams, two yokes of oxen and 3 pairs of horses. He says he has about 700,000 thousand feet of logs. You say in your letter that Miss Polly [Dommett] was to be married about Christmas, wishing her much happiness and comfort. I think you will miss very much for she must have been a great deal of help and comfort to you. The weather here has been poor for lumbering. It has been very mild and thawing. We had a very heavy snowstorm 2 weeks ago for 2 days. The third day it blowed as to block the roads so as to make it impassable. At the present for 3 days it has thawed most of the snow, but yesterday it rained and froze and tonight it snowed a little which is

good sleighing and still freezing and snowing a little at the present time and is very cold. 14 of February Thomas's mother [Charlotte Jennings Pipe Pillar] is living with Elizabeth Pillar [Bowron] which was married 1 year last November. She has a son about 3 months old. I hear that [James] Pillar is married again to a young girl [Eliza Morgan]. He had a divorce from grandmother [Charlotte Jennings Pipe Piller]. They went to law [court] about the matter and the Judge granted her 2 thousand dollars which made him draw a very long face. He carried it to a higher court but all to no use only more expenses for him to pay.

Grandmother [Charlotte Jennings Pipe Pillar] kept house for me last winter as I went in the woods to cook for 12 of us for Thomas's camp which they have to pay 30 or 35 dollars a month for board and he thought it would be saving a little as expenses are very large in the lumbering wood so much waste with men cooks. Tom our 2nd boy is cooking this winter. He has been home for tonight for the first time since November and has now gone to the

woods again. I ask him how he got along very well. He says he have pork, beans, fried cakes, and tea for breakfast, fried pork, potatoes, pudding sometimes soups, cookies, tea for dinner. Fried port buckwheat pancakes, fried potatoes or cold beans warmed up and tea for supper. You see they don't use any butter in the woods for a substitute molasses for every meal, bread all the time.

Mary Elizabeth [Pipe] had a letter from my sister [Mary Stickland] about Christmas, not a very long one but no news in it only that John's [Stickland] little boy was very sick. She never said a word about any of our relations or friends only John's [Stickland] family and mother [Elizabeth Wall Stickland Bartlett] which she said was enjoying good health for her age. I must now conclude with best respects to all friends not forgetting Mr. [William] Jennings and yourself and little daughter. How is your brother Richard's [Coleman] wife? What family has she? Does she go to your brother John's [Coleman?] often? Is John Mathews still living at Hay Farm [Yarcombe, Devon]? I should like to write a longer letter but there is no one here that your acquaintance will nor nothing you would feel interested about in America as we do when we have a letter from England. Is your brother William Coleman in America? If you have his directions if not intruding Thomas like to have it.

[other way]

when you next write we are all well [mostly too faint to read]

Your affectionate

Elizabeth Pipe

Letter Number 59, Page 1

Wanfell Feb 14th [illegible]

My Dear Uncle & Aunt
I am happy to
inform you that yours of Sept 24
has been duly received, with the draft
for 54.18.0 for the Rent due up
to March 25th 1868, for which I
give you a thousand thanks for the
present, I am sorry to hear that
Mr G. Bonfield does not give you
better satisfaction as a Tennant
I hope to hear of his improvement
by the next Spring,
now as winter is comin on I am
about to return to the woods where
I shall remain untill the Spring
I take with me 12 men & 4 Teams
I intend to put in to the river
from 1000000 to 1200000 feet of Logs
before the snow leaves in the Spring
as I am very hurried I must leave
this letter for my Wife to finish

Letter Number 59, Page 2

Dear Mrs Jennings

As Thomas has
left this for me to finish which was begun
some little time since he wrote his,
He has been home since for more
men and another team of horses
he has [illegible] 5 teams,
2 yoke of oxen and 3 span of horses
he says he has in about 700 000 thousand
feet of logs. You say in your letter that
Miss Pole has to be married about Christmas
wishing her much happiness and comfort.
I think you will miss her very much for
she must have been a great deal of help
and comfort to you. The weather
here has been very poor for lumbering
it has been very mild and thawing we
had a very heavy snow storm 2 weeks ago
for 2 days the snow drift blowed as to blockade
the roads so as to make it impassable
at the present for 3 day it has thawed most
of the snow but yesterday it rained and froze
and tonight it snowed a little which is

Letter Number 59, Page 3

good sleighing and still freezing and snowy
a little at the present time which is very cold
14 of February Thomas Mother is living with
Elizabeth Pillar which was married 1 year
last November she has a son a bout 3 months
old I see that Pillar is married again
to a young girl he had a divorce from
Grandmother they went to law a bout
the matter and the Judge granted her
2 thousand dollars which made him
draw a very long face he carried it
to higher cort but all to no use only
more expences for him to pay
Grandmother kept house for me last
winter as I went in the woods to cook
for 12 of us for Thomas camp which they
have to pay 30 or 35 Dollas a month for
a hand and he thought it would be
saving a little as expences is very large
in the lumbering woods so much wast with
men cooks, Tom our 2nd boy is cooking this winter
he has been home for 6 nights for the first
time since November he is now gone to the

Letter Number 59, Page 4

woods again I ask him how he got a long
very well. he says he have Pork Beans Fried
cakes and Tea for Breakfast. Fried Pork Potatoes Puddin
some times soups Cookies, tea for dinner. Fried Pork
Buck wheat Pancakes Fried Potatoes or cold Beans
warmed up and pie Tea for supper. you see
they dont have any butter in the woods for
a substitute Mollasses for every meal.
Bread all the time

Mary Gray hath had a letter from my
Aunt [illegible] about christmass not a very long
one but now news in it only that Johns
little Boy was very sick she never sayed
a word bout any of our relations or
friends only Johns family and Mother
which she said was enjoying good health
for her age. I must now concluded with
[illegible] to all friends [illegible]
[illegible] and your self and little daughter
How is your Brother Richards Wife what family
has she does she go to Brother Johns often
is John Mathews still living at Hey Farm
I would like to write a longer letter but their is
no one there that your acquainted with nor nothing
you would feal interested about in a measure [illegible]
we do when we have a letter [illegible] from England
is your Brother William in America if you have his
directions if not to intending Thomas would like to have it

Letter Number 60

Date: Before 1 May 1868
Writer: Thomas & Elizabeth Stickland Pipe
Recipient: William & Elizabeth Coleman Jennings
Sent from: Waupaca, Waupaca County, Wisconsin, USA
Sent to: Northay Farm, Whitestaunton, Chard, Somerset County, England

Key Ideas

- Elizabeth Stickland Pipe writes to tell that Thomas Pipe has an opportunity to buy the best and largest farm in the county at a great bargain. The old man who owned it died, and his son, who is not a farmer, wants to sell it.
- The son offered the farm to Thomas Pipe for $6,500.
- Elizabeth Stickland Pipe wants to know whether they have sufficient collateral with William Jennings or in Pithayne Farm, Yarcombe, Devon, to secure William or anyone else to borrow £300 or £400 plus interest. Right now, the exchange rate is favorable: £1 is worth $2. Thomas has $2,500 of his own. He wants to pay at least $4,500. The son will let him pay as he goes.
- Thomas Pipe continues the letter by saying that this farm is the only one that has interested Elizabeth Stickland Pipe. The farm has taken first place at three county fairs.
- Thomas wants to buy the farm for his family. It would be a home for their children. The four boys would help do the work.
- Thomas puts more value on this farm than Pithayne Farm, Yarcombe, Devon. Thomas will let Mr. Mumbrude know by May 1, (1868), whether he will buy the farm.

Waupaca 8th/[18]68

Dear Uncle & Aunt [William and Elizabeth Coleman Jennings]

I suppose that you will be surprised to receive a letter from us so soon after the other, but now we have speculation flavour on. Thos. has an opportunity to buy the best and largest farm in the county at a great bargain. The farm is 570 acres with 175 under the plough and 160 of meadow, 40 of heavy woods, a hop yard of 7 acres, the balance is in the state of nature. It has the best farm buildings complete of any in the county with the best orchards and garden with 300 fruit trees. It has 7 miles of cedar rail fence on the farm. The old man that owned it is dead, and the son wants to sell it as he is no farmer. He has been to Thomas and offered the farm to him for 6,500 dollars, six thousand five hundred dollars with 15 cows 2 yoke of oxen, a grain drill, one wagon, plough drags, and all light tools on the place. Now the question is this, have we sufficient interest [collateral] with you or in that farm Pithayne [Yarcombe, Devon] to secure you or any person that you might borrow 300 or 400 pounds of by paying a good little interest for it which we should be willing to pay as there is a double chance to make money, the first place Thos. thinks the property is worth 2,000 so buying the next thing English exchange is worth a big premium at the present one pound is worth two,

but I expect it is to come down very soon. But it is the general impression that it would come below 1¾ or 1½ at the farthest for the next year. Thos. says that he do not want you to think this to be some wild project of his. It is the wish of a number of his best friends who is good financiers as well as good businessmen. They all claim it to be the best prospective chance of anything, they have been especially for us on account of the family. Thos. says that he can make out 2,500 dollars on his own account and there is teams with other stock left which he will want on the farm. This man wants Thos. to take the farm and pay what he can and pay the balance as he make it off the farm, but Thos. won't touch it without he can pay at least 4,500 dollars on it at the start. He has also offered if Thos. will close the bargain this spring to allow him 10 percent on the whole for the use of the farm this summer as he has it let [rent] on shares or we might take it as it is let [rented] or if we could take possession before spring's work commence we might.

Dear Uncle, I left this letter for Elizabeth [Stickland Pipe] to write which I see she has done so far, now she is hustling and there is not time to lose. It is necessary that I should finish it which I will do. This farm is the only one that I have seen her taken up with in this section. This farm has taken the premium as the first at three county fairs, now if it possible for you to find me the above amount of money I should be very glad for you to take the pay for all the trouble that you might be to.

Now as to the state of that property, I am not posted. I suppose though that it is in a shape that you can give the necessary security for what you might get. If there is anything that you might need, if not you shall have it at the quickest opportunity as should you need any security on the property then you shall have it.

I want to buy this place on account of the family. It will make a home that they all will naturally want to stay at. The boys are now getting grown up, to do me a great good. They are good quiet boys, and I believe they often referred to by the people of the town so as template for other boys. Four of them will make a pretty strong team.

Now as to the times in this county for the future I think we shall not have very glorious times perhaps for some time to come but I think a good farm must pay especially a farm that is adapted to anything. Stock must pay for years to come as it is all cleared out of the country and the grain is pretty well cleared out. First from the shortness of the crops for they have not two or three years. Second there has been such a vast portion of the country that is from consumers where they ought to be producers. As to our own taxes I think the heaviest portion new are through with, that is what we call the war tax. I am inclined to think we have men enough in the field to wipe out this rebellion. Now as to this money assure it will be necessary to do what can be done forthwith for two reasons, first to secure the premium on exchange and second the farm. I should put more value on this farm than the Pithayne Farm.

I have promised Mr. Mumbrude that I will give him an answer about the first of May [1868]. Please write the first opportunity that I might decide one way or the other. May this find yourself and family in good health and spirits as it leaves us all at present.

From your affectionate nephew and niece

Thos. and Elizabeth Pipe

P.S. Please give the kindest love to all enquiring friends not forgetting yourself and family.

Letter Number 60, Page 1

Waupacca 8th /68

Dear Uncle & Aunt

I suppose that you will be
surprised to Receive a letter from us so soon after the
other but now we have speculation fearing on
Thos has an opportunity to buy the Best and largest
Farm in the county at a great Bargin the Farm is
570 Ackers with 175 under the Plow and 160 of Meadow
40 of heavey Woods a Hop yard of 7 ackers the Balance is
in the state of nature it has the Best Farm Buildings
compleit of any in the county with the Best Orchard and Garden
with 300 Fruit Trees it has 7 Miles of Seder Rail Fence on the
Farm The Old Man that owed it is dead and the Son wants
to sell it as he is no Farmer He has being to Thomas and
offered the Farm to him for $6500 Dollars Six Thousand
five Hundred Dollars with 15 Cows 2 Yoke of Oxen a Grain
Drill one Wagon Plows Drag's and all light Tools on
the place now Sir the question is this have we sufficient
Intrest with you or in that Farm Perhaps to secure you
or any Person that you might Borrow 300 or 400 Pounds
of by Paying a good liberal Intrest for it which we should
be willing to pay as their is a Double chance to make
money the first Place Thos thinks the Property is worth
2000 to Buying the next thing English exchange is worth
such a big Breanum [Premium] at the present one Pound is worth two

Letter Number 60, Page 2

but I expect it is to come down very soon But it is
the general impression that it wont come below 1 3/4 or 1 1/2
at the farthest for the next year Thos sayes that he x do
not want you to think this to be some wild project
of his, it is the wish of a number of his Best friends
who is good financiers as well as good Business men they
all claim it to be the best Prospective Chance of any thing
they have seen especaly for us on account of the family
Thos sayes that he can make out 2500 Dollars on his own
account and have is team's with other Stock left which
he will want on the Farm This man wants Thos
to take the Farm and Pay what he can and Pay
the Balance as he make it off the Farm But Thos wont
tuch it without he can Pay at least $500 Dll on it at
the start he has also offered if Thos will close the Bargin
this spring to alow him 10 Percent on the whole for the
use of the Farm this Summer as he has it let on Share's
or we might take it as it is let or if we could take Posetion
before Spring's Work commence we might

Dear Uncle, I left this letter for Elizabeth to wright
which I se she has don sofar, now she is busily and
there is no time to lose it is necisery that I Shold
finish it which I will do, This Farm is the only
one that I have seen her takenup with in this Section
This Farm has taken the Premnum as the best at three
County Fairs, now if it posabell for you to fiend
me the above amount of Money I Shold be very glad for
you to take the Pay for all the trouble that you might be to

Letter Number 60, Page 3

Now as to the State of that Property I am not posted
I Sopose thee that it is in a Shape that you can give
the necesary Security for what you Might get, if there
is any thing that you Might need of me you Shall have it
at the quickest opportunity, or Shold you need any Security
on the Property Here you Shall have it,
I want to buy this Place on acount of the Family
It will Make a Home that they all will natuerly want
to Stay at, the Boys ar now getten grown up to do me
a great good they ar good quiet Boys and I believe they
they often refered to by the people of the Town as Sample
for other Boys. Two of them will Make a pretty Strong team
Now as to the times in this Cuntery for the futcher I think
we Shall not have very glowin times perhaps for Som time
to com but I think a good Farm Must pay especially
a Farm that is adapted to any thing, Stock Must pay
for years to com as it is all Cleaned out of the Contry
and the Grain is pretty well cleaned out first from the
Shortness of the Crops for the last two or three years Second there
has been sutch a vast portion of the Cuntery that has ben
Consumers where they ment to be Producers, As to our
Taxes I think the heaviest portion we ar through with
that is what we Call the war tax I am inclined
to think we have Men a nough in the Field to wipe out
this Rebelion, Now as to this Money affair it will be
necesary to do what can be don forthwith for two
reasons first to Secure the premium on Exchange and Second
the Farm. I Shold post More value on this Farm than the
Pitthain Farm

Letter Number 60, Page 4

I have Promised Mrs Mummbrude that I will give them
an answer about the first of May Pleas wright the
first opportunity that I might decide one way or the other
May this find your Self and Family in good Health
and Spirits as it leaves us all at present
From your Affct Nephew & Niece

Thos & Elizabeth Sipe

P.S.

Pleas give our kindest love to all inquiring
Friends not forgetten your Self and Family

Letter Number 61

Date: 4 May 1869
Writer: Williams Jennings
Recipient: Thomas & Elizabeth Stickland Pipe
Sent from: Northay Farm, Whitestaunton, Chard, Somerset County, England
Sent to: Waupaca, Waupaca County, Wisconsin, USA

Key Ideas

- William Jennings has sent Thomas and Elizabeth Stickland Pipe a receipt showing John Stickland received his annuity.

Yarcombe, May 4th, 1869

Received from Mr. George Bondfield [Bonfield] half years annuity twelve pounds

£12 0s 0d

Stamped receipt John Stickland May 1st 1869

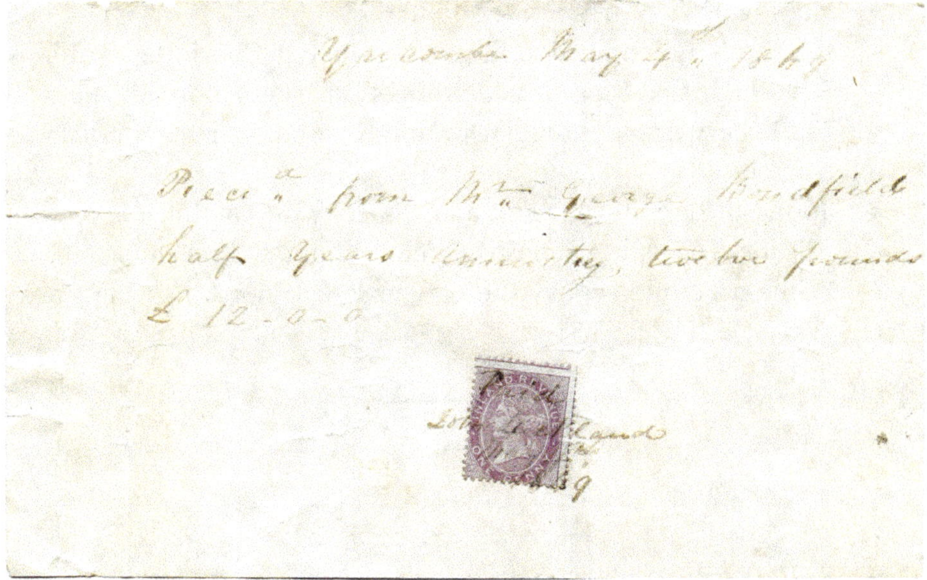
Yarcombe May 4th 1869

Recd from Mr George Bondfield
half years Annuity, twelve pounds
£ 12-0-0

Letter Number 62

Date: Between fall 1869 and 25 March 1870
Writer: Elizabeth Coleman Jennings
Recipient: Thomas Pipe
Sent from: Northay Farm, Whitestaunton, Chard, Somerset County, England
Sent to: Waupaca, Waupaca County, Wisconsin, USA

Key Ideas

- Uncle John Jennings is ill at Birch Oak Farm, Membury, Devon. He will not be turned out. He complains about not having cash, but he has only himself and his wife to support.
- Uncle William Jennings has bought a small farm near Broadwindsor, Dorset, ten minutes from his sister Mary Ann Jennings Dommet. William and Elizabeth Coleman Jennings are not yet living there. They are thinking of building a new house there.
- The Jennings are 2 ½ miles from daughter Mary Ann Jennings Davy who has two little boys. Daughter Nellie (Ellen) is there visiting on her midsummer holiday.
- Elizabeth Coleman Jennings asks to tell Charlotte Jennings Pipe Pillar that Mary Ann Jennings Davy gets more like her.
- Aunt Mary Ann Jennings Dommett's son, William, is not to be trusted.
- John Stickland is living on a farm below the estate.
- Elizabeth Coleman Jennings includes undated receipts.
- William Jennings says the expenses will not be so high next year.

[crosshatched]

Dear Thomas

Your Uncle John is ill at Birch [Oak Farm, Membury, Devon]. I think it likely he will remain there as long as he like. That is they will not turn him out. I have not seen him for a long time, he complains if he had reasons very much. Cash always seem short with them and no one to keep but themselves. His health is better. Your Uncle Wm. has bought a small farm near Broadwindsor [Dorset] about a ten minute walk from his sister Mrs. [Mary Ann Jennings] Dommett. We are not going there to live this winter as we are thinking

of building a new house. It's about 21 acres of good pasture land and about 2 ½ miles from our daughter Mrs. [Mary Ann Jennings] Davy. She has two little boys, Nellie [Ellen] is there visiting to spend her mid-summer holidays. Tell your dear Mother [Charlotte Jennings Pipe Pillar] that old Mary Ann [Jennings Davy] get the more she is like her aunt Charlotte [Jennings Pipe Pillar]. Your aunt [Mary Ann Jennings] Dommett's health is much improved, but I am sorry to say her son [William Dommett] is anything but shady, which I know is a very great trial to them. He has every comfort at home a young man can wish to have.

[Accounts undated]

Received Mrs. Bonfield half year's rent due Michaelmas

[September 29]	£36 0s 0d
Mr. Singleton	£4 10s 0d
	£40 10s 0d

Disbursements

Mr. [John] Stickland's annuity	£12 0s 03
Fire insurance	£1 5s 0d
56 sheaves seed	£1 2s 6d
Thatcher's bill	12s 0d
Chard newspaper ¼ year	2s 2d
	£15 1s 8d
Half year's rent	£40 10s 0d
Mr. [John] Stickland's annuity	£12 0s 0d
Land tax	3s 0d
8 gates	£2 0s 0d
	£14 3s 0d
Year's rent	£81 0s 0d
Paid out	£29 4s 8d
Balance	£51 15s 4d

[other way]

but still he leaves it all for the public. I trust he will very soon see his errors

With our very fondest love to you all once more goodbye. Mr. J. [John] Stickland is living in a farm below Estate [Pithayne Farm?]. He has had a very trying year being so dry.

Letter Number 62, Page 1

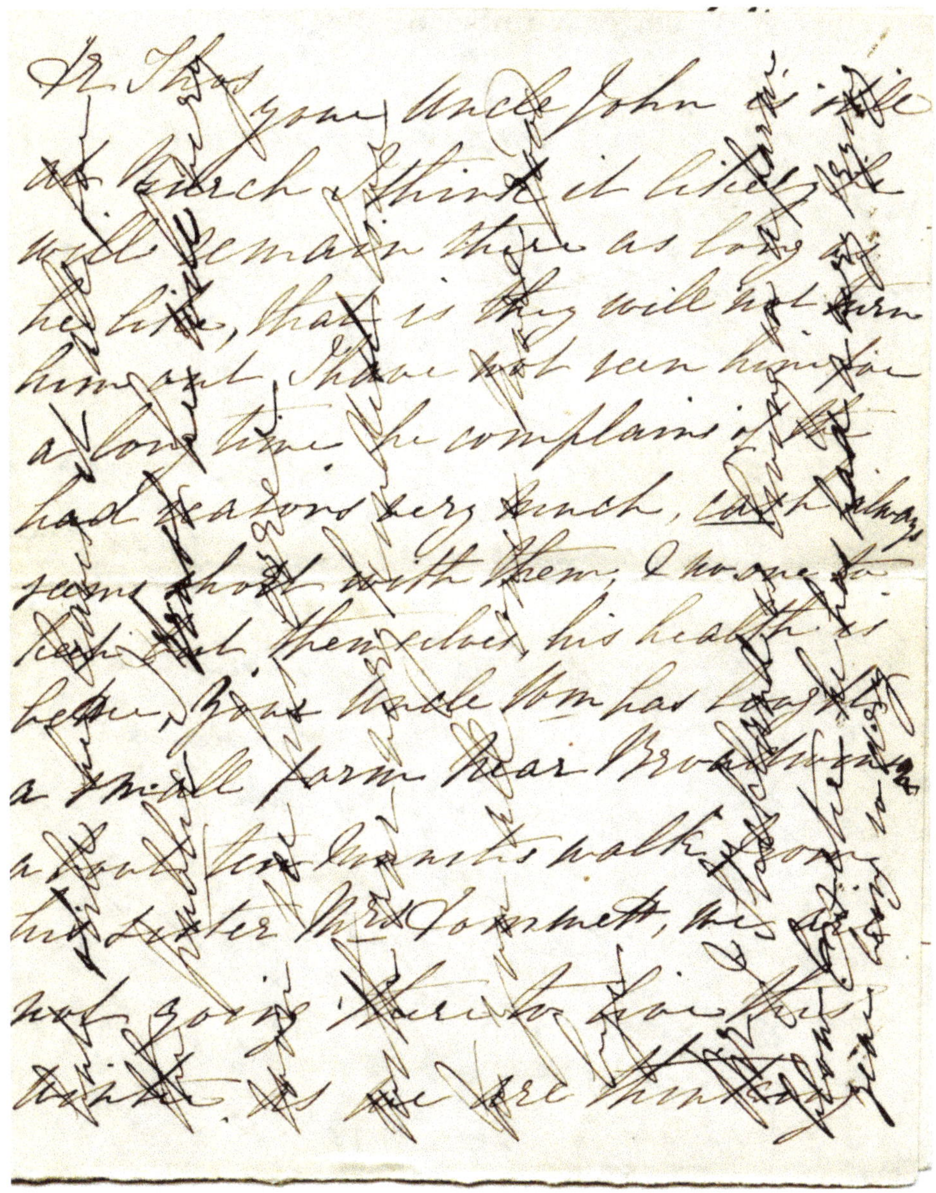

Dr Thos

your Uncle John is still at Church I think it likely he will remain there as long as he likes, that is they will not turn him out. I have not seen him for a long time he complains of the bad seasons very much, cash always seems short with them, & no one to keep out themselves, his health is better. Your Uncle Tom has bought a small farm near Broadway about ten minutes walk from his Sister Mrs Tommett, we are not going there to live this winter, as we are thinking

Letter Number 62, Page 2

of building a new house
its a bout 21 acres of good
pasture land & a bout 2 1/2
Miles from our daughters
Mrs Saby she has two little boys
Nellie is there visiting to spend
her Midsummer holidays, tell your
dear Mother the older Mary Ann
gets the more she ~~[illegible]~~ is like her
Aunt Eh. your Aunt Tommotts
health is much improved, but
I am sorry to say her son is any
thing but steady, which I know
is a very great trial to them
he has every comfort at home
a young man can wish to have

Letter Number 62, Page 3

Sept 1 Reced Mrs Bondfield half years
rent due Michlemas last £ 36..0..0
Mr Singleton 4..10..0
£ 40..10 0

disbursments
Mr Sticklands annuity -- 12..0..0
fire insurance 1..5..0
56 Sheaves Reed -- 1..2..6
Thatchers Bill 12..0
Chard News paper 1/4 year 2..2
£ 15..1..8
half years rent -- 40..10..0
£ s d
Mr Sticklands annuity 12..0..0
Land Tax -- 3..0
8 Gates -- 2..0..0
14..3..0

years rent 81..0..0
pd out 29..4..8
balance £ 51..15..4

Letter Number 63

Date: 9 July 1870
Writer: Elizabeth Coleman Jennings
Recipient: Thomas & Elizabeth Stickland Pipe
Sent from: Forton, Chard, Somerset County, England
Sent to: Waupaca, Waupaca County, Wisconsin, USA

Key Ideas

- William is still unhappy with Mr. Bonfield. Mrs. Bonfield's mother, Mrs. White, lived with them until her death in early spring 1870.
- The Fever has been to Yarcombe. Those who have died include Mrs. Wyatt of Pithayne Farm, John Harford of Manning's Common, Sir Trayton Drake, and the old keeper J. Palmer.
- Brother John Stickland is leaving his place near Axminster (Somerset) for a farm closer to Exeter (Devon).
- Uncle John Jennings at Marsh (Yarcombe, Devon) has twelve or fourteen acres now.
- William and Elizabeth Coleman Jennings left Northay (Farm) last Lady Day (25 March). Their landlord died in spring. The new landlord raised the rent so high that they had to leave. They are now living in Forton (Somerset).
- Polly Dommett, who is now Mrs. Wm. Wyatt, lives about 2 miles from the Jennings at Winsham (Somerset). Mrs. (Mary Ann Jennings) Dommett is better.
- Brother Richard Coleman has two farms.
- Brother William Jennings Pipe is still in Heathcote, Victoria, Australia.

[crosshatched]

Forton, Chard

Somerset

July 9th, 1870

Dear Mr. & Mrs. Pipe

Enclosed is a draft for £48 14s a year's balance on your estates. I must tell you as I did last time Mr. Bonfield the tenant don't give your uncle satisfaction at all in his mode of farming. Sometimes he has a mind to give them notice to leave. He then argues he don't like doing it. They have a very numerous family, eleven or twelve children. Mrs. Bonfield's mother Mrs. White lived with them up to her death.

She died early in the spring. The Fever has been to Yarcombe for some time, some have died of it. Mrs. Wyatt of Pithayne [Farm, Yarcombe, Devon], John Harford of Manning's Common [Yarcombe, Devon], Sir Trayton Drake is no more, the old keeper J. Palmer, those three was all taken about the same time months ago, your brother J. [John] Stickland is leaving his place near Axminster [Somerset], then he has taken a farm close Exeter [Devon]. We very seldom hear anything of them. We are having very dry weather. The hay crop is very bad. Uncle John [Jennings] at Marsh [Yarcombe, Devon] has twelve or fourteen acres now at all in it. You have heard

ere now I presume we left Northay last Lady Day [25 March]. Our old landlord died the spring before and the young one rose the rents so high we thought it best to give up while it was well with us, so now we are quite out of business. We are living at Forton, the parish of Chard [Somerset]. We have a nice little house, stable, dairy house, and good, nice garden. We are very happy and comfortable. I am glad we are away from Northay [Farm] as my health is so much better here than there. Pollie Dommett that was now Mrs. Wm. Wyatt lives about two miles

from us at Winsham [Somerset]. Last Monday your uncle and myself went to visit them. She is very comfortably married. She has a little girl about six weeks old. We met your Aunt [Mary Ann Jennings] Dommett there and one daughter and her husband, that is Mr. & Mrs. [William and Mary Ann Jennings] Davy. They brought Aunt [Mary Ann Jennings] D. [Dommett] on in their carriage as they pass her house on their way there. Aunt [Mary Ann Jennings] Dommett is better than she has been for a long time. She can now dress herself without help. They have a very nice housekeeper. The eldest of the Miss Wyatts there, once lived at Chilworthy near Combe [Somerset]. I have ordered you a Chard newspaper to be sent from the office weekly. I hope you will like it. I get it regular. I can assure we have had a great bore to sell out and get settled again.

[other way]

My brother Richard [Coleman] has one farm with his I think I have told you before he succeeded my father [Richard Coleman, Sr.], now he has the two farms which makes a very good business. My father [Richard Coleman, Sr.] and mother are still living and my youngest brother [Frank Coleman] with them. I hope to write to your dear mother [Charlette Jennings Pipe Pillar] next week She was very glad to get a letter from him. Please give our love to him when you see her, your uncle Wm. Will write to you soon. He is very poorly now

[other way]

taken a cold this weather. At present is very hot and we are all apt to sit in the draught to get a little air. We heard from your brother Wm. [Jennings Pipe] last month. He seem to be getting on very well as working in an office still in the same place Heathcoat, Victoria [Australia]. I hope to write to him soon. With our kind love to you all, hope to hear from

[other way]

you soon.

From your affectionate

Aunt E. [Elizabeth] Jennings

Letter Number 63, Page 1

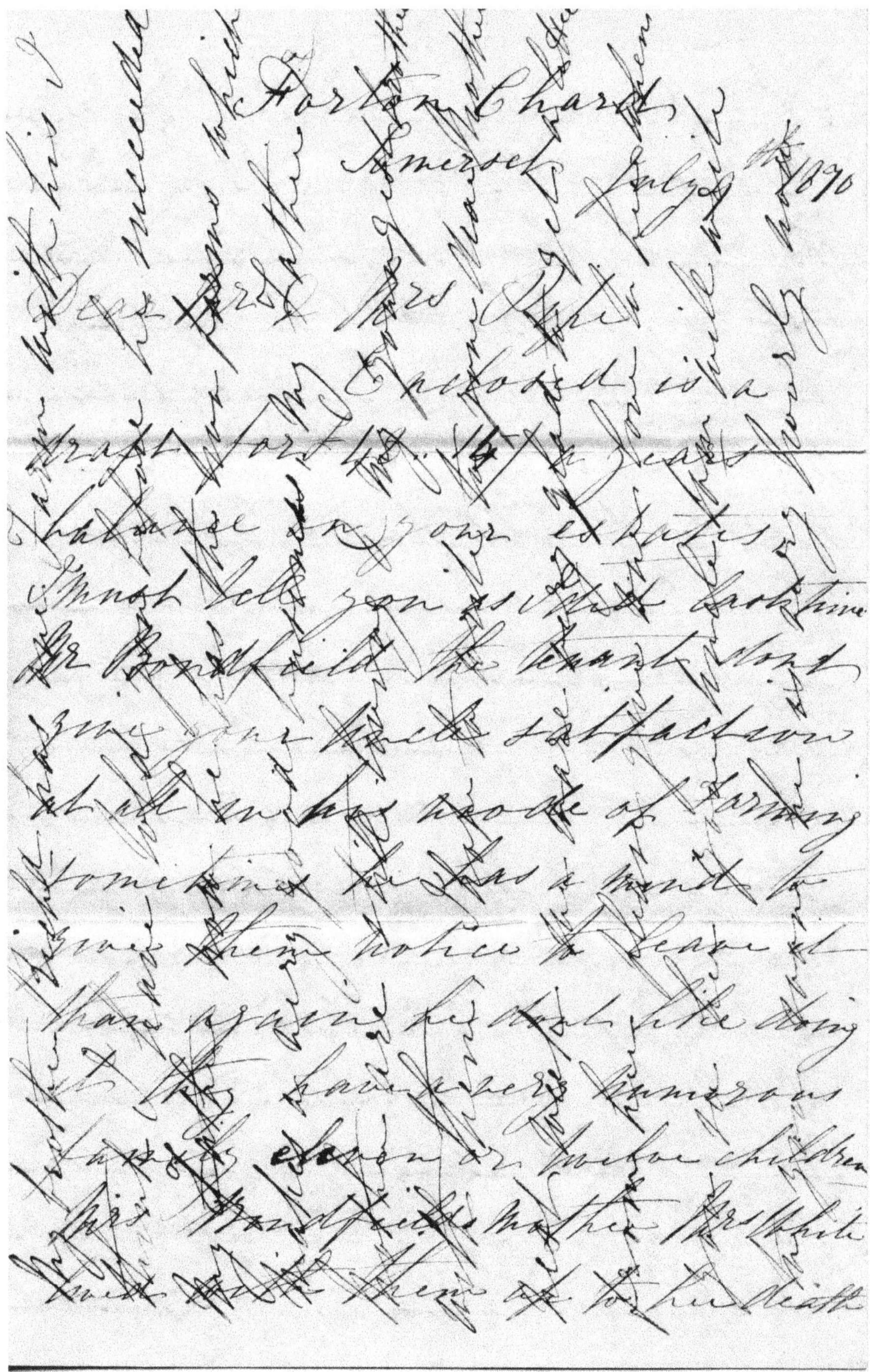

Horton Chard,
Somerset July 4th 1870

Dear Mrs Pipe

Enclosed is a
draft for £48.14 to clear
balance on your estates
I must tell you as I did last time
Mr Bondfield the tenant dont
give you little satisfaction
at all in his mode of farming
sometimes he has a mind to
give them notice to leave it
than again he dont like doing
it they have a very numerous
family eleven or twelve children
Mrs Bondfield's mother Mrs White
lived with them up to her death

Letter Number 63, Page 2

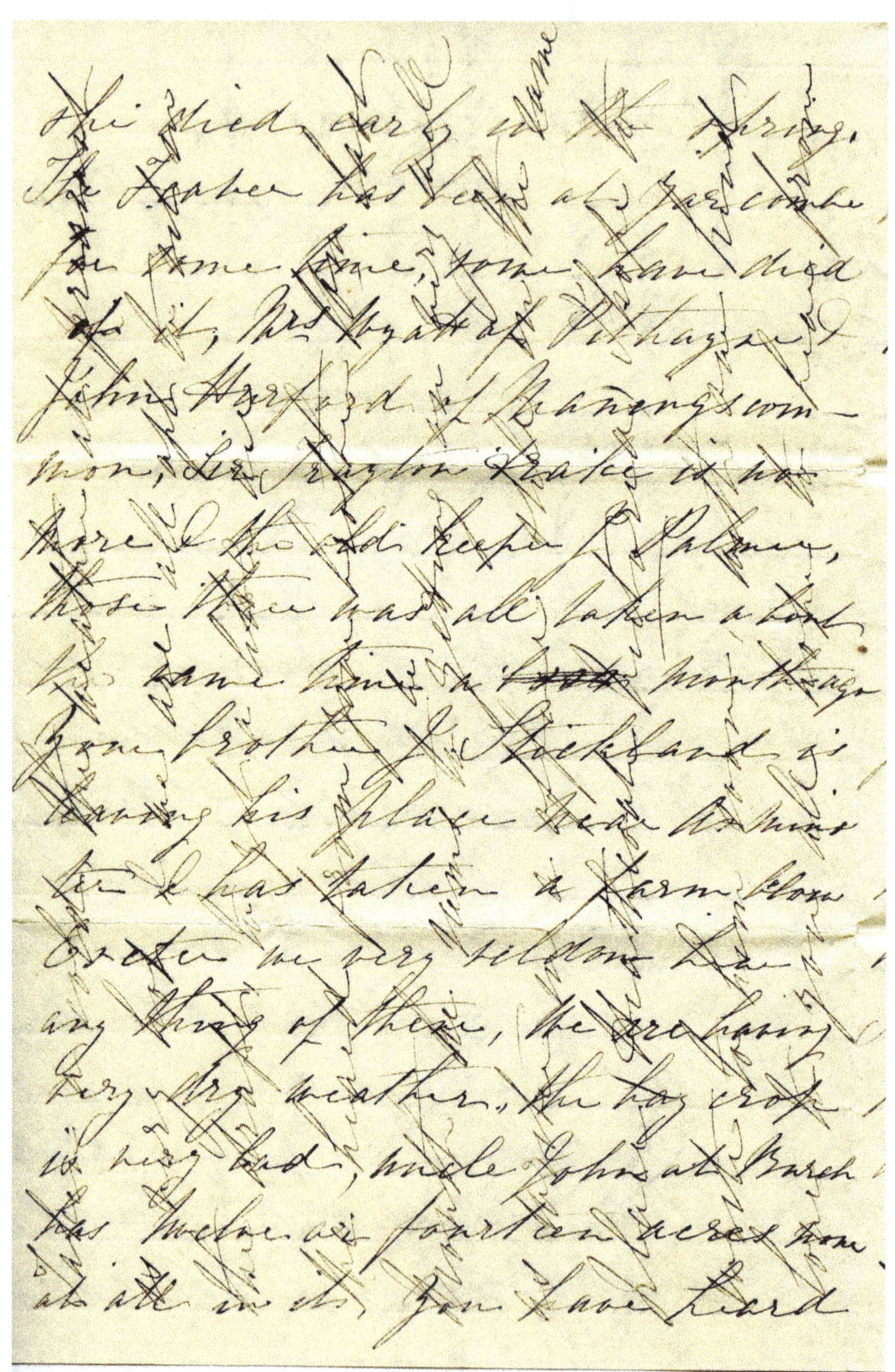

she died early in the spring.
The fever has been at [illegible]
for some time, some have died
of it, Mrs Wyatt of [illegible] &
John Harford of [illegible]com-
mon, Sir Taylor Blake is no
more & the old keeper [illegible] Palmer,
those three was all taken about
the same time a few months ago
your brother J. Strickland is
leaving his place near Axminis-
ter & has taken a farm close
Exeter we very seldom see
any thing of them, we are having
very dry weather, the hay crop
is very bad, uncle John at Burch
has twelve or fourteen acres mown
[illegible] in it, you have heard

Letter Number 63, Page 3

ere now I presume we left
Worthy last lady day, our
old Landlord died the spring
before & the young one rose
the rents so high, we thought
it best to give up while it
was well with us, so now
we are quite out of bussness
we are living at Forton in the
parish of Chard we have a
nice little house Stable & coach
house & good size garden,
we are very happy & comfortable
I am glad we are away from
Worthy as my health is so much
better here than there. Pollie
Hammett that was, now Mrs Wm
Wyatt lives about two miles

Letter Number 63, Page 4

from us (at Birnham) last Monday your Uncle & myself went
to visit them she is very comfortably married she has a little girl
about six weeks old, we met your
Aunt Dommett there, & one daughter & her husband, that is
Mr & Mrs Davy, they brought
Aunt D— on in their carriage
as they pass her house on their way there
Aunt Dommett is better than she
has been for a long time, she can
now dress herself without help
they have a very nice housekeeper
The eldest of the Miss Moyatts that
once lived at Chilworth near
Combe, I have ordered you a Chard
news paper to be sent from the office
weekly I hope you will like it
& get it regular, I can assure
you we have had a great bore
to sell out & get settled again

Letter Number 63, Envelope Front

Letter Number 63, Envelope Back

Letter Number 64

Date: 8 July 1871
Writer: Elizabeth Coleman Jennings
Recipient: Thomas Pipe
Sent from: Forton, Chard, Somerset County, England
Sent to: Waupaca, Waupaca County, Wisconsin, USA

Key Ideas

- George Bonfield was thrown from his trap, horse-drawn carriage, returning from Chard Market and died. The horse was on his head. He died in the early part of October at age 46. The incident is in the Chard, Somerset, newspaper.
- Bonfield left 12 children, one child is two months old. Several of the children are set out on rotation.
- William Jennings will collect the late rent from a sale they are having. Mrs. Bonfield begs to stay.
- Elizabeth Stickland Pipe's mother, Elizabeth Wall Stickland Bartlett, is living with her sister Mrs. Henry Fowler of Thorncombe, Dorset. Brother John Stickland and sister Mary Stickland keep her between them. The Jennings do not see or hear from them. They do not know the reason, but they speculate that the reason is Uncle William Jennings supported Elizabeth Stickland Pipe's rights to Pithayne Farm, Yarcombe, Devon.
- Elizabeth Wall Stickland Bartlett is looking better. John Stickland lost his eldest son last summer because of fever.
- Edwin Jennings died last February 13, 1870. His eldest daughter is living with her Aunt Mary Ann Jennings Dommett. The youngest who teaches their four children is with her brother Frank Jennings.
- George Bond is living near Crewkerne, Somerset, with seven children.
- William Coleman had a daughter married last October. He still lives in Kansas City, Missouri, and is in butchery. (The Kansas City Stockyards opened there in 1871.)

- Thomas Pipe's little girl, Charlotte (Lottie), died in Waupaca, Wisconsin. Smallpox is prevalent in some places in Devon.
- Elizabeth Wall Stickland Bartlett visited Elizabeth Coleman Jennings' brother, Richard Coleman, for a few days in May.
- Aunt Elizabeth (Betsey) Coleman is still living on Crock Street, Ilminster, Somerset. (Verified in *1871 U.K. Census)*

[Crosshatched] [the right side of the letter is missing]

Forton, July 8th, 1871

Dear Thomas

The amount enclosed is due to you from your estates £51 15s. They are very backwards with their payments. Did you see the account of Mr. George Bonfield's death in the Chard [Somerset] paper. He was thrown from his trap [horse-drawn carriage] returning from Chard Market and died from the effects a week after. The horse was on his head.

He left eleven children. His wife has since had another. It's now about two months old. He died the early part of October aged 46. They have a son, a young man. The eldest he manages the farm. Several of the others since their father's death are sent out in rotation. They cannot stop there for the want of means. They had a sale to sell the sheep the 1st of June, by chance your uncles had hears of it. I had an order from the attorney. He demands the

last half year's rent from the auction. He your uncle would not allow horses to be fed on the sheep sold as he con[sidered] it injured, the land. The poor widow begs to be allowed to remain a little longer there. The seasons will be better such a very dry summer last year. They made but little and had no hay for the winter to keep the stock. It was the case with every one. We have had a very hard winter quantity of cattle has died for the want of better food, which now makes it sell high, many

little farmers cannot stock their farm for the want of money laying out so much to keep their stock through the winter.

Your uncle [William] says he will do the best he possibly can for you. There is a great deal of repairs wanted. The house and buildings all want to be done up. I don't know anything of your sister Mary [Stickland], but your mother [Elizabeth Wall Stickland Bartlett] is living with her sister Mrs. [Henry] Fowler of Thorncombe [Dorset]. I believe your brother John [Stickland] and sister [Mary Stickland] keep her between them. They don't come near us as we don't know the reason more than this, your uncle stuck out for your rights of Pithayne [Farm, Yarcombe, Devon], Mrs. [Elizabeth Wall Stickland] Bartlett was

[other way]

at my brother Richard [Coleman] for a few days last May. They said she was looking very well, indeed your brother John's [Stickland] wife [Elizabeth Mathews Stickland] was with him. They lost their eldest son last summer, died of fever, since we left Northay [Farm, Somerset] we hear but little of Yarcombe [Devon], but I have again paid a quarter in advance for the Chard paper to be sent to you if you

[other way]

prefer Crewkerne [Somerset] that we could ask it to be sent. It is a half penny a week. How is your dear mother [Charlotte Jennings Pipe Pillar]. She has heard of her brother Edwin's [Jennings] death. He died last February. His eldest daughter is at present living with her Aunt [Mary Ann Jennings] Dommett. The youngest is with her brother Frank [Coleman], She teaches the children, They have four, another expected soon. He is in a first rate farm and getting on well. George Bond is living near Crewkerne [Somerset] in a very pretty farm. They have seven children. They seem to be getting on very well. We do not see much of them. My brother Wm. [Coleman] had a daughter married last October. He is still living at Kansas City, Missouri in the butchery business. He were sorry to hear of the death of your dear little girl [Charlotte (Lottie) Pipe]. Many children had been carried off about now with the same complaint. Now the

[other way]

smallpox is very prevalent in some places. We have not heard from your brother Wm. [Jennings Pipe] for some time. I wrote to him last fall.

With our kindest love to you all

From your ever-loving Aunt

E. [Elizabeth Coleman] Jennings

My love to your dear mother [Charlotte Jennings Pipe Pillar]. Your Aunt [Elizabeth (Betsy)] Coleman is still living at Crock Street [Ilminister, Somerset]. I have not seen her for years.

Letter Number 64, Page 1

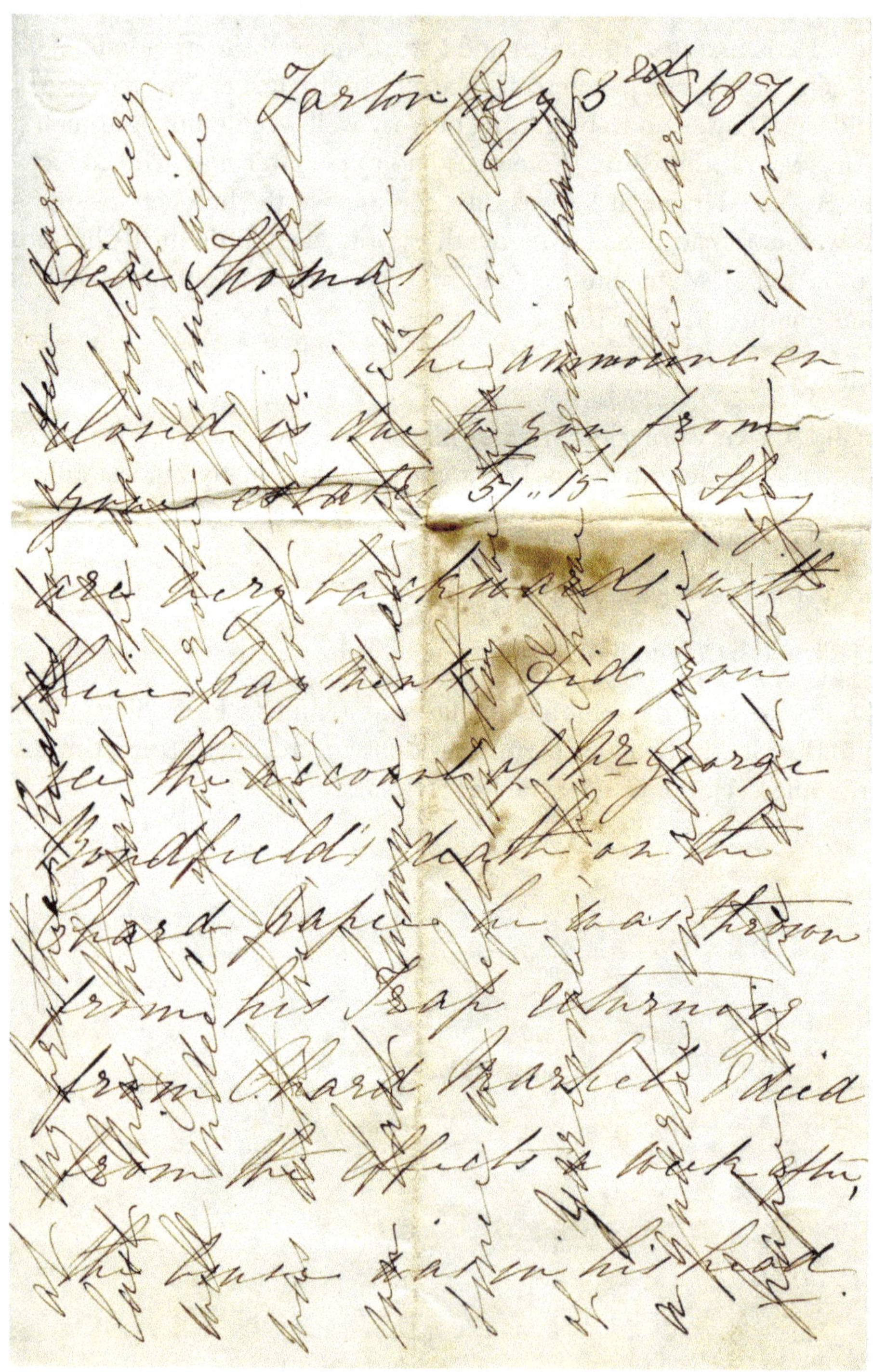

Tarton July 3rd 1871

Dear Thomas

The ammount en-
closed is due to you from
your estate 37"15 they
are very backward with
their payment. Did you
see the account of Mr George
Broadfield's death on the
Chard paper he was thrown
from his trap returning
from Chard Market & died
from the effects a week after,
the bruise was on his head.

Letter Number 64, Page 2

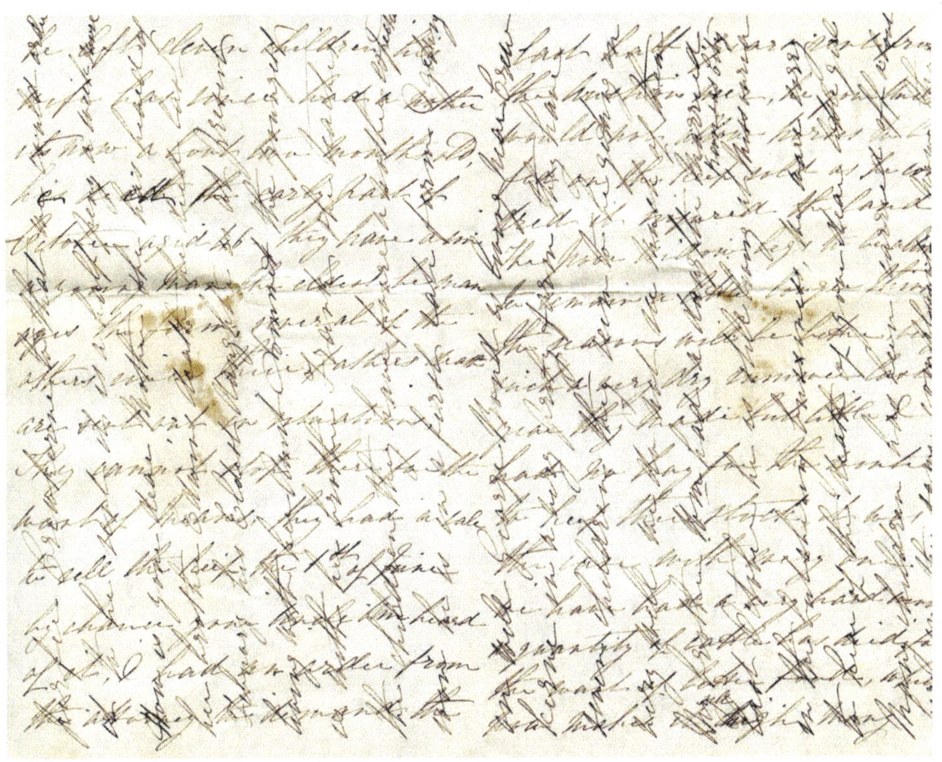

Letter Number 64, Page 3

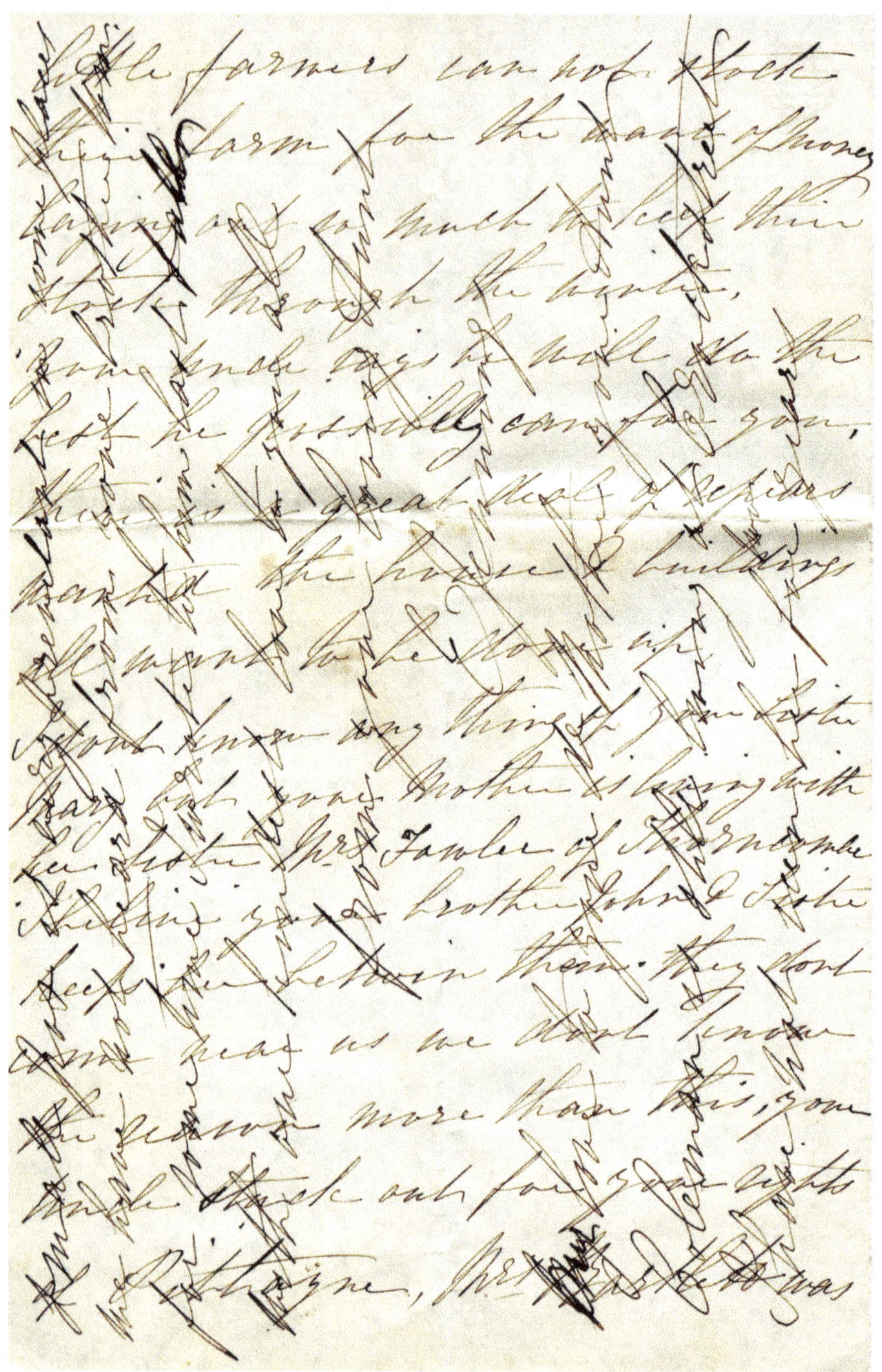

little farmers can not stock
their farm for the want of money
having out so much to keep their
stock through the winter.
Your Uncle says he will do the
best he possibly can for you.
there is a great deal of repairs
wanted on the house & buildings
all want to be done up
I dont know any thing of your letter
says but your Mother is living with
her sister Mrs Fowler of Thornecombe
I believe your brother John & Fisher
keep [illegible] between them. they dont
come near us as we dont know
the reason more than this, your
uncle struck out for your rights
at Rithayne, Mrs [illegible] was

Letter Number 64, Envelope Front

Letter Number 64, Envelope Back

Letter Number 65

Date: 15 August 1872
Writer: Mary Ann Jennings & Elizabeth Coleman Jennings
Recipient: Thomas & Elizabeth Stickland Pipe
Sent from: Hursey, Burstock, Beaminster, Dorsetshire County, England
Sent to: Waupaca, Waupaca County, Wisconsin, USA

Key Ideas

- Mrs. Bonfield is still on the farm with the house needing numerous repairs.
- Uncle John Jennings at Birch Oak Farm is dangeroulsly ill with an abscess in the bowels. Mr. and Mrs. Mary Ann Jennings Dommett and William Jennings visited him. William has been lending money to the Dommett's over the last five years.
- William and Elizabeth Coleman Jennings like their new house. Nellie (Ellen) left school midsummer. She is now visiting cousin Frank Jennings in Kingsbury Episcopi, Somerset. Elizabeth Coleman Jennings took Nellie (Ellen), and Jennie Jennings back with her for a visit.
- The Jennings live near Mrs. Dauncey, who was Lizzie (Elizabeth) Dommett, daughter of William and Mary Ann Jennings Dommett. She has a three-year-old girl.
- The Jennings are about two miles from their daughter, Mrs. Mary Ann Jennings Davy, who is expecting their third child.
- Elizabeth Coleman Jennings has heard that Mary Stickland had been in Yarcombe recently.
- William Jennings nearly rented Pithayne Farm, Yarcombe, Devon, to Sir Francis Drake. The farm was rented to Mr. Bonfield for 60 years.
- Elizabeth Coleman Jennings' aunt Elizabeth died July 20.
- Aunt Betsey, Elizabeth Coleman, is still living on Crock Street, Ilminister, Somerset, with William Coleman.

[crosshatched]

Hursey
Burstock
Beaminster
Dorsetshire

August 15th, 1872

My dear niece and nephew [Elizabeth Stickland and Thomas Pipe]

We have at last sent you a draft for a year's rent of £52 10s and they owe us now about two pounds on the last year but we have sent you the ten seventy [illegible, crossed out or written over] it seems very low times

still with Mrs. Bonfield, but she is in hopes it will soon be better. Your uncle Wm. was there about a fortnight ago. Their crops are looking pretty well. The house wants a thorough repairing such as painting and whitewashing but I fancy it would be soon made shabby again with so many children.

Your uncle John [Jennings at Birch Oak Farm, Membury, Devon] is dangerously ill. Mr. & Mrs. [William and Mary Ann Jennings] Dommett and Wm. [Jennings] went to see him last Monday. We heard again yesterday. He was then

about the same. He is so very weak, not able to stand. They had a physician from Taunton [Somerset]. He says it is abscess in the bowels and think there is a chance of recovery. None of his friends think he will recover, but I trust he may be spared yet a few years. We have known but little of them this last five years. Wm. has been lending them money at many different times when we gave up business. Wm. wished to have things put straight. It has never been done, so they have kept away from us and treated us

very coolly ever since, and of course we visit there but seldom. We like our new home very much. We have a nice house and about twenty acres of pasture lands of our own, just a little amount for us. We have thirteen beasts, forty more sheep. We keep one man and one servant girl. Nellie [Ellen] left school midsummer. She is at present at Kingsbury [Episcopi, Somerset] visiting her cousin Frank Jennings. Him and his wife made us a visit last week. They took her [Ellen (Nellie)] and her cousin Jennie Jennings back with them. We are living very near

[other way]

Mrs. Dauncey that was Lizzie [Elizabeth] Dommett. She has one little girl nearly three years old. Mr. & Mrs. [William and Mary Ann Jennings] Dommett are pretty well, but I fancy Mrs. [Mary Ann Jennings] Dommett ages fast. We are about two miles from our daughter Mrs. [Mary Ann Jennings] Davy. She is expecting an increase in her family soon that will be three. Have you heard from your mother [Elizabeth Wall Stickland Bartlett] or sister Mary [Stickland], lately. I heard the latter had been at Yarcombe [Devon] some little time ago.

[other way]

I should have told you in the beginning of my letter that Wm. had nearly let [rented] your farm to Sir Francis Drake. He would be then share of the rent. He has a deal of trouble to get it from the Bonfields. If you remember it was let [rented] in the first place to Mr. Bonfield for 60 years. They said it was too high. the neighbouring farms said the same so they have as you know been paying off

[other way]

per year, until last year everything has and still is selling so very high, Wm. told them they must pay the old rent, if Sir Francis [Drake] takes it he is to give 60 per year for it. Hope to tell you particulars next letter. How is your dear mother [Charlotte Jennings Pipe Pillar]. Please give her our very kindest love and thanks for her second letter to me, Tell her my aunt Elizabeth [?] died the 20th July last after

[other way]

short illness age 66 years. All the family are gone but Uncle Francis [Coleman?] three of them since my dear father [Richard Coleman, Sr.] in less than two years. With love trusting you are all well and happy.

From your affectionate

Aunt and Uncle

Wm. & E. [Elizabeth Coleman] Jennings

Your Aunt Betsey [Elizabeth Coleman] is still living at Crockstreet [Ilminister, Somerset] with Wm. Coleman and is generally pretty well.

Letter Number 65, Page 1

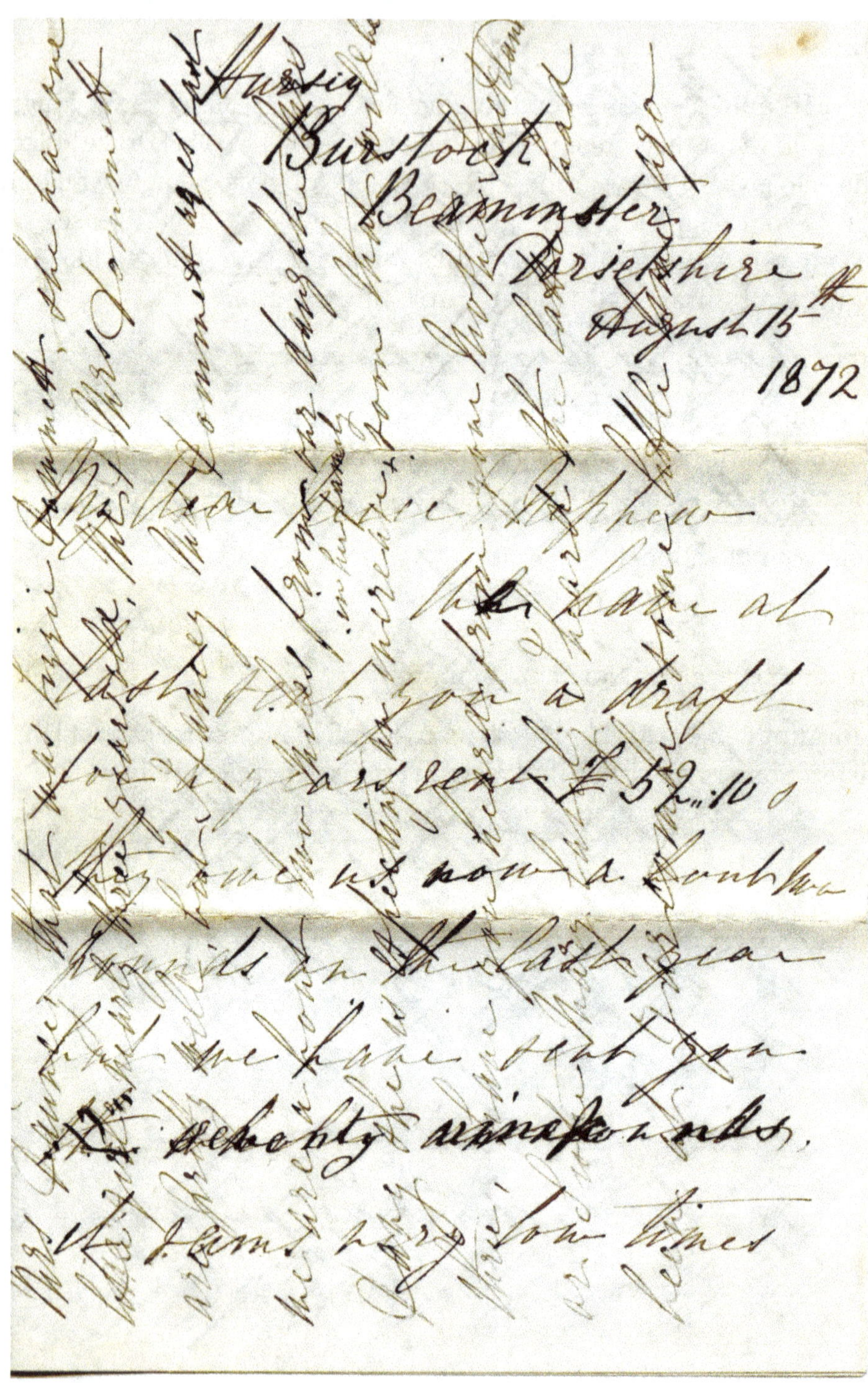

Hursey
Burstock
Beaminster
Dorsetshire
August 15th
1872

My dear Niece & Nephew

We have at last sent you a draft for 2 years rent £52..10s they owe us now a [illegible] pounds in the last year [illegible] we have sent you [illegible] seventy [illegible]. It seems very low times

Letter Number 65, Page 2

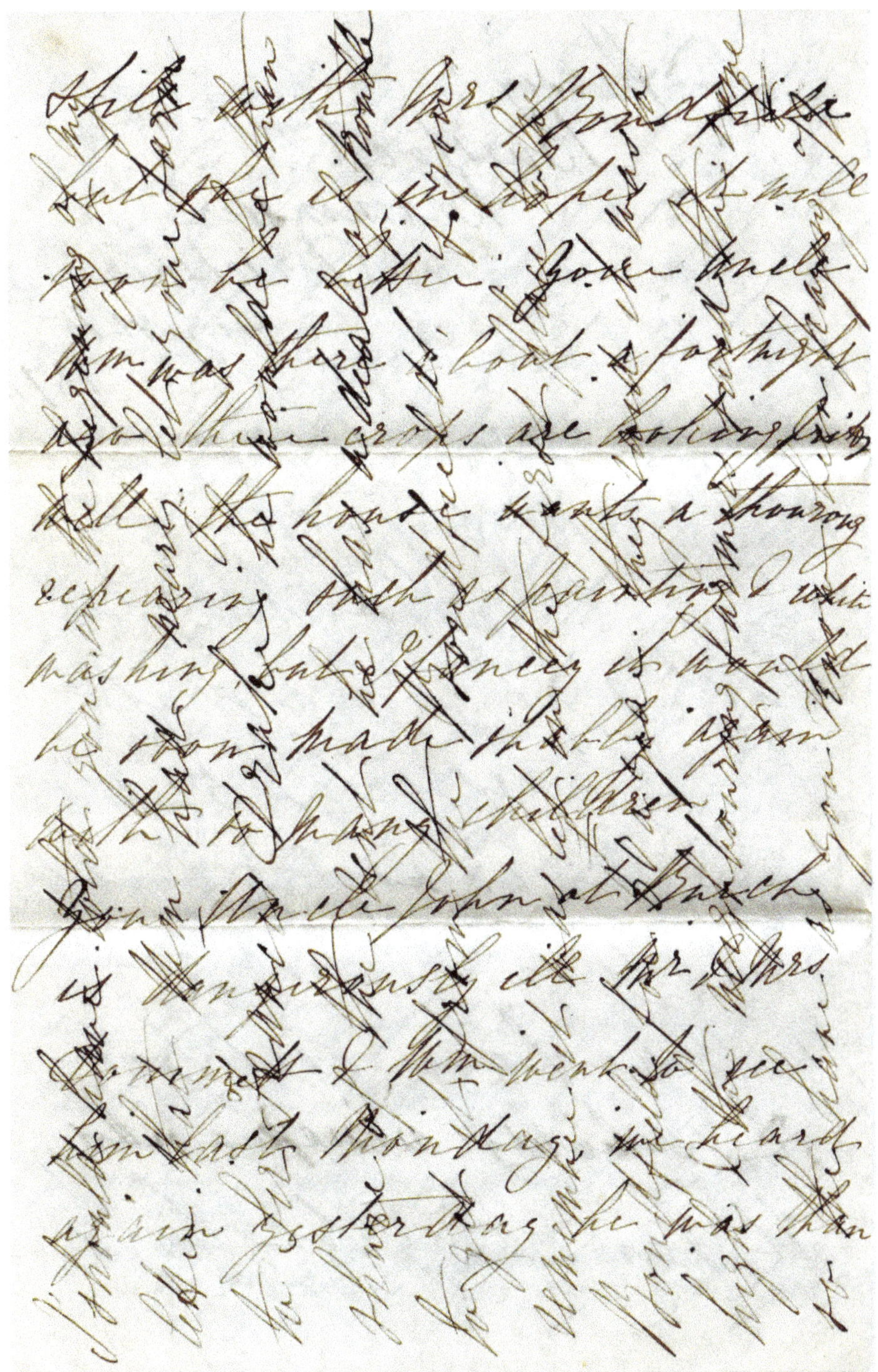

still with Mrs [illegible]
but [illegible] it is [illegible] hoped she will
soon be better. Your Uncle
Wm was here about a fortnight
ago their crops are looking pretty
well the house wants a thorough
repairing such as painting & white
washing, but I fancy it would
be soon made shabby again
with so many children
Your Uncle John at [illegible]
is dangerously ill Mr & Mrs
[illegible] & Wm went to see
him last Monday, we heard
again yesterday he was then

Letter Number 65, Page 3

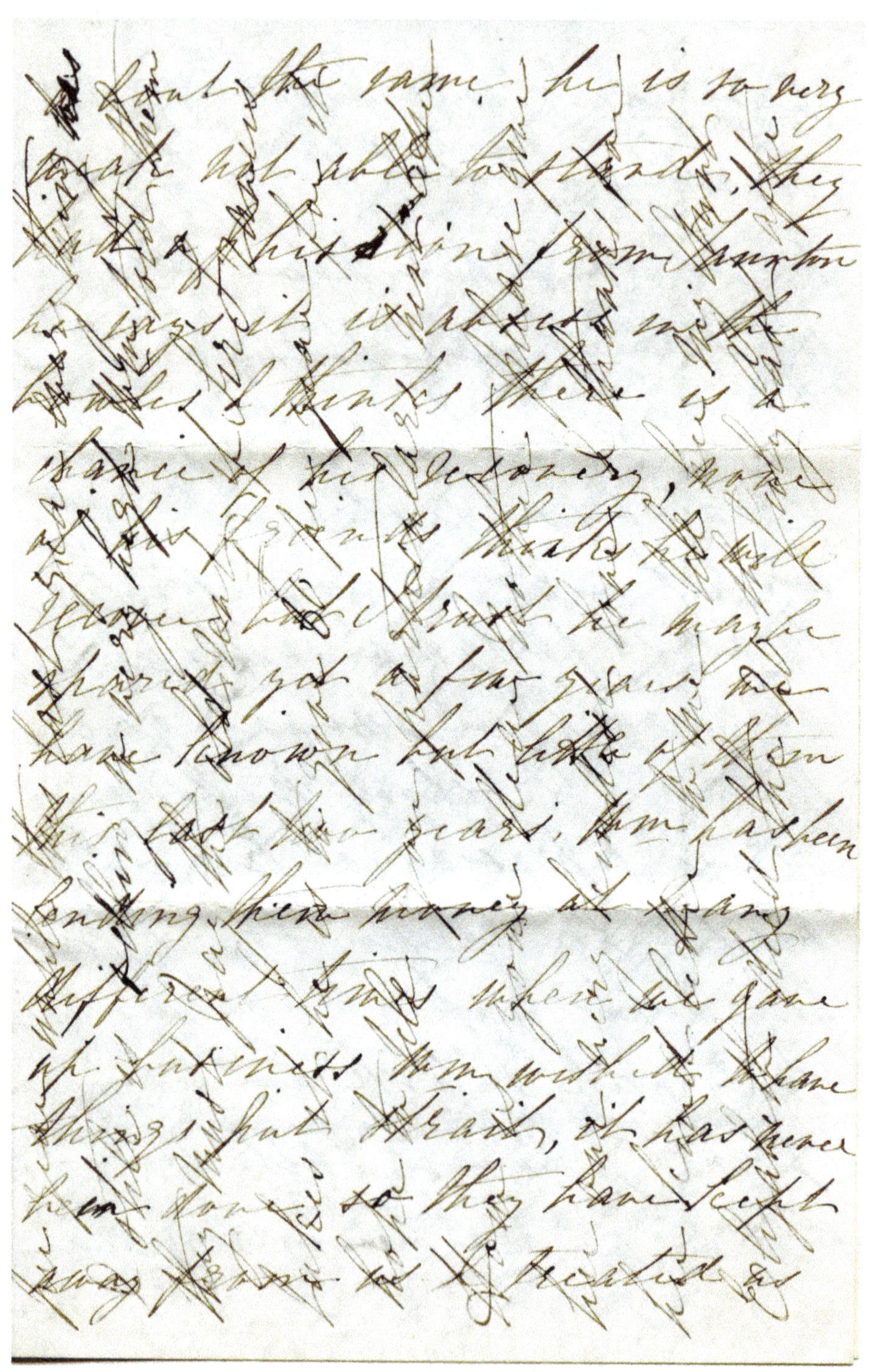

[illegible] the same, he is so very
weak not able to stand, they
had a physician from Taunton
he says it is [illegible] with the
bowels & thinks there is a
chance of his recovery, none
of his friends thinks he will
recover but it must be maybe
spared yet a few years, we
have known but little of them
this last two years, Tom has been
lending there money at many
different times when he gave
up business [illegible] to have
things put straight, it has never
been done so they have kept
away [illegible] [illegible] as

Letter Number 65, Page 4

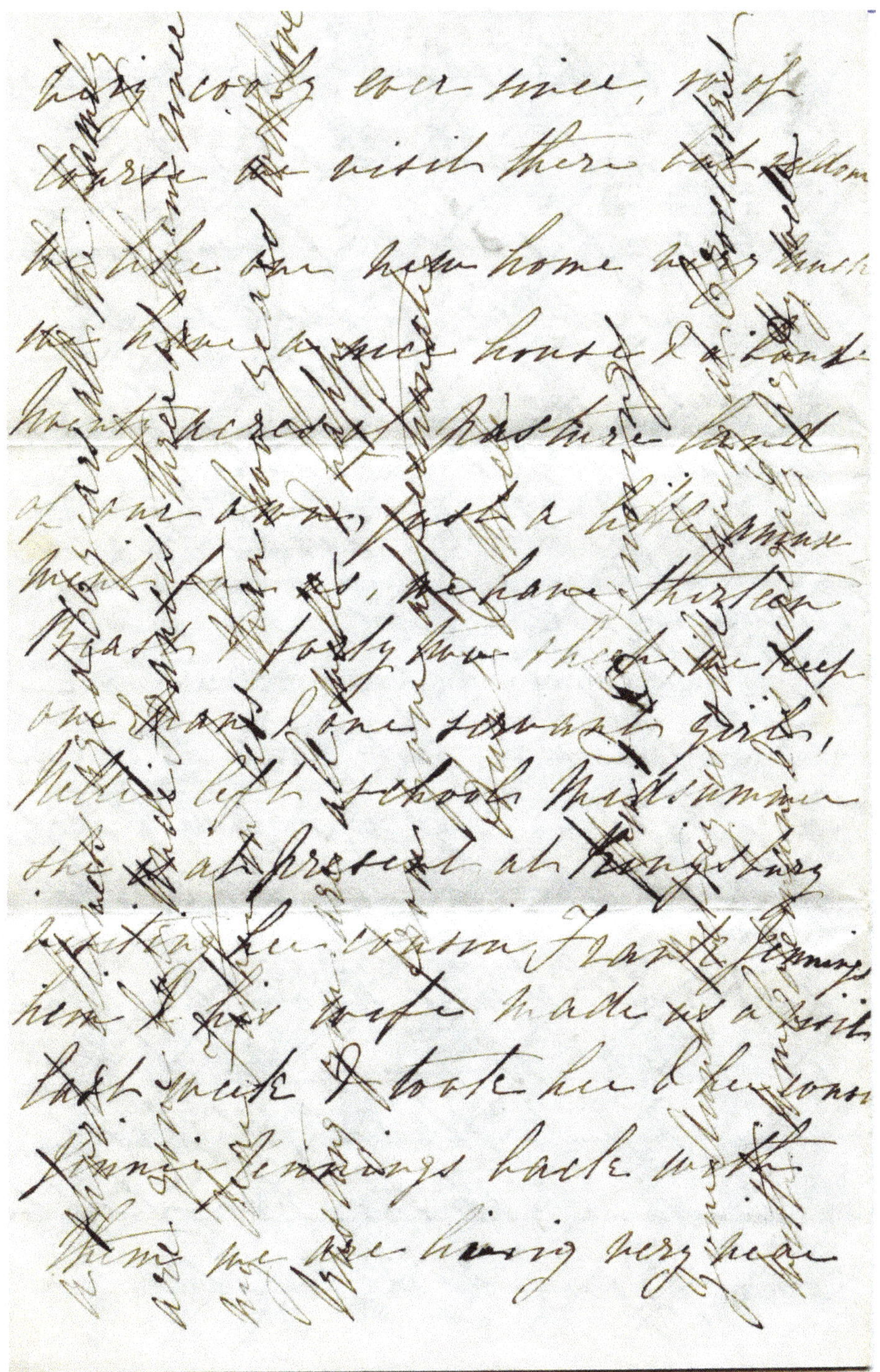
very cosy ever since, so of
course we visit there but seldom
We like our new home very much
we have a nice house & a hand-
some [illegible] acres of pasture land
of our own, just a little more
[illegible], we have thirteen
[illegible] & forty two [illegible] we keep
one man & one servant girl,
Nellie left school Midsummer
she is at present at [illegible]
[illegible] her cousin, Frank Jennings
here & his wife made us a visit
last week & took her & her cousin
Jennie Jennings back with
them we are having very near

Letter Number 65, Envelope Front

Letter Number 65, Envelope Back

Letter Number 66

Date: 8 September 1872
Writer: Thomas & Elizabeth Stickland Pipe
Recipient: William & Elizabeth Coleman Jennings
Sent from: Waupaca, Waupaca County, Wisconsin, USA
Sent to: Hursey, Burstock, Beaminster, Dorsetshire County, England

Key Ideas

- Thomas and Elizabeth Stickland Pipe acknowledge the receipt of William and Elizabeth Coleman Jennings' letter and the rent money.
- The Pipes are happy to hear the Jennings are feeling better.
- The Pipes are sorry to hear about Uncle John Jennings' poor health. Thomas would like to see him once more to thank him for his friendship.
- Thomas remarks that he and Elizabeth Stickland Pipe would like to visit England next summer to see family and friends while they are still living.
- Thomas Pipe gives an account of his children: John Stickland, Tom, and Frank have all reached the age of majority. Mary Elizabeth is almost 19, William is almost 17. Florence is 14, Effie is 10.
- Thomas Pipe states that he does not hear from the Stickland family. He supposes they are angry with him about something. He does wish them well.
- Thomas Pipe will dispose of all his land in Waupaca this fall, if possible.
- Thomas Pipe states William is about to rent Pithayne Farm to Sir Drake. He supposes he will not want to return and live there.
- Thomas Pipe asks to be forgiven for his handwriting. He says he has rheumatism.

Waupaca, Sep 8th, 1872

My dear Uncle and Aunt [William and Elizabeth Coleman Jennings]

It is with pleasure that I write to acknowledge the receipt of your kind letter containing the draft for £52 10s 0d the amount of the last year's rent. We was very much pleased to hear that you are all well and so comfortable in your new home. Aat the same time so sorry to hear of poor Uncle John's [Jennings] sickness. I do hope that he might be spared a few years yet to come. I so much want to see him once more to thank him for the kindness that I have received from him. May the Lord bless him if I have not the opportunity to thank him, should my present ?? work favourable this fall

I might perhaps make you all a visit the coming summer, in company with my wife. We both feel that if we ever do make England a visit now is the time, whilst there is so many of our dear friends left alive. I have never seen my wife so anxious as she has been this summer to return to England. Our family is gotten pretty well grown up. The three oldest boys [John Stickland, Tom, and Frank] are just now of age. Mary Elizabeth is almost 19. William [Edwin] my eldest is almost 17, Florence 14, Effie is in her 10 year but she is a little thing for the age. We do not hear a word from the Stickland family and have not for some years past. I suppose that they are all angry with us for something, but we are not with them, and one wishes all that they are doing well. I should like

to get Mr. John Stickland's address when you write again as I suppose you have it by you. Mother [Charlotte Jennings Pipe Pillar] has been at Oshkosh for the last two months. I was down last week after getting your letter. I did not see Mother [Charlotte Jennings Pipe Pillar] as she was out in the country on a visit. I think she is taking more enjoyment now than for the last 25 years. She has her two homes to go to which she pleases and when she pleases, with lots of acquaintances to visit with. She finally makes her home with us through the winter and a month or two in the summer. I suppose that she will be gotten around again with cold weather. A great many of our English acquaintance has been home this summer and their appearance indicates that they enjoyed themselves, which they say they did. I am about to dispose of all my property in Waupaca this fall, if it is possible. Then I think of going to farming the balance of my life somewhere, but I do not know where it will be yet. You say that you are about to let [rent] Pithayne [Farm] to Sir Drayton Drake. I suppose that that is all right, for I do not think it could be a place that I should want to live. It is not enough of it I think. When you write tell me what amount of stock it will or ought to carry. Please to give our kindest respects to all our uncles and aunt and to all our cousins, and accept some yourselves.

From your affectionate nephew and niece

Thomas and E [Elizabeth] Pipe

P.S. Please excuse all blunders and mistakes as I am suffering very much with the rheumatism and have for the last few months

Letter Number 66, Page 1

Waupace Sept 8th 1872

My Dear Uncle & Aunt

It is with ~~pleasure~~ pleasure that I wright to acknowledge the receipt of your kind letter containing the draft for 52..10..00 the amt of the last years rent, We was very much pleased to hear that you are all well and so comfortable in your new home, at the same time so sorry to hear of poor Uncle John's sickness I do hope that he might ~~that he might~~ be spared a few years yet to live, I so much want to see him once more to thank him for the kindness that I have recd from him, May the Lord Bless him if I have not the opportunity to thank him, Should my present plans work favorable this fall

Letter Number 66, Page 2

I Might perhaps Make you
all a visit the coming Sumer
in company with My Wife.
We both feel that if we ever do
make England a visit now is the
time whilst there is so Many
of our dear friends yet alive
I have never seen My Wife so anctious
as She has been this Sumer to Return
to England, Our family is getten a
prety well groon up, the three Oldest
boys are just now of age, Mary
Elizabeth is almost 19 William
My Oldest is almost 17 Florance
14 Effie is in her 10 year but
She is a little thing for her age
We do not hear a word from the
Strickland family and have not
for som years past I sopose
that they are all angery with us
for somthing, but we are not with
them, and our wishes are that they
are doing well, I Should like

Letter Number 66, Page 3

To get Mrs John Strickland
Adress when you wright again
as I supose you have it by your
Mother shes ~~been~~ been at Oshkosh
for the last two Months, I was
down last weke after geting your
letter I did not see Mother as
She was out in the Country on
a Visit, I think She is taken
more injoyment now then for the
last 25 years, She has her two
homes, to go to which she plese
and when She plese, with lots of
of aquaintence to visit with
She jenerly makes her home with
us through the winter and a
Month or two in the Summer
I supose that She will be getin
around again with cold wether
A great Meney of our English
aquaintance has been home this
Summer and there aperance,

Letter Number 66, Page 4

Indicate that they injured
them selves, which they say they did
I am about to dispose of all my property
in Wanfleet this fall if it is
possible, Then I think of goin
to farming the ballance of my life
somewhere that I do not know where
it will be yet, You say that you
are about to let Pitmayne to Sir
Drayton Drake I suppose that that
is all right for I do not think
it would be a place that I should want
to live, It is not a rough of it I think
when you wright tell me what amt of
stock it will be ought to [illegible] —
Please to give our kindest respects to
all our Uncles and Aunt also to all our
Cousins, and accept some yourselves From your Affct Nephew & Niece
Thos & E. Pipe
P.S. please excuse all blunders and
mistakes as I am suffering very much
with the Rumatism and have for the last
three months

Letter Number 67

Date: circa December 1872
Writer: William & Elizabeth Coleman Jennings
Recipient: Thomas Pipe
Sent from: Hursey, Burstock, Beaminster, Dorsetshire County, England
Sent to: Waupaca, Waupaca County, Wisconsin, USA

Key Ideas

- Elizabeth Coleman Jennings' daughter, Mrs. Mary Ann Jennings Davy, has died on September 30, 1872.
- Elizabeth Coleman Jennings and William Jennings have been at Horn Park, Beaminster, Dorset, with Mr. William Clement Davy, husband of the late Mary Ann Jennings Davy.
- Both Uncle John Jennings (December 2, 1872) and Uncle Thomas Jennings (December 12, 1872) died only 10 days apart. There was a sale yesterday at Birch Oak Farm, Membury, Devon.
- Mr. Dommett (Dommett & Canning) and George Bond are trustees for the estate.
- Elizabeth Coleman Jennings hopes that Tom Jennings' wife and children can stay in the little cottage.
- Elizabeth Coleman Jennings and William Jennings never hear anything from the Sticklands. Matthews receives John Stickland's annuity and sends it to him.

[start not included]

We should have written to you before but had I very bad bereavement has quite unfiled us. I mean the death of our darling daughter Mrs. [Mary Ann Jennings] Davy. Mrs. [Mary Ann Jennings] Dommett has told you, I think. I believe I may say she was everything you could wish in a daughter, wife, or mother. She had a devoted husband, every comfort this world could afford. We have been at Horn Park [Farm, Dorset] with Mr. [William Clement] Davy most of our time since her death, the 30th Sept. The dear children are getting along nicely. Our greatest comfort

is her end was peace. We do not intend having them long at a time. You know ere now the death of your uncles John [Jennings] and Thomas [Jennings] only ten days apart.

There was a sale at Birch [Oak Farm, Membury, Devon] yesterday, a fearful rough day. I don't know anything, how the property is left, in fact we know but little of them. Mr. Dommett [Dommett & Canning] was there. He very often goes down. Him and George Bond are the trustees.

I have not heard who is to have the farm. I suppose it will pass out of the family. It is finally considered to have been rented very cheap as farms are now rented. I hope your uncle Tom's [Jennings] wife and family will be able to remain in the little place. We were both there at the funeral. Mrs. [Tom] Jennings bears it up wonderfully. He was ill about two months, so you see we all suffer bereavements trials and afflictions in our turn How is your dear Mother [Charlotte Jennings Pipe Pillar]. I trust she is quite recovered of her late illness.

I fancy Mrs. [Mary Ann Jennings] Dommett ages fast, but still she seems pretty well with the exception of rheumatism. We never hear anything of the Stickland family. The Matthews receive John's [Stickland] annuity, sends it to him. I will endeavour to get his address. I send it to you with our kindest love to your all wishing you all a happy new year from your affectionate

Aunt and Uncle

Wm. [and] E.[Elizabeth] Jennings

Letter Number 67, Page 1

We should have written to
you before but our sad &
very sad bereavement has
quite unfitted us. I mean the
death of our darling daughter
Mrs Davy Mr Tommett has
told you I think, I believe
I may say she was every think
you could wish in a daughter
wife or Mother, she had a devoted
husband & every comfort this
world could afford, we have
been at Horn Park with Mr
Davy most of our time since
her death the 30th Sept the
dear children are getting
on nicely our greatest comfort

Letter Number 67, Page 2

is her end was peace,
we do not intend leaving
them long at a time,
you know ere now the death
of your uncles John & Thomas
only ten days apart,
There was a sale at Barch
yesterday, a fearfull rough
day, I dond know anything
how the property is left
in fact we know but little
of them, Mr Commett was
there, he very often goes
down, him & George Bond
are the trust,

Letter Number 67, Page 3

I have not heard who is to
have the Farm suppose it
will pass out of the family
it is generally considered to have
been rented very cheap as farms
are now rented, I hope your
Uncle Toms wife & family will
be able to remain in their
little place, we were both
there at the funeral Mrs Jennings
bears it up wonderfully, he was
ill about two months,
so you see we all suffer bereavements trials & afflictions in
our turn, how is your dear
Mother I trust she is quite
recovered of her late illness

Letter Number 67, Page 4

I fancy Mrs Commett ages
fast but still she seems
pretty well with the exception
of Rheumatism,
we never hear any thing of
the Strickland family the
Mathews's receive Johns
annuity sends it to him
I will endeavour to get his
address & send it to you
with our kindest love
to you all wishing you
all a happy new year
from your affectionate
Aunt & Uncle
Wm E Jennings

Letter Number 67, Envelope Front

Letter Number 67, Envelope Back

Letter Number 68

Date: 22 May 1874
Writer: W. Dommett
Recipient: Elizabeth Stickland Pipe
Sent from: Chard, Somerset County, England
Sent to: Waupaca, Waupaca County, Wisconsin, USA

Key Ideas

- Dommett requests that Elizabeth Stickland Pipe sign the enclosed lease with Sir Francis Drake. If possible, Elizabeth should have the lease notarized. (See Appendix G.)
- Dommett also encloses papers for her children to sign in case of her death. The paper assigns William Jennings liability in case of Elizabeth's death.
- Dommett estimates a sale price of at least £2500.

Chard, May 22, 1874

Dear Madam

It is necessary that you should sign the accompanying paper to confirm the lease Mr. Jennings has agreed to make to Mr. Francis Drake. Please do so and return it to us as soon as you can. If you will sign it in the presence of a Justice of the Peace, it will be enough instead of doing to Notary.

So many of your children as are of age might also sign the enclosed paper. Mr. Jennings has guaranteed ten years certain but you can only lease so long as you live. The children should therefore sign the confirmation to return Mr. Jenning's liability in case of your death. There is no doubt that

the property will sell well but I cannot say for how much as in a place like Yarcombe there is none to be competition but should fetch at least £2,500.

Please send these papers back to me as soon as possible.

Yours truly

W. Dommett

For Dommett & Canning

Mrs. Pipe

Letter Number 68, Page 1

Chard May 22-1874

Dear Madam

It is necessary that you should sign the accompanying paper to confirm the Lease Mr Jennings has agreed to make to Mr Francis Drake - please do so & return it to us as soon as you can - if you will sign it in the presence of a Justice of the peace it will be enough instead of going to Notary -

So many of your children as are of age might also sign the enclosed paper - Mr Jennings has guaranteed ten years certain but you can only Lease so long as you live the Children should therefore sign the confirmation to relieve Mr Jennings ~~from~~ liability in case of your death - there is no doubt that

Letter Number 68, Page 2

the property will sell well but I cannot say for how much as in a place like Yarcombe there is sure to be competition and should fetch at least £2500.

Please send these papers back as soon as possible.

Yrs Truly

H Donnell

for W H Manning

Mrs Pipe

Letter Number 69

Date: 30 May 1874
Writer: Thomas Pipe
Recipient: Dommett & Canning
Sent from: Waupaca, Waupaca County, Wisconsin, USA
Sent to: Chard, Somerset County, England

Key Ideas

- Thomas Pipe wrote a letter last February 1. He has not heard back from the firm.
- Thomas Pipe enclosed certificates of baptisms for Frank and Mary Elizabeth Pipe. John Stickland and Tom Pipe were baptized in England.
- Thomas and Elizabeth Stickland Pipe intended to travel to England, but now they defer the trip until November.

Childrens baptism May 30th 1874 [Written later by a descendant.]

Waupaca, May 30th, 1874

Messrs. Dommett and Canning

Solicitors Chard

Dear Sirs

As I wrote you a letter on the 1st February last and have received no reply from you in any way, I thought I would drop you a line again fearing that there might have been a letter lost. In my letter I enclosed to you the certificates of baptism of the two youngest children Frank and Mary Elizabeth, the two older boys being baptised in England. I concluded that you might perhaps procure the certificates in less time and with less expense that what I could. It was our intention to have started for England about this time but

shall have to defer it now until the latter part of November next.

Letter Number 69, Page 1

Waupaca May 30th 1874

Messers Sommett & Canning
Solicitors Chard
Dear Sirs

As I wrote you a letter on the 1st day of February last, and have received no reply from you in any way, I thought I would drop you a line again fearing that there might have been a letter lost, In my letter I inclosed to you the certificates of baptisem of the two youngest Children Frank & Mary Elizabeth the two older Boys been baptised in England I concluded that you might perhaps procure the certificates in less time and with less expence then what I could I was our intention to have started for England about this time but

Letter Number 69, Page 2

Shall have to defer it now until
the latter part of November next

Anderson Dayton
May, 30, 1874

Letter Number 70

Date: November 1874
[envelope stamped Chard 15 January 1875]
Writer: William & Elizabeth Coleman Jennings
Recipient: Thomas & Elizabeth Stickland Pipe
Sent from: Hursey, Burstock, Beaminster, Dorset County, England
Sent to: Waupaca, Waupaca County, Wisconsin, USA

Key Ideas

- William Jennings told Thomas Pipe that he saw Mr. Dommett of Dommett & Canning, who wants papers signed and sent back to him. (See Appendix G.)
- William Jennings does not think anyone but Sir Frances Drake will buy the property. (See Appendix D.)
- Elizabeth Coleman Jennings' mother turned 75 on November 6, 1874.

Hursey, Nov 9th, 1874

Broadwindsor

Dear Thomas

I saw Mr. Dommett on Wednesday. He wished one to write to you for the papers he sent, to be signed as directed by him and returned to him without delay. It will make no difference in selling the property. I don't think anyone will buy it only Sir Francis Drake. I should wish you to enquire something about it as soon as you can

as I understand you are home for that purpose. I should recommend you to send the papers or he will be writing to you again and they don't write without being paid.

Please to acknowledge the last half year's rent that I sent and I will send the other.

From your affectionate

Uncle

Wm. Jennings

[Crosshatched]

My dear Mrs. Pipe

I thought I must just say a few words to you to inquire how you all are. I hope well and happy as it leaves us at present. My dear little grandchildren are growing nicely. Nellie [Ellen] stays with them most of the time. She is now away writing. She is far from strong. Cousin Pollie Jennings received a long letter from Wm. [Jennings] Pipe last Wednesday. He has two sons. He seems to write very cheerful. How is dear Mrs. [Charlotte Jennings Pipe] Pillar? Please give my love to her. My mother is still living very strong, here and there about with her children. On the 6th of this month she was 75, older than Mrs. [Charlotte Jennings Pipe] Pillar

[other way]

I have sent you the paper *Bridport* for you to see the account of poor Mr. [William] Dauncey that is her late husband and of your cousin E. [Elizabeth] Dommett after the sale she will go home with her parents again. She has one dear little girl who will live there with her. Now I must wish you goodbye with love to you all.

From your loving

Aunt E. J. [Elizabeth Coleman Jennings]

Letter Number 70, Page 1

Hursey Novr 9th 1874
Broadwinsor

Old Thomas
I saw Mr Dommett
on Wednesday he wished me
to write to you for the papers
be sent, to be signed as directed
by him
+ and returned to him without
delay, it will make no difference
in selling the property I don't
think any one will by it unless
Sir Francis Drake I should
wish you to enquire something
about it as soon as you can

Letter Number 70, Page 2

as I understand your are coming home
for that purpose, I should
recommend you to send the
~~th~~ papers or he will be writing
to you again and they don't
write without been paid

Please to acknoledge the
last half years rent that
I sent and I will send
the other

From your affectionate
Uncle
Wm Jennings

Letter Number 70, Page 3

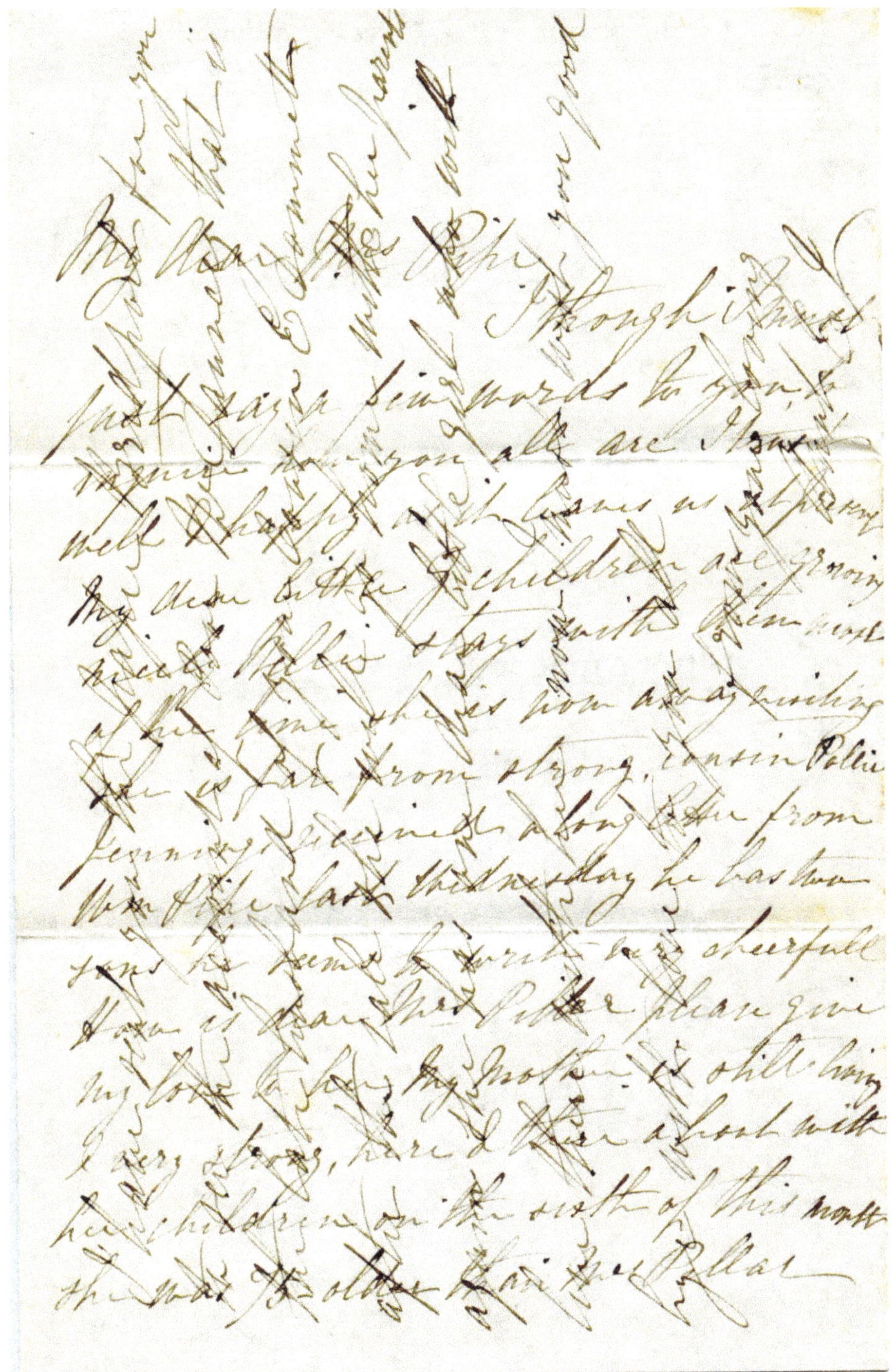

My dear Mrs Pipe,
Though it must [illegible]
just say a few words to you, to
enquire how you all are. I am
well & happy [illegible]
My dear little children are growing
nicely. Willie stays with them most
of the time [illegible] visiting
she is far from strong. Cousin Pollie
Jennings received a long letter from
Wm Pipe last Wednesday he has two
sons he seems to write very cheerfull
[illegible] Pipe please give
my love to [illegible] my mother & [illegible]
[illegible] very strong, [illegible] school with
her children on the sixth of this month
[illegible] other [illegible] Pollar

Letter Number 70, Envelope Front

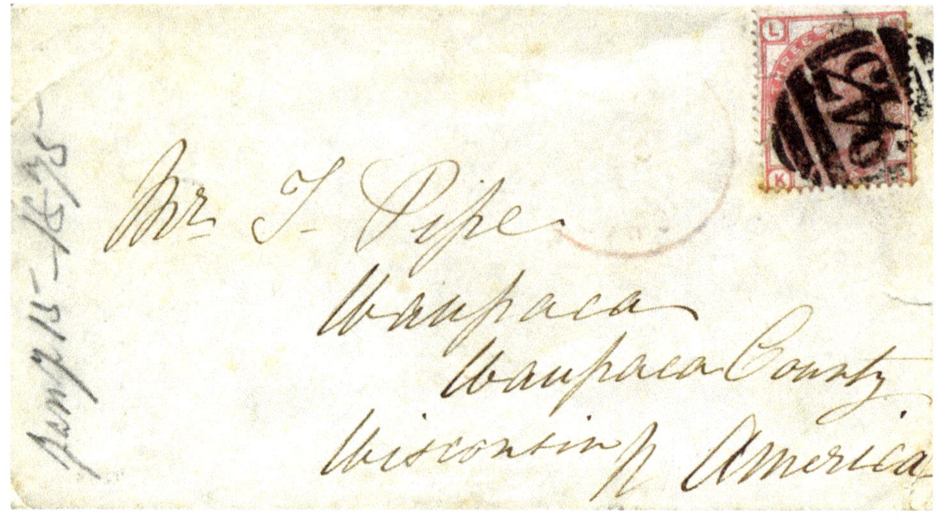

Letter Number 70, Envelope Front

Letter Number 71

Date: 17 November 1874
Writer: Dommett & Canning
Recipient: Elizabeth Stickland Pipe
Sent from: Chard, Somerset County, England
Sent to: Waupaca, Waupaca County, Wisconsin, USA

Key Ideas

- Dommett & Canning state Elizabeth Stickland Pipe has not acknowledged their letter of May 22, 1874.
- Mr. Henry Mathews appears to think Elizabeth desires the law firm to take steps to sell the estate. However, the firm is not authorized until her youngest child is of age.
- Dommett & Canning request that Elizabeth ask her brother John Stickland and Henry Matthews to go over the estate to determine how the estate should be divided for the sale.
- Dommett & Canning advise the pieces of land away from Pithayne Farm should be sold separately.
- Dommett & Canning will analyze how to handle the annuities payable out of the property. They say they will do their best for Elizabeth (Stickland Pipe). They will not do anything without the advice of John Stickland and Henry Matthews.
- Dommett & Canning do not think Sir Francis Drake will bid on the property because of his illness. (See Wellcome Library, Ticehurst House Hospital Papers, Patient List b29146719; Patient Certificates and Notices, MS6245/6326/6326/6327/120 .)

Chard, Nov 17, 1874

Dear Madam

We send you copy of a letter that we wrote to you on the 22nd day of May 1874 to which we have been waiting for a reply. Mr. Henry Matthews appears to think that you expected us to take some steps about the sale of the estate but we did not feel authorised to do so without first hearing from you again nor until your youngest child [Mary Elizabeth Pipe] was of age.

If it is now your wish that we should do so, we will ask your brother John [Stickland] and Mr. Matthews to go over the

estate with us and determine in how many lots it shall be sold. The pieces of land that lie away from the main bulk of Pithayne [Farm] should be sold separately. We will arrange what best to be done as to the annuities payable out of the property and do the best for you as if you were here and not act in anything without the advice of John [Stickland] and Henry Matthews, unless you wish us.

Yours truly

Dommett & Canning

Sir Francis Drake being out of his mind [on March 4, 1873, admitted to Ticehurst Asylum, Sussex, England] we fear the Drake family will not bid.

Mrs. Pipe

Letter Number 71, Page 1

Chard Nov 17. 1874

Dear Madam -

We send you copy of a letter that we wrote you on the 22nd day of May 1874. to which we have been waiting for a reply. Mr Henry Matthews appears to think that you expected us to take some steps about the Sale of the Estate but we did not feel authorized to do so without first hearing from you again nor until your youngest child was of age

If it is now your wish that we should do so we will ask your Brother John and Mr W Matthews to go over the

Letter Number 71, Page 2

Estate with us and determine in how many
Lots it shall be sold. The pieces of Land
that lie away from the main bulk of Pitkayne
should be sold separately - we will arrange
what had best be done as to the Annuities
payable out of the property and do the best
for you as if you were here and not act in
any thing without the advice of John and
Henry Matthews unless you wish us -

Yrs truly
Bennett Harmins

Mrs Pope

Sir Francis Drake being out of his
mind we fear the Drake family will not bid -

Letter Number 71, Envelope Front

Letter Number 71, Envelope Back

Letter Number 72

Date: 8 December 1874
Writer: H. Dommett
Recipient: Elizabeth Stickland Pipe
Sent from: Chard, Somerset County, England
Sent to: Waupaca, Waupaca County, Wisconsin, USA

Key Ideas

- Dommett & Canning sent a parcel to Greece, New York. They did not know anything about Pithayne Farm, Yarcombe, Devon, except what William Jennings has told them.
- William Jennings always told Dommett & Canning that Elizabeth Stickland Pipe gave him (William Jennings) the rent.
- The Pithayne Farm lease was £85 for rent and £15 for game. The solicitors believed it was all with Elizabeth Stickland Pipe's approval.
- The solicitors do not believe the Drakes will buy Pithayne Farm.
- The solicitors did not know that John Valentine Pipe had died at sea in 1854. Either they were not told, or they do not remember.

Dommett & Canning, Solicitors

Chard, Somerset
December 8, 1875

Dear Madam

We have today received your letter and regret that our former parcel should have been directed to Greece [Monroe County, New York]. We have never had anything to do with Pithayne [Farm, Yarcombe, Devon] except under Mr. [William] Jennings instructions, and we thought he was acting for you and fully on your behalf and with your consent and we never knew the terms except what he told us upon which he acted.

He [William Jennings] always told us you gave

him the rent of the Game for his trouble a [blank] in making Mr. Francis Drake's lease he put down the game at £15 a year and the rent at £85 and not knowing but that it was all with your approval we prepared the lease. Before you get this, you will have heard from us and will see that we have acted according to your wishes. John [Stickland] won't sell his annuity, but we can sell the estate subject to that. Mr. Dommett saw him at Mrs. Matthews' funeral and talked it over. She has promised when we have heard from you to come up and meet us on the

farm and arrange how to make the best of it. You will have heard from our letter the state of the Drake's health. We don't expect he or Lady Drake will buy but the person who comes next to the property will no doubt bid for it and if he does not there will be plenty of others who will. You are quite right in saying it would have been better if no lease had been granted if you thought of selling when the children [John Stickland, Tom, Frank, and Mary Elizabeth Pipe] became of age but that cannot be helped now and it could not have been done whilst the children [John Stickland, Tom, Frank, and Mary Elizabeth Pipe] were underage nor whilst your

husband lived. We had forgotten or else we never heard of your first husband's [John Valentine Pipe] death [in 1854].

If you send the papers back (both lots we sent you) we will at once make all necessary arrangements for the sale and send you one of the hand bills.

It is a stormy time for you to come over and if you don't you may rely upon everything possible being done, but you can well imagine it would be pleasanter for us to have you here to cancel if things go crop [crop up]. I think all the other points are answered in our letter sent out 5 weeks ago.

Your very best for [ult naming?]

H. Dommett
Mrs. Pipe
Waupaca
Wisconsin
America

Letter Number 72, Page 1

DOMMETT & CANNING,
SOLICITORS.

Chard. Somerset.

December 8 1874

Dear Madam

We have today received
your letter and regret that our
former parcel should have been
directed to Greece. We have
never had any thing to do with
Pitkayne except under Mr Jennings
instructions and we thought he
was acting for you and fully
on your behalf and with your
consent and we never knew
the terms except what he told
us upon which he acted.
He always told us you gave

Letter Number 72, Page 2

him the Rent of the Game for
his trouble a in making Sir
Francis Drakes Lease he put down
the game at £15 a year and
the Rent at £85 and not knowing
but that it was all with your
approval we so prepared the
Lease. before you get this you
will have heard from us and
will see that we have acted
according to your wishes. John
wont sell his Annuity but we
can sell the Estate subject to
that. Mr Dommett saw him at
Mr Matthews's funeral & talked
it over he has promised when
we have heard from you to
come up and meet us on the

Letter Number 72, Page 3

farm and arrange how to make
the best of it - you will have
heard from our letter the state
of Sir J Drakes health we dont
expect he or Lady Drake will
buy but the person who comes
next to the property will no
doubt bid for it and if he
does not there will be plenty
of others who will - You are
quite right in saying it would
have been better if no lease
had been granted if you thought
of selling when the children became
of age but that cannot be helped
now & it could not have been
done whilst the children were
under age nor whilst you

Letter Number 72, Page 4

Husband lived - we had
forgotten or else we never heard
of your first-Husbands death

If you send the papers back
(both lots we sent you) we will
at once make all necessary
arrangements for the Sale and
send you one of the Handbills -

It is a stormy time for you to
come over but if you dont you may
rely upon every thing possible being
done but you can well imagine
it would be pleasanter for us
to have you here to consult as
things go crop. I think all the
other points are answered in our
letter sent out 3 weeks ago -

Yrs very truly
for self & Company
H Connell

Mr Pipe
Waupaca
Wisconsin America

Letter Number 72, Envelope Front

Letter Number 72, Envelope Front

Chapter 8

Lanark, Portage County, Wisconsin
1875 - 1880

Chapter 8 includes letters dated 1875 to 1880 while Thomas and Elizabeth Stickland Pipe and their children are living in The Pipe House in the town of Lanark, Portage County, Wisconsin. This chapter focuses on Thomas and Elizabeth Stickland Pipe's seven-month trip home to England to visit family and friends and settle family business. Nine letters are written by family and friends in Waupaca, Neenah, and Woodville, Wisconsin, and Chicago, Illinois. These letters highlight local news, including the "biggest of the biggest" fires in Oshkosh, Wisconsin, in April 1875. Mary Stickland writes three letters to her sister, Elizabeth Stickland Pipe, while the Pipes are in England. John Stickland's daughter Anna writes to Thomas and Elizabeth Stickland Pipe with family news. Two letters are from William Jennings Pipe, who discusses family and friends in Australia. One letter is from cousins in Dorset after the Pipes return from their trip. Another is from a friend from Norfolk County in England. Five letters involve business matters in England and in Wisconsin. Chapter 8 ends with the death of Thomas Pipe in November 1880.

Letter Number 73

Date: 22 March [1875]
Writer: Giles Rendell
Recipient: Thomas Pipe
Sent from: 103 West Madison St., Chicago,
Cook County, Illinois, USA
Sent to: Pipe House, Lanark, Portage County, Wisconsin, USA
[Sheridan, Waupaca County, Wisconsin,
USA Post Office]

Key Ideas

- Giles Rendell cannot visit this spring. He will possibly be able to visit this fall.
- He asks to be remembered by Francis Gillingham.
- Giles Rendell mentions that he has land in the Waupaca area.
- He wonders when the Pipes will go to England. The letter was likely written in 1875 because the Pipes leave for England in April 1875.

---

103 West Madison St.

Chicago, March 22nd, [1875]

Mr Pipe

Dear Sir

I regret that I shall not be able to pay you a visit this spring as I anticipated. I do not see how I can get away from my business long enough not having any one to leave in charge, although I feel very anxious to see my land and to know its value, under existing circumstances I must defer it until towards the fall or such time when my wife is sufficiently recovered to superintend in the business during my absence. I should enjoy the trip very much and

hope when I come to be able to spend a few days amongst you. When do you intend leaving for England. Do not fail to call on us. We shall be very pleased to have you and Mrs. Pipe spend a few days with us. My wife is getting along nicely now, she has not been out yet, but if the weather continues fine, I am going to take her for a drive next Sunday.

Remember us kindly to Mr. [Francis] Gillingham. Hope they are all well, also yourself and family.

And with our kind regards

I remain

Respectfully Yours

Giles Rendell

Excuse haste

Letter Number 73, Page 1

103 West Madison St
Chicago. Mar. 22nd

Mr. Pipe,
Dear Sir,
I regret that I shall not be able to pay you a visit this spring as I anticipated. I do not see how I can get away from my business long enough not having any one to leave in charge, altho. I feel very anxious to see my land and to know its value, under existing circumstances. I must defer it until towards the fall, or such time when my wife is sufficiently recovered to superintend in the business during my absence. I should enjoy the trip very much, and

Letter Number 73, Page 2

hope when I come to be able to
spend a few days amongst you.
When do you intend leaving for
England. do not fail to call on
us, we shall be very pleased to
have you and Mrs Pipe spend
a few days with us. — My wife is
getting along nicely now, she has
not been out yet, but if the weather
Continues fine I am going to
take her for a drive next Sunday.
Remember us kindly to Mr
Gillingham, hope they are all
well, also yourself and family
and with our kind regards

I Remain

Respectfully Yours
Giles Rendell

Excuse Haste

Letter Number 74

Date: 9 April 1875
Writer: H.C. Mead
Recipient: Charles Francklyn, Esq.
Sent from: Exchange and Savings Bank,
Waupaca, Waupaca County, Wisconsin, USA
Sent to: 111 Broadway, New York, New York, USA

Key Ideas

- The letter introduces Thomas Pipe to the Great Cunard Lines. H.C. Mead of the Exchange and Savings Bank of Waupaca has written to the Great Cunard Lines in New York regarding cabin tickets for Thomas and Elizabeth Stickland Pipe's trip to England. Thomas likely carried a copy of the letter with him and presented it upon his arrival.
- The Pipes are on their way to England.

Letter Number 74, Envelope Front

Return to
H. C. MEAD & CO.'S EXCHANGE & SAVINGS BANK,
WAUPACA, Wis ,
If not delivered within 5 days.

Chas G Francklyn Esq
Agent Cunard Line
111 Broadway
New York

Exchange and Savings Bank of Waupaca

H.C. Mead & Co Bankers

Waupaca, Wis., April 9th, 1875

Chas. G. Francklyn Esq.

Agent Cunard Line

111 Broadway

New York

Dear Sir

That Thos. Pipe the bearer of this is on his way to England and may wish to purchase tickets of you to London for his company (some half dozen) provided you can give him information that will assure him that the Cunard Line has advantages equal or better than others. We have represented you here for past two years by distributing circulars and posting but have no certain tickets. So we made this line of introduction to Mr Pipe wishing you success in selling him tickets

Respectively [or Respectfully] yours

H.C. Mead

Letter Number 74

Exchange and Savings Bank of Waupaca.

H. C. MEAD & CO., Bankers.

Waupaca, Wis., April 5th 1875

Chas. B. Francklyn Esq
Agent Cunard Line
111 Broadway N.Y.

Dear Sir—

Mr. Thos. Pope the bearer of this is on his way to England, and may wish to purchase Tickets of you to London for his company (one half dozen). Provided you can give him information that will assure him that the Cunard line has advantages equal or better than others — we have represented your line for past two years by distributing Circulars and posters, — but have no Cabin Ticket, — so we make this line of introduction to Mr. Pope, wishing you success in selling him Tickets —

Respy Yours
H. C. Mead & Co

Letter Number 75

Date: 30 April 1875
Writer: Francis Gillingham
Recipient: Thomas Pipe
Sent from: Neenah, Winnebago County, Wisconsin, USA
Sent to: Thorncombe, Dorset County, England
[envelope sent to Chard, Somerset, England]

Key Ideas

- Francis Gillingham relates events of the largest fire Oshkosh, Winnebago County, Wisconsin, has ever known. He includes a diagram and a detailed description of the damage and locations of burned down buildings.
- (The Oshkosh Public Library provides a video about the fire from their series "Librarian Learn" at https://www.youtube.com/watch?v=wWZYZBq02f4 .)
- Alma Gillingham, Francis Gillingham's daughter, returned home the previous week.
- Francis Gillingham hopes the Pipes had a good trip across the Atlantic to England.

Neenah, April 30, 1875

Friend Pipe

I am not going to wait until I hear from you as that would be too long. I am sorry to relate to you another big fire in Oshkosh the biggest of the biggest it is thought more than all the fires Oshkosh ever had put together right here. I will give you a diagram as near as possible.

You will see by diagram it took all of Main St. from where the side track crosses Main Street on the south of fire limits to 5 stores north of the Beckwith House on one side of the Harding's Store Opera house on the other east through to the lake except the Court House which is standing in the midst of the ruins alone, every bank, every printing house, every large store of any kind except what had moved up town in those new stores just built. Pages Foundry was saved, he having a hose attached to his engine kept his building wet the whole time or everything to the water's edge must have burned so that saved Jim's shop and the few remaining stores below the RR crossing, Boles Clothing store and Hutchinson Hardware is left about the RR crossing on the north of it. I mean on west side of Main St.

I went down yesterday to see it. I think it the most distressing sight I ever saw, so much property burned and all the business portion of it, with the exception of Algoma St., all the best residences in the city it seems that it can never be built up again. Oshkosh seems to be doomed any way. Some lumber firms claim to have lost 100,000 dollars, the whole loss estimated at two million. It was supposed to start from a spark in Peck & Spauldings [Spaldings] mill, a very strong west wind blowing all the time and blew it into Morgan's Mill, they were not running. The bookkeeper [Thomas Davis] runned into the mill to get the books and got burned so his flesh dropped from his bones when he came out. He only lived a few moments. One Mare got killed by the falling of the walls of Harding's Opera House, was very little property saved as the wind was so strong. The fire leaped from building to building, probably one mile all burning at one time.

Francis Gillingham's sketch of damage from the great Oshkosh fire

You can form some idea. Jem and Sam started after dinner for the shop. He stopped by Harding's Opera House and bought some trees while he was paying for them the fire bell rang. He sent Jem home with the trees. By the time Jem came back the fire had reached Main St. so as he could not get through to the shop, I tell you the people of Oshkosh Feel blue and I do not know as I can blame them. My family is well as usual, Alma [daughter] got home last week I think better than when she left. Our spring is backward, heavy frost again this morning, I have sold 45 acres of wheat this week up to Friday morning. I meant to have got through this week but have one sick horse. I hope you had a pleasant trip across the old ocean and that you and Mrs. P. [Pipe] is enjoying the balmy clime of Old England among your friends. I have written this in a hurry, as I knew you would be anxious to know the contents of the fire. No doubt you have read newspaper accounts before this. I remain your well-wisher and friend Francis Gillingham

Neenah, Wis[consin].

Letter Number 75, Page 1

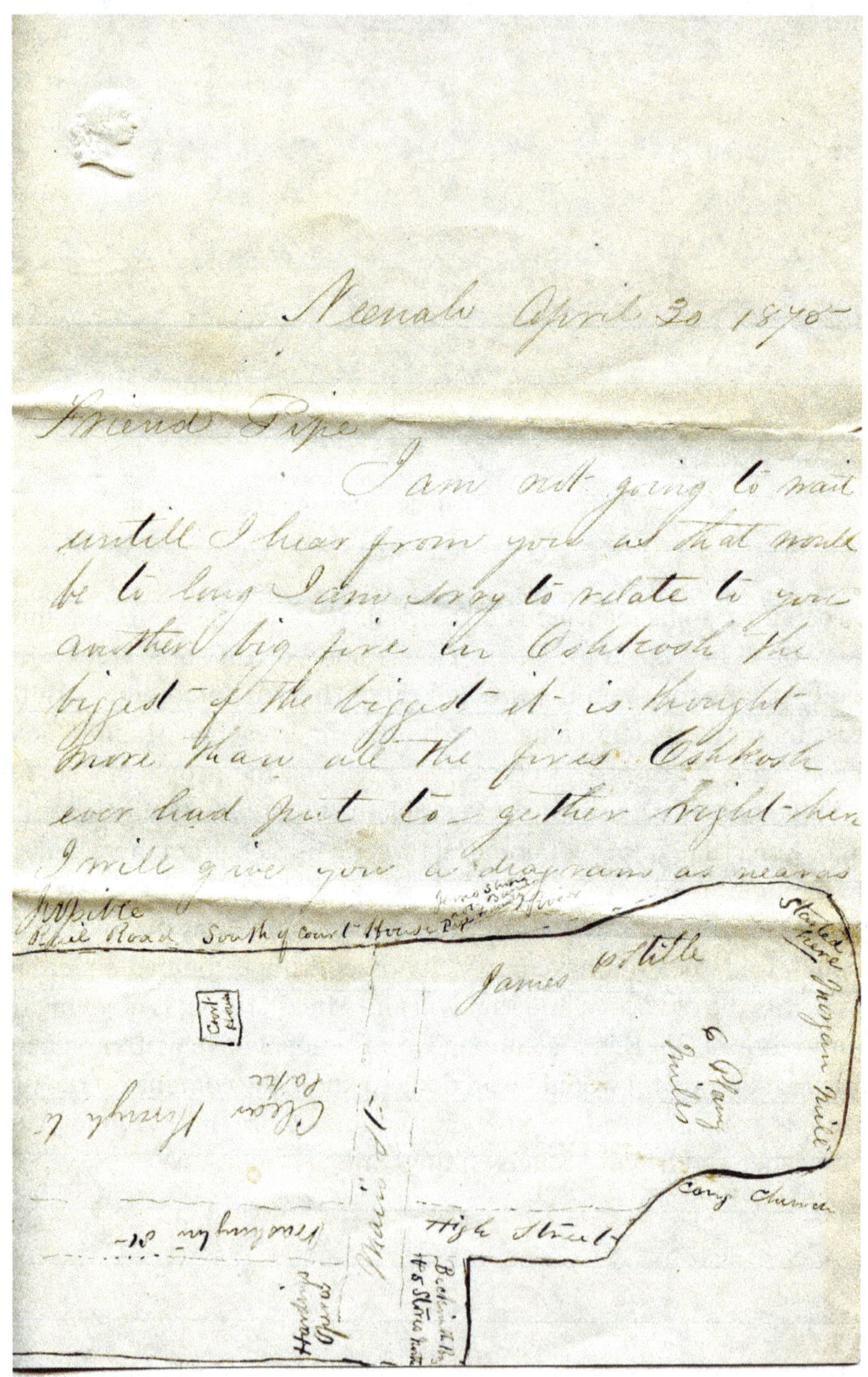
Neenah April 20 1875

Friend Pipe

I am not going to wait untill I hear from you as that would be to long I am sorry to relate to you another big fire in Oshkosh the biggest of the biggest it is thought more than all the fires Oshkosh ever had put to gether Right here I will give you a diagram as near as

Letter Number 75, Page 2

you will see by diagram it took
all of Main St from where the side
track crosses Main Street on the
South of fire limits to 5 Stores north
of the Beckwith House on one side
~~Hastings Store Opera house on the other~~
East through to the lake except the
Court house which is standing in
the middle of the ruins alone, every Bank every
printing House every large store of
any kind except what had moved up
town in those new stores just built.
Pages Foundry was saved he having
Hose attached to his Engine kept his
Building wet the whole time or every
thing to the waters edge must have
Burnd so that saved Jims shop
and the few remaining stores below
the R R Crossing Boles clothing store
& Hutchinson Hardware is left above
the R R Crossing on the North of it I
mean on west side of Main St

Letter Number 75, Page 3

I went down yesterday to see it I
think it the most distressing sight
I ever saw so much property Burned
and all the Buisness Portion of it with
the exception of Algoma St all the best
residences in the City it seems that
It can never be Built up again
Oshkosh seem to be doomed any way
Some lumber Firms Claim to have lost
\$110000 Dollars the Whole loss estimated
at Two Million it was supposed to
Start from a Spark in Peck & Spaldings
Mill a Very strong West wind blowing all
the time and blew it into Morgans Mill
they were not running the Book keeper
run into the mill to get the Books and
got Burnd so his flesh droped from his
Bones when he came out he only lived a
few moments one Man got Killed by
the falling of the Walls of Hardings Opera
House was vary little property saved as
the wind was so strong the fire leaped
from building to Building probaly one mile all
burning at one time

Letter Number 75, Page 4

you can form some Idea Jem and Tom
Started after dinner for the shop he stoped by
Hardings Opera House and Bought some trees
while he was paying for them the fire
bell Rang he sent Tom home with the trees
by the time Tom came back the fire had
reached main St so as he could not get things
to the shop, I tell you the People of Oshkosh feel
blue and I do not know as I can blame them

my family is as well as usal Alma
got home last week I think better than
when she left, our Spring is backward
heavy frost again this morning I have
sowed 45 acres of wheat this week up to now Friday morning I meant
to have got through this week but have
one sick horse I hope you had a pleasant
trip across Old Ocean and that you
and Mrs P is enjoying the balmy Clime
of Old England among your friends
I have written this in a hurry as
I knew you would be anxious to know
the contents of the fire no doubt but
you have read Newspaper Acct before
this I remain your well wisher
& Friend Francis Gillingham
Neenah
Wis

Letter Number 75, Envelope Front

Letter Number 75, Envelope Back

Letter Number 76

Date: 27 May 1875
Writer: Dommett & Canning
Recipient: Thomas Pipe & William Jennings
Sent from: Chard, Somerset County, England
Sent to: Hursey, Broadwindsor, Dorset County, England

Key Ideas

- The attorney, Thomas Pipe, and William Jennings will meet on Tuesday at Yarcombe Club (social gathering at Yarcombe, Devon) to determine whether the estate should be sold in lots or otherwise.
- The attorney suggests inviting Hussey to meet with them.

Dommett & Canning, Solicitors

Chard Somerset

May 27th, 1875

Dear Sir

I shall go to Yarcombe Club [social event at Yarcombe, Devon] on Tuesday and if you will meet me there soon after, I will go over the estate with you and so will determine whether it shall be sold in lots or otherwise.

Don't you think it would be well for us to ask Hussey to meet us, if so please write him. I have done so.

Yours sincerely

Dommett & Canning

Mr. Pipe

Mr. W. Jennings

Hurcol [Hursey]

Broadwindsor

Letter Number 76

DOMMETT & CANNING,
SOLICITORS.

Chard, Somerset.

May 27th 1875

Dear Sir,

I shall go to Yarcombe Club on Tuesday and if you will meet me there soon after 9 I will go over the Estate with you and we will determine whether it shall be sold in Lots or otherwise — Dont you think it would be as well for us to ask Hussey to meet us. If so please write him — (I have done so)

Yrs truly
Dommett & Canning

Mr Pope
Messrs Jennings
Hurcot
Broadwinsor

Letter Number 76, Envelope Front

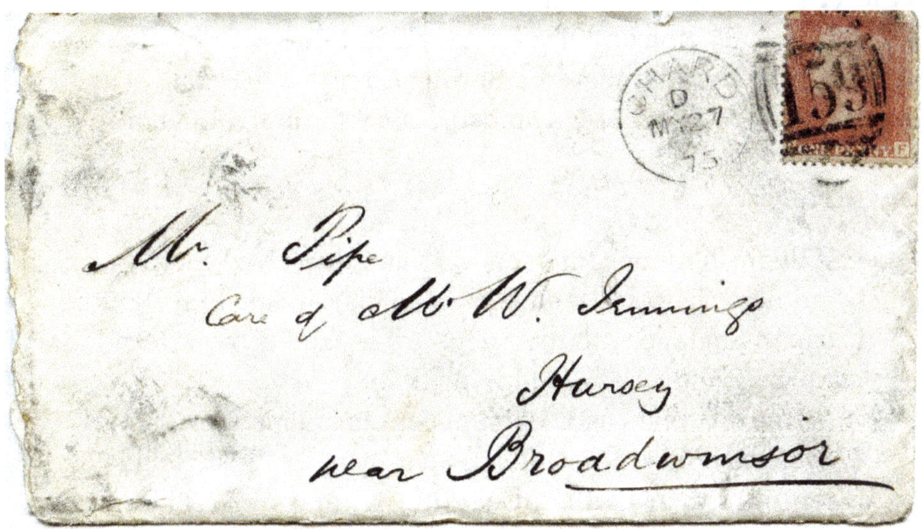

Letter Number 76, Envelope Front

Letter Number 77

Date: 31 May 1875
Writer: William Jennings Pipe
Recipient: Thomas & Elizabeth Stickland Pipe
Sent from: Stawell, Victoria, Borung County, Australia
Sent to: Hursey, Broadwindsor, Dorset County, England

Key Ideas

- William Jennings Pipe reports that he received a letter from his mother, Charlotte Jennings Pipe Pillar, telling him about Pipe's trip to England with their departure scheduled for the middle of April arriving at the beginning of May.
- About two years ago, William Jennings Pipe sent Thomas Pipe a letter about Uncle William Jennings' conduct. He mistakenly sent it to their mother, Charlotte Jennings Pipe Pillar, in Oshkosh.
- William Jennings Pipe presumes that Thomas Pipe will find out what William Jennings has done while he is in England. He feels getting restitution will be difficult. William Jennings Pipe says that William Jennings has been "netting a very pretty thing at Thomas's expense all these years."
- Thomas Pipe is thinking of going to Australia to start over in farming. Brother William Jennings Pipe does not think that is a good idea at his point in his life.

Stawell, Victoria

Australia 31st May 1875

My dear brother and sister [in-law]

The mail from England this morning brought me a letter from Mother [Charlotte Jennings Pipe Pillar] dated March the 1st in which she informs me that you were to leave for Europe in the middle of April reaching there I presume about the early part of the month, of which this is the last day. You have my dear brother learnt in this that I was not quite so neglectful as you must have thought me not replying to your letter of nearly two years back. The fact of the matter is I presume that I must have got in a fog with reference to your address and sent to Oshkosh [Wisconsin], Mother's [Charlotte Jennings Pipe Pillar] place, instead of yours. I don't know that such as such was the case but can only account for its not reaching you on such a supposition, without it miscarrying through the blundering of the P. [Post] Office people. My dear Thomas I am really sorry that the letter miscarried as I spoke out pretty freely in it concerning Uncle William's [Jennings] conduct in the treatment of your affairs, however re[garding] this I presume you will be in a position to know what I may suspect, that he has been netting a very pretty thing at your expense all these years. If so, I trust you will see an easy way of getting restitution. It is so messy in such cases to allow roguery to reap its due reward. Little of the milk of human kindness finds its way to William

[Jennings].

I regret that my letter did not reach you as I replied to some of your queries in it, relative to farming in Australia. I have not much of an opinion of it unless a man has a fair capital and carry on grazing as well as cultivating, still there are many farmers that have done well. New South Wales [Australia] has now the preference over Victoria [Australia], of course you know there is only the River Murray divides the two colonies. The former has greatly the advantage in mileage and her population is nothing like proportionate thereto. I think the place is too hot, and water too scarce, ever to be a good farming country. There is another thing my dear Thomas that is worth a little consideration, which is that it is not worth while at your time of life to begin to make a new house, distant from all your bairns [children]. Have you any good steady boys, industrious and with a tack [natural inclination] for business. I do believe Australia must be as good as America. I think in fact my dear Thomas that, had your net been cast for Australia instead of America you would now have been in a better position than you are. That is all past and is not worth thinking about now. Twenty-four or five years taken out of the prime of one's life leaves little but fragments on either side of it. So far as health is concerned, I believe the climate to be as good as any in the world, and perhaps with a nice little farm, if you could make yourself contented you could eke out the remainder of your days very comfortable. The idea of going back into new selections is to me rather repugnant, especially in one's old days, but there are a good few of the people selling out their old holdings and going back, and if a man could drop into one of them for a few hundred pounds, a year or two's rest should put them in good order again, I should say, and this could be done easily no doubt. But I do not anticipate the pleasure of seeing you in Australia so perhaps it is scarcely worth going into. I know the children in America will have a natural attraction. I can recommend the climate aye [yes] and the country too for an enterprising young man, with not too much regard to old world honesty.

Letter Number 77, Page 1

Stawell Victoria
Australia 31st May 1875

My Dear Brother and sister,
The mail from England this morning brought me a letter from Mother, dated March the 1st, in which she informs me that you were to leave for Europe in the middle of April, reaching there I presume about the early part of the month of which this is the last day – You have my dear Brother learnt ere this that I was not quite so neglectful as you must have thought me not replying to your letter of nearly two years back. The fact of the matter is I presume that I must have got in a fog with reference to your address and sent the ~~it~~ to "Oshkosh" ~~Mothers~~ place instead of to yours. I don't know that such was the case but can only account for its not reaching you on such a supposition, without it miscarried through the blundering of the P. Office people. My dear Thomas, I am really sorry that the letter miscarried as I spoke out pretty freely in it concerning Uncle Williams conduct in the treatment of your affairs; however, ere this I presume, you will be in a position to know what I only suspect, that he has been making a very pretty thing at your expense all these years. If so I trust you will see an easy way of getting restitution; it is no mercy in such cases to allow roguery to escape its due reward – Little of the milk of human kindness finds its way to William

Letter Number 77, Page 2

I regret that my letter did not reach you as I replied to some of your queries in it relative to farming in Australia. I have not much of an opinion of it unless a man has a fair capital and carry on grazing as well as cultivating. Still there are many farmers that have done well. New South Wales has now the preference over Victoria. Of course you know there is only the River Murray divides the two colonies. The former has greatly the advantage in mileage and her population is nothing like proportionate thereto. I think the place is too hot and water too scarce, ever to be a good farming country. There is another thing my dear Thomas that is worth a little consideration, which is that it is not worth while at your time of life to begin to make a new home, distant from all your 'bairns'. Have you any good steady boys, industrious with a tack for business. I do believe Australia must be as good as America. I think, in fact my dear Thomas, that had your lot been cast for Australia instead of America, you would now have been in a better position than you are. That is all past and is not worth thinking about now. Twenty four or five years taken out of the prime of one's life leaves little but fragments on either side of it. So far as health is concerned I believe the climate to be as good as any in the world, and perhaps with a nice little farm, if you could make yourself contented, you could eke out the remainder of your days very comfortable. The idea of going back into new selections is to me rather repugnant, especially in one's old days, but there are a good few of the people selling out their old holdings and going back, and if a man could drop in to one of them for a few hundred pounds, a year or two's rent should put them in good order again I should say, & this could be done easily no doubt. But I do not anticipate the pleasure of seeing you in Australia so perhaps it is scarcely worth going into. I know the children in America will have a natural attraction. I can recommend the climate aye, & the country too for an enterprising young man, with not too much regard to old world honesty

Letter Number 77, Page 3

Jennings's bosom. and I dont think I should study him much. in such a case if I found a neat way of making him dub up. The man has become something less than man through his inordinate love of money - but perhaps he has done things in such a manner that you are powerless. Please write me a long letter giving me the full particulars. now Good bye to William Jennings

I hope you all found a benefit from your trip, and that you find Old England agreeable - though my dear Brother & Sister greatly changed since you left, and many that you left behind you hail and well gone to their long homes - Still hope you will find enough in the Old place to make it pleasant -
Had I not been married I should have endeavoured to run home for a month or two to meet you, but with a wife & a couple of youngsters it requires a little consideration before incurring an expense of such magnitude however I have not given up all hopes yet of seeing you again some day, should things prosper. In your last letter you said I think that you were taking two of your Children to England with you - leaving the others in America. You must have some marriageable are they yet married? any of them, and how many

Letter Number 78

Date: 1 June 1875
Writer: Mary Elizabeth Pipe Woodnorth
Recipient: Thomas & Elizabeth Stickland Pipe
Sent from: Pipe House, Lanark, Portage County, Wisconsin, USA [Sheridan, Waupaca County, Wisconsin, USA Post Office]
Sent to: Likely Hursey, Broadwindsor, Dorset County, England

Key Ideas

- Mary Elizabeth Pipe asks the reason she has not heard from her parents, Thomas and Elizabeth Stickland Pipe. They have been gone eight weeks and only two letters have arrived. She complains that the letters received are only about a dozen words. The Roberts' family has heard from Mrs. Roberts three times, and Mary Elizabeth Pipe has heard only once from her parents, Thomas and Elizabeth Stickland Pipe. Even Grandmother Charlotte Jennings Pillar Pipe is out of patience.
- Jack (John Stickland Pipe) thinks his parents are off and do not care about their children. They take turns going to the post office, but there are no letters from them. Grandmother Charlotte Jennings Pipe Pillar thinks the next letter they receive from them will be when they are coming home.
- Mary Elizabeth Pipe asks whether her father Thomas Pipe has "danced on the green" yet? She gives an update on the crops.
- Mary Elizabeth Pipe has lost thirteen pounds since her parents have left. Mr. Lea stopped in after going to town. Hugo (Lea) is down on a visit. Mr. and Mrs. Grand have not heard from the Pipes either.
- Mr. Baump has moved back to Waupaca. They will live in Mr. Vantassel's shop.
- Charlotte Jennings Pipe Pillar is visiting Mr. Lea.
- A train burned between Waupaca, Wisconsin, and Rochester, New York. Now, the family thinks that is why they have not heard from their parents. (Letters were carried by rail.)

- Libbie Dutton married Mr. Howlett's brother.
- Tom Pipe, Jr., has moved his market between Mr. Brown's office and Denmerest furniture store.
- Winthrop (Chandler) Lord bought the old Hutchinson house. (According to *The Story of Waupaca and Its Railroads*, Winthrop and his brother George Lord founded Waupaca Star Mills in 1851.)
- The Lords are meeting at Armstrong's house to reorganize the Episcopal Church. Mary Elizabeth Pipe thinks they will do away with dancing.
- Mary Elizabeth Pipe comments on her letter: "Don't this look like an English letter?"

[Crosshatched]

Waupaca, June 1st, 1875

Tuesday evening

My dear father and mother,

Why is it we do not hear from you. I hear you have been gone for almost eight weeks and we have only had two letters and my they were not worth calling letters, about a half a dozen words in each. Roberts's people have heard from Mrs. [Elizabeth Jones] Robert[s] three times and us only once. Where are you and what are you doing, do let us know. We are all out of patience even my grandmother [Charlotte Jennings Pipe Pillar], we did all say we would all sit down and write and scold at once. If you were [to] get such a letter, you know we are all feeling bad, Jack [John Stickland Pipe] thinks you are off and that is

all you care. He thinks it is a good way getting away from a lot of children. We all have taken turns going to the [post] office but that did no good. Grandmother [Charlotte Jennings Pipe Pillar] thinks the next letter we get you will be coming home.

Well, I guess I have scolded almost enough for a little while anyway. Perhaps I shall scold more before I get through. Father, have you danced on the green yet? If not when you do I hope you won't dance too much. Jack [John Stickland Pipe] has sold one of the cows, he thought one was enough. She gives lots of milk, he is pasturing three cows here by the house for seventy-five cents per head a week. The clover grew so fast that ours could not begin to eat it all, everything is looking lovely. The apple trees are not near as full of blossoms as

they were last year. Almost all of the trees around here were winter killed. It is raining very fast and has been all day today and part of yesterday. Mr. Lea came from buying goods today. Hugo [Lea] is down on a visit.

Everyone tells me I am getting poor. I begin to think so. When I find out that I have lost thirteen pounds since you left. Mr. and Mrs. Grant were down a week ago today. They hadn't heard a word from you till they came down, tried to but no one up there had heard anything about whether you were there or not. Mr. Baump has moved back to Waupaca, they are fitting up Mr. Vantassel's shop to live in, the other side of Cooledges.

Miss Josephine Murry and Mr. Clark went off last night on the cars.

[other way]

Wednesday afternoon. I will finish your letter soon. It is raining again today, and Grandmother [Charlotte Jennings Pipe Pillar] has gone to Mr. Leas visiting today. She just received your letter from Cib and Pake and they say there was a train of cars burned between here [Waupaca, Wisconsin] and Rochester [New York], so we have come to the conclusion that is why we do not get a letter from you. I have just made butter, and it is the yellowest ever seen. I have to churn twice a week. I think if we had kept the other cow I should have to four times a week. Libbie Dutton was married this morning to Mr. Howlett's brother. Jack [John Stickland Pipe] says there is one more out of the way that won't bother him to be married. I believe Miss Emerson went to the depot to collect her mash bill of him. Just as they were starting away just been asking

Grandmother [Charlotte Jennings Pipe Pillar] what to fill my letter out with. She says to tell you she often thinks who you have seen that she knows and what you are doing but have most made up her mind that she is not going to hear till you come back. Tom [Pipe] has moved his market between Mr. Brown's office and Denmerest furniture store. The clock has just struck nine and that is my bedtime especially when I am tired so I guess I shall have to bring my letter to a close for tonight. Write soon on everything, goodbye

From your affectionate daughter

Mary E. [Elizabeth] [Pipe

All join in kindest love to all

[other way]

Before I forget, Tom caught a large trout yesterday morning, and we had it for supper—everyone declared it was the best we'd tasted this season. The garden is coming along nicely. The peas will be ready for picking next week, and I've started training the beans up the stakes just as you showed me last year. There's talk in town of organising a picnic by the river if the weather clears up, and everyone hopes you'll be back in time to join us.

[on left side]

Mr. Winthicke [Winthrop Chandler] Lord has bought the old Hutchinson house. Mr. G. [George] L. Lord is fixing his one, tearing it all to pieces making a new one of it. The Lords of the Episcopal Church meet at Mr. Armstrong this afternoon to reorganise their society, as it is running a little too high at present. I think they will do away with dancing hereafter.

All for today

Mary [Elizabeth Pipe]

Don't this look like an English letter!

Letter Number 78, Page 1

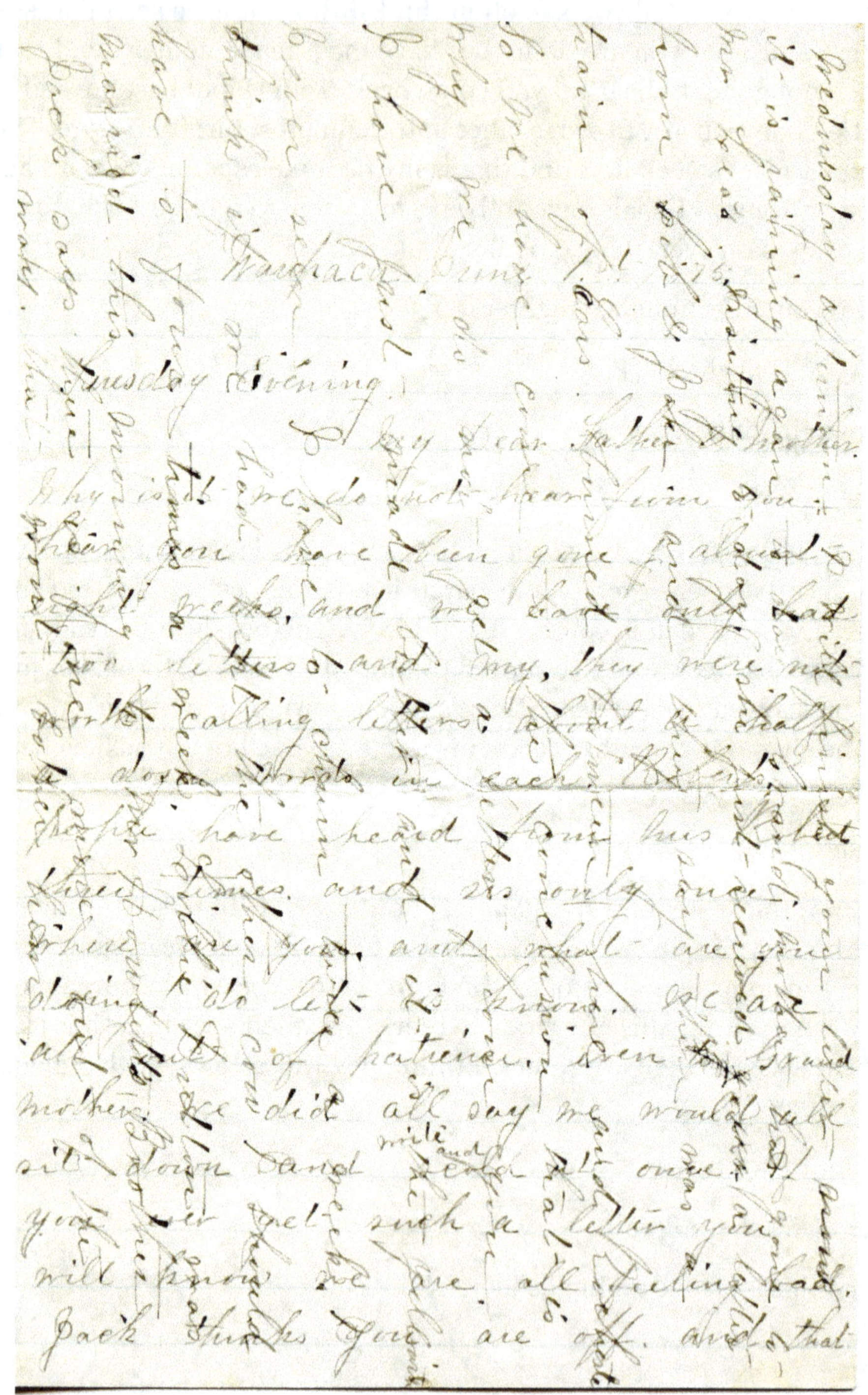

Tuesday Evening.

My Dear Father & Mother.

Why is it we do not hear from you? I hear you have been gone for about eight weeks, and we have only had two letters and my, they were not worth calling letters, about a half a dozen words in each. Bigelow's people have heard from him [illegible] three times, and us only once. Where are you, and what are you doing, do let us know. We are all out of patience, even to Grandmother. We did all day we would all sit down and write and scold at once. If you ever get such a letter you will know we are all feeling bad. Jack thinks you are off. and that

Letter Number 78, Page 2

and that is all you care. he thinks
it is a good way getting a way from
a lot of children. we all have taken
taken turns going to the office but
that did no good. Grand mother
thinks. the next letter we get you
will be coming home.
Well I guess I have scolded almost
enough. for a little while any way.
prehaps I shall scold more before I get through
Father have you danced on the green
yet. if not. when you do. I hope
you wont dance to much.
Jack has sold one of the cows.
he thought one was enough. she
gives lots of milk. he is Pastureing
three cows here by the house. for
seventy five cts per head a week. the clover
grew so very fast that ours could
not begin to eat it all. every thing
is looking lovley. the apple trees are
not near as full of blossom as

Letter Number 78, Page 3

they were last year. all most all of the trees around here were Winter killed. it is raining very fast. and has been all day. to day and part of yesterday. Mr Lea came from buying goods to day. Hugo is down on a visit.

every one tells me I am getting poor. I begin to think so. when I find out that I have lost thirteen pounds since you left. Mr and Mrs Grant were down a week a go to day. they hadent heard a word from you till they came down. tried to but no one up there had heard any thing about whether you were there or not. Mr Bump has moved back to Wanpaca. they are fitting up Mr Vantassels shop to live in. the other side of Cooledge's.

Miss Josephene Merry and Mr Clark went off last night on the cars

Letter Number 78, Page 4

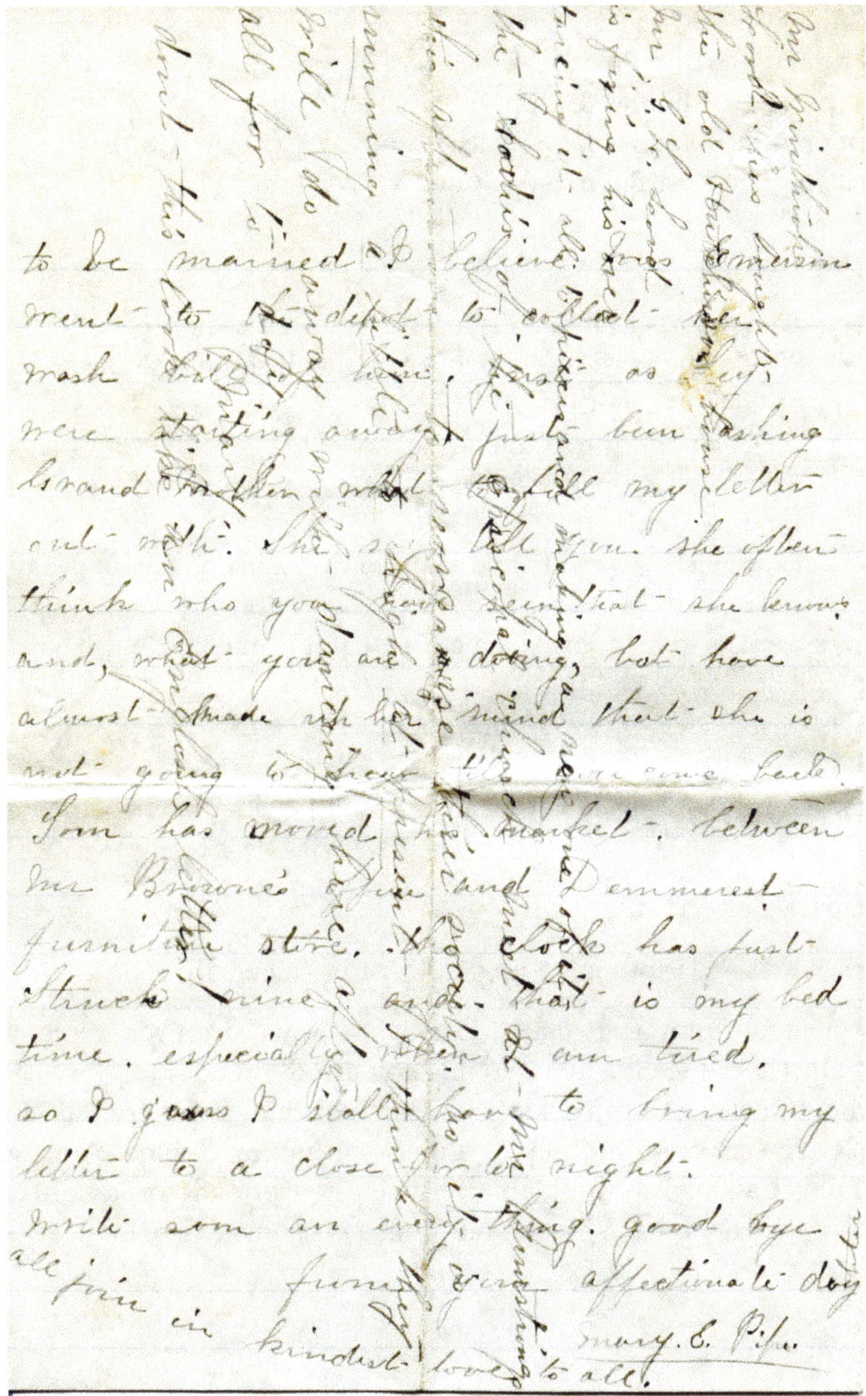

to be married I believe. Mrs Emerson
went to the depot to collect her
wash bill of him, just as they
were starting away. I just been asking
Grandmother what to fill my letter
out with. She says tell you she often
think who you have seen that she knows
and, what you are doing, but have
almost made up her mind that she is
not going to know till you come back.
Tom has moved his market, between
Mr Browne's office and Demmerest
furniture store. the clock has just
struck nine, and that is my bed
time. especially when I am tired.
so I guess I shall have to bring my
letter to a close for to night.
write soon an every thing. good bye
all join from your affectionate daughter
in kindest love to all. mary. E. Pipe.

Letter Number 79

Date: 9 June 1875
Writer: Tom Pipe
Recipient: Thomas & Elizabeth Stickland Pipe
Sent from: Waupaca, Waupaca County, Wisconsin, USA
Sent to: Chard, Somerset County, England

Key Ideas

- Tom reports that Calkins is putting up a nice house.
- Winthorpe Lord has bought the Hutchinson house. Bronson is going to live in it.
- Lewis has left the Tuttle house.
- Tom recounts a personal situation between Mr. and Mrs. Thorn and their boy.
- Tom tells his parents that he is getting married. He hopes they will approve. He does not want to be trouble for them.
- He asks them to bring a nice present for Amelia. He will pay for it.

Uncle Tom to Mother & Father in England [Written later by descendant.]

Waupaca, June 9th, 1875

Dear Father and Mother [In England written in pencil]

Having a few minutes to spare, I thought I would drop you a line. We are all well and feeling good hoping you are the same. It is very cold. Spring things are very backwards, plenty of rain. It is very dull here times are very close but hoping things will improve some. Some are building. Calkins is putting up a very nice house. Winthorpe Lord has bought the Hutchinson house and Bronson is going to live in it.

Lewis is gone out of the Tuttle house and Sibbers and Warner the restaurant fellow has gone into it, great old Handhards you bet. Thomas came home last Saturday and when getting ready for bed went into the room with his wife Mrs. Thom [Thomas]. She asking him what he was going to do. He said that he was going to bed. She says you can go and sleep with the boy, and he said not. He thought he would try her [body or butt]. He said that he had not slept with her for one year and he thought he would just try her

for she seemed to shun him. So he said he could not sleep in that bed. He could not sleep in the garret. She said he could not. He told her to come down and open the door, and he went to the hotel to sleep. He is going to take the boy with him and give the place to her, so I have understood they are watching all Mead Close. Well, Father and Mother, I am going to tell you something. I do not know whether you will be surprised or not. I am going to get married in August. I do not know what you think about it, but it is time. We calculated to before you went away but could not get around to it but hoping you will think it is all right and for the best, for I think I have been a burden to you for a long time and want to not trouble anyone any more than possible hoping you think it is for the best. Write and let me know. Write to me individually, what you think about it. Mother, I want you to fetch back a nice present for Amelia, and I will pay you for it. I must come to a close. Write soon.

Amelia sends her best love to you both.

And receive the same from me

From you beloved son

Tom Pipe

Letter Number 79, Page 1

Uncle Tom to Mother + Father in England

Waupaca June 9th 1875

Dear Farther + Mother In England

haveing a few minutes to spair I thaught I would
drop you a line, ~~we~~ we are all well and feeling good
hoping you are the same, it is very cold spring thing are
very backward plenty of rain it is very dull here times
are very close but hopeing thing will improve some
some are building Calkins is puting up a very nice
house Winthrop Leard has baught the Buckingham house
and Bronson is going to live in it
Lewis is gone out of the Tuttle house and Gibbens
& Warner the restrurant fellow has gone into it
great old Hand Cards you bet. Thorn came home
last Saturday and when getting ready for bed went into
the room with his wife Mrs Thorn she asking him
what he was going to do he sayed that he was going
to bed she says you can go and sleep with the boy
and he said not he thaught he would try ~~her~~
for he said that he had not slept with her for one
year and he thaught he would just try her

Letter Number 79, Page 2

for she seemed to shun him so he said if he could
not sleep in that bed he could not sleep in the house
she said he could not he told her to come down and open
the door and he went to the Hotell to sleep he is going to
take the boy with him and give the place to here so
I have understood they are watching all Mead Closes
Well Father + Mother I am going to tell you something I do
not know whether you will be surprised or not I am
going to get Married in August I donot know what you
think a bout it but it is time we calculated to before you
went a way but could not get a round to it but hoping you
will think it is all wright and for the best for I think I have
been a burden to you for a long time and want to not trouble
any one any more than possible hoping you think it is for the
best. write and let me know write to me individually what
you think a bout it Mother I want you to fetch back a nice
present for Millie, and I will pay you for it I must come
to a close Write soon

Amelia send here best Love to you both
and receive the same from me

From your beloved son
Tom Pipe

Letter Number 79, Envelope Front

Letter Number 79, Envelope Back

Letter Number 80

Date: 6 July 1875 [Postmarked Chard 6 July 1875]
Writer: Anna Stickland age 16 [John Stickland's daughter]
Recipient: Thomas & Elizabeth Stickland Pipe
Sent from: Brydon, Highamption, Devon County, England
Sent to: Hursey, Broadwindsor, Dorset County, England

Key Ideas

- Anna Stickland's older sister, Elizabeth, received a letter from Thomas and Elizabeth Stickland Pipe.
- Mrs. Blackmoor of Bloomers Farm Upottery, Devon, is a friend of one of John Stickland's cousins. She enclosed a letter to Thomas and Elizabeth Stickland Pipe.
- Mrs. Blackmoor was Miss Smith of Middle Farm not far from Askworth (likely Ashwick, Somerset).
- Anna Stickland thinks she will pay all relations a visit. She comments that America is too far. She has heard there are unbelievably bad times there. She thinks that perhaps John Stickland Pipe or William [Edwin] Pipe, both sons of Thomas and Elizabeth Stickland Pipe, will come to England for her.
- Last Thursday everyone but mother, Elizabeth Mathews Stickland, and the two little ones, Katie aged 5 and Mary aged 7, went to the races at Blacktofrington (Black Torrington, Devon)
- Sister Elizabeth Stickland has gone to Mrs. Martins. William is well. Mother and father (Elizabeth Mathews and John Stickland) are quite well.

[Crosshatched]

Brydon

Highampton

July 1875

Dear Uncle and Aunt [Thomas and Elizabeth Stickland Pipe]

????? .... Be under ... to you..

I thought I would write and tell you a little news.

Sister [Elizabeth Stickland] was very much pleased to have a letter from you and to think you are both well. You seem to be spending a very pleasant time with all of our friends.
Well to learn the subject we had a letter from one of father's [John Stickland] cousins viz Mrs. Blackmoor of Bloomers Farm Upottery [Devon], in it was enclosed a letter for you. She wrote to Uncle Henry for your address but he not knowing your place of abode sent it over and so she asked Father [John Stickland] if you were not staying with us to forward it on. She was once a Miss Smith of Middleton Farm [Devon], it appears that she does not live very far from Askworth [likely Ashwick, Somerset].

It will be well for her daughter and for you too just think how anyone's relations pop up. She must be my 4 cousin as Father [John Stickland] says he set much regard of her. He thinks she must be getting old, I think I shall go and pay all my relations a visit someday if they allow me but I rather think America is too far, at least for some years to come. They tell me it is very bad times there. I must leave that

for some future day until John [Stickland Pipe] or William [Edwin Pipe] come to England for me.

Have you had very much rain where you have been to. The newspaper tells of horrid floods in Willes Geneva Manchester and various other places, but we have not had ¼ so much here.

I hope Grandmother [Elizabeth Wall Stickland Bartlett] will get down all safe, I'm she will be rejoiced to see you both over

[other way]

You will give all of my love to her. On Thursday last was the Races at Blacktofrington [Black Torrington, Devon], all of us went with the exception of Mother [Elizabeth Mathews Stickland] and the two little ones [Katie and Mary]. We tell all enjoyed it very much. I wish you had been here, there which are you [?] down again September, write soon.

[other way]

Have you heard from any of the cousins yet

Sister [Elizabeth] is gone down to Mrs. Martins this evening, William is quite well

Mother and father [Elizabeth Mathews and John Stickland] are quite well and send much love to you

I must close as it is late and dark.

[other way]

We send you our fond love to you and accept from them the largest share from me.

Ever I remain

Your fond niece

Anna Stickland

P.S. the enclosed is to show you I am not quite comfortable, write soon

Letter Number 80, Page 1

Letter Number 80, Page 2

Letter Number 80, Page 3

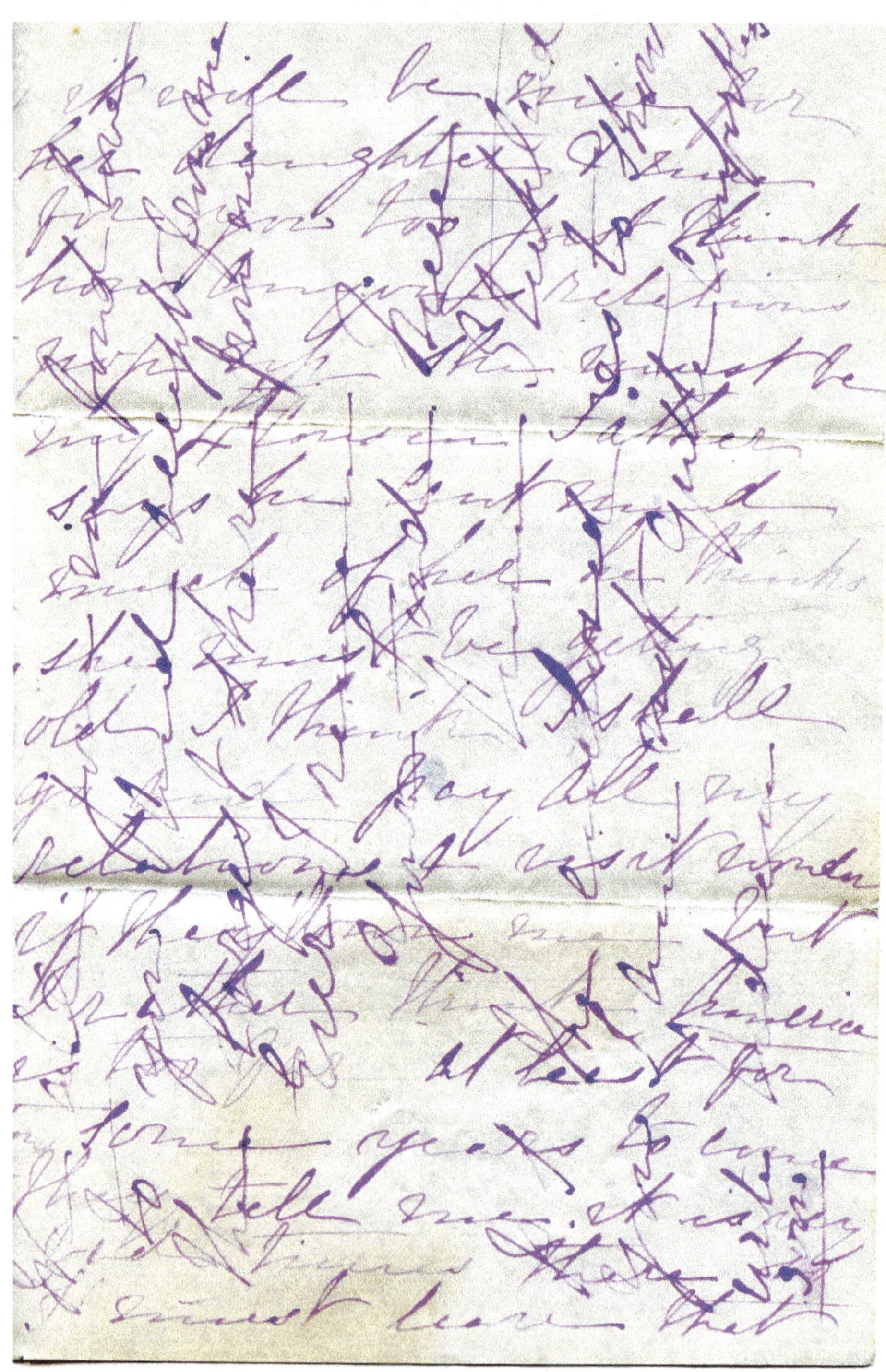

Letter Number 80, Page 4

for some future they
until John or Willif
come to England for
me
Have you had very
much rain where you
have been too the
newspaper tele's of
horrid Floods in
Wales Geneva Manchester
and various other
places but we have
not had 1/4 so much
here
I hope Grandmother
will get home all
safe I am sure she
will be rejoiced to
see you both once

Letter Number 80, Envelope Front

Letter Number 80, Envelope Front

Letter Number 81

Date: 8 July 1875 [envelope stamp]
Writer: Mary Stickland
Recipient: Elizabeth Stickland Pipe
Sent from: Manchester, Lancashire County, England [envelope stamp]
Sent to: Post Office, Chard, Somerset County, England

Key Ideas

- Mrs. Kirkpatrick is ill and will not be able to visit.

Saturday morning

My dear Sister [Elizabeth Stickland Pipe]

I have just got a note from Mrs. Kirkpatrick to say she is prevented through illness from going down the country the early part of next week, and she fears she won't be able to leave next week but will let me know

then as soon as she can arrange it. I have only time to catch the post so can't stop to say more, but I thought you would be sure to send to the post on Monday all being well. You shall have a long letter from me the middle of the week, so please send to the post.

Letter Number 81, Page 1

Saturday morning

My dear Sister,

I have just got a note from Mrs Kirkpatrick says she is prevented through illness from going down the Country the early part of next week - & she fears she won't be able to leave next week but will let me know

Letter Number 81, Page 2

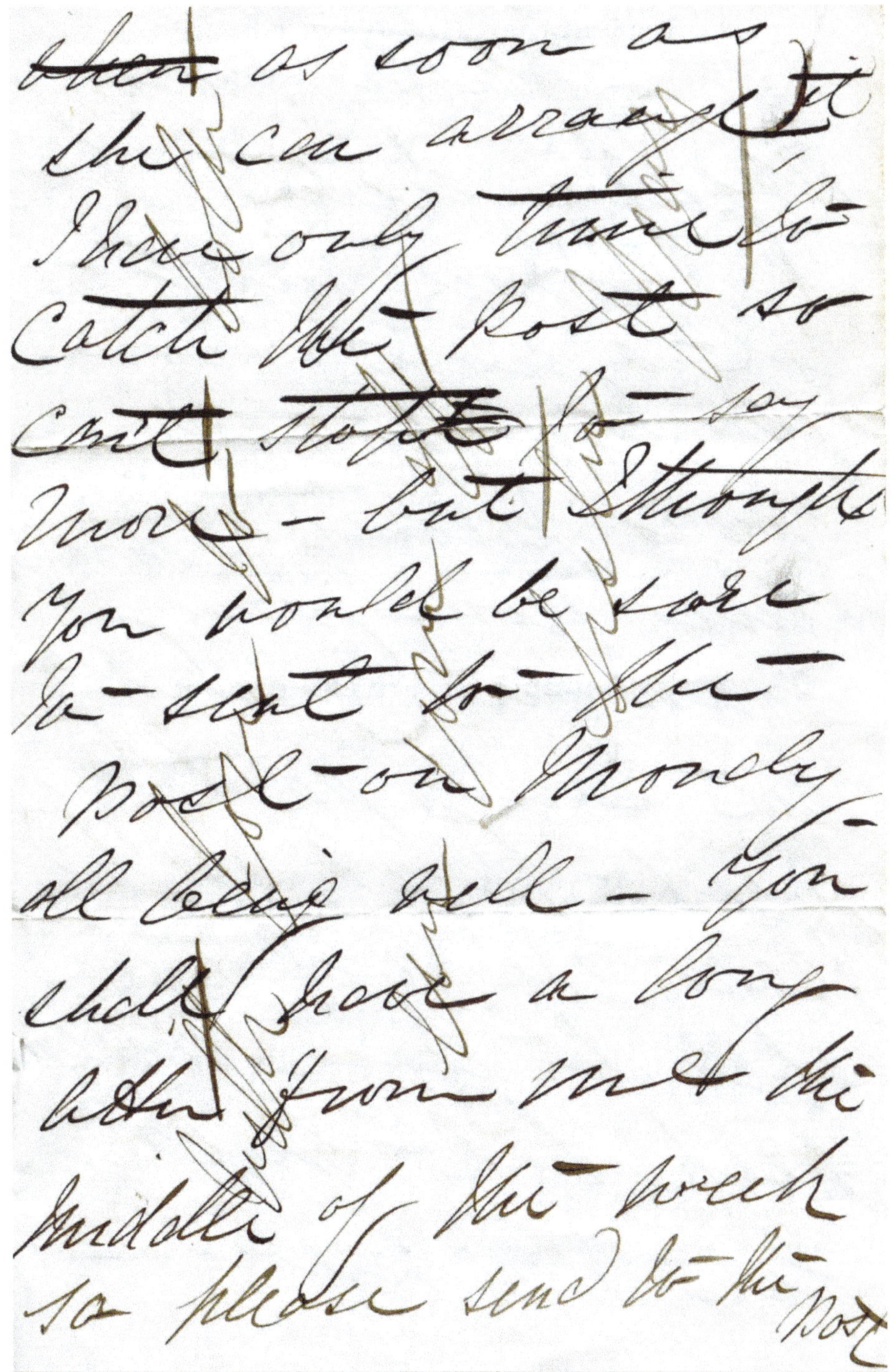

~~then~~ as soon as she can arrange it. I have only time to Catch the post so can't stop to say more - but I thought you would be sure to send to the post on Monday all being well - You shall have a long letter from me the middle of the week so please send to the post

Letter Number 81, Envelope Front

Letter Number 81, Envelope Front

Letter Number 82

Date: 12 July 1875
Writer: Alfred Poll
Recipient: Thomas Pipe
Sent from: Hilgay near Downham, Norfolk County, England
Sent to: Chard, Somerset County, England

Key Ideas

- Poll writes to Thomas Pipe to find out whether he is dead or alive. He has not heard from him.
- Poll hopes he has not offended Thomas Pipe. He wishes to hear from him.

Hilgay, July 12th, 1875

Friend Pipe

I write to hear if you are dead or alive. I wrote to you and I have never received an answer. I hope I have not offended you. I should so like to hear from you and hear whether you are enjoying yourself.

Yours truly

Wm. Thos.

[back of letter]

Alfred Poll

Hilgay

Near Downham

Norfolk

England

Letter Number 82, Page 1

Hilgay July 12th
1875

Friend Pipe

I write to hear if you are dead or alive I write to you and I have never recieved a aunser I hope I haive not affended you I should so like to hear from you. and hear weather you are enjoying your self.

Yours Truly
[illegible]

Letter Number 82, Page 2

Alfred Poll
Hilgay
Near Downham
Norfolk
England

Letter Number 82, Envelope Front

Letter Number 82, Envelope Back

Letter Number 83

Date: 18 July 1875 and 23 July 1875
Writer: Effie Pipe Alexander & Charlotte Jennings Pipe Pillar
Recipient: Thomas & Elizabeth Stickland Pipe
Sent from: Pipe House, Lanark, Portage County, Wisconsin, USA [Sheridan, Waupaca County, Wisconsin, USA Post Office]
Sent to: Post Office, Chard, Somerset County, England

Key Ideas

- Mary Elizabeth Pipe Woodnorth has told Florence Pipe McCunn and Effie Pipe Alexander they must write now.
- They received a letter from their parents, Thomas and Elizabeth Stickland Pipe, dated the 26th of this week.
- Effie Pipe Alexander mentions Belle Barnum, John Goodland, Lizzie Bomen (Elizabeth Pillar Bowron), Mary Sessions, and Nellie Haywood are visiting.
- Charlotte Jennings Pipe Pillar has a sore eye.
- Effie Pipe Alexander notes that something got her hen last night.

Charlotte Jennings Pipe Pillar continues:

- Bramley came home on the 3rd.
- Mrs. Elizabeth Jones Roberts wishes to be home.
- Charlotte Jennings Pipe Pillar asks for a blessing when Thomas and Elizabeth Stickland Pipe leave the shores of England.

Charlotte Jenning Pipe Pillar continues dated July 23:

- Charlotte Jennings Pipe Pillar asks whether Thomas and Elizabeth Stickland Pipe are aware that their son Tom Pipe is getting married next Thursday. They will take a trip to Oshkosh, Wisconsin.
- Charlotte Jennings Pipe Pillar states that Elizabeth Stickland Pipe's mother, Elizabeth Wall Stickland Bartlett, will meet her in Heaven and spend a day together.

Dear Mother [Elizabeth Stickland Pipe]

Mary [Elizabeth Pipe Woodnorth] says that Florence [Pipe McCunn] and I [Effie Pipe Alexander] has got to write this time, and so I thought I would commence. We received your letter that was written on the 26 this week. Belle Barnum and I had a picnic yesterday afternoon there was 15 there. We had a good time. Have you seen John Goodland yet. Lizzie Bomen [Elizabeth Pillar Bowron] has come home, and Mary Sessions is here and Nellie Haywood. I guess that all of the girls are coming back. Grandmother [Charlotte Jennings Pipe Pillar] has got a very sore eye. Something caught my hen last night I heard a noise and so

I got out of bed and looked out of the window and saw nothing and then went to bed again then the dog barked and something barked and this morning when I got up there was feathers all over where she was. I guess that Florence [Pipe McCunn] will write. Goodbye from your affectionate daughter, Effie Pipe

[*Copied with original spelling as it is endearingly childish*]

Dear Mother [Elizabeth Stickland Pipe] Mary [Elizabeth Pipe Woodnorth] says that Florence [Pipe McCunn] and I [Effie Pipe Alexander] has got to write this time and so I thogh I would commence. we received your letter that was written the 26 this week. Belle Barnum and had a picnic yesterday afternoon there was 15 there we had a good time. Have you seen John Goodland yet. Lizzie Bomen [Elizabeth Pillar Bowron] has com home & Mary Sessions is here to & Nellie Haywood. I Guess that all of the Girls are coming back Grandmother [Charlotte Jennings Pipe Pillar] has got a very sour eye. something caught no hen last night I heard a noise and so I got out of bed and looked out of the wingo and saw nouthing and then went to bed agan then the dog barked and something barked and this morning when I got up there was fethers all over where she was. I guess that Florence [Pipe McCunn] will write. good by from your fainant daughter Effie Pipe

Charlotte Jennings Pillar Pipe continues:

My dear children [Thomas and Elizabeth Stickland Pipe]

I expect to hear of your coming home. I pray God that you both may commit yourselves to God's care and keeping by prayer and all will be well. God plants his footsteps in the sea and rides upon the storm.

Bramley came home the 3 [third] isn't he says it was very, very cold on the ocean, many icebergs. I understand Mrs. [Elizabeth Jones] Roberts is wishing herself home now my dear children with my best love wishes and prayers to yourselves and every dear creature you leave behind you and my dear native land.

When you leave her shores ask a blessing to rest upon her your mother.

C. [Charlotte Jennings Pipe] Pillar

We all can meet in heaven. Christ have died for us that we might live but if we are too proud to ask we shall never receive.

Waupaca July 23, [18]75

My dear children [Thomas and Elizabeth Stickland Pipe]

I see Effie [Pipe Alexander] have not quite filled out her letter so I will just say a few words of course you are aware of your son Tom's [Pipe] wedding next Thursday and their trip to Oshkosh [Wisconsin], of course you think all are preparing for the great event. I so pray God they may be united in love to each other and God their heavenly father or all will go wrong, daughter give me thy heart and all will be well. We receive not because we ask not or ask amiss. Are those weddings you have visited sanctified by divine grace or is the [??] gold worshipped. I pray God these dear girls and their companions may give their souls to God and ask his blessing on all they do. They know not how soon their Lord and master may call for them to be ready and all is well. I long to see your home all right.

Left top: I should have said John [Stickland Pipe] is happy the weather is bountiful, all are well.

Upside down: Tell your dear Mother [Elizabeth Wall Stickland Bartlett] I hope to meet her in heaven and spend a day together.

Letter Number 83, Page 1

Waupaca July 18th 1875

Dear Mother Mary says
that Florence and I has got
to write this time and so I
thogh I would comence. we
received your letter that was
written on the 26 this week.
Belle Barnum and I had a picnic ~~yesty~~ yesterday afternoon there was 13 there we
had a good time. have you
seen ~~A~~ John Goodland yet.
Lizzie Bomen has com home.
& Mary Sessions is here to &
Nellie Haywood. I Guess that
all of the Girls are comming
back Grandmother has got
a very sowr eye. something
caught mo hen last night
I heard a moise and so

Letter Number 83, Page 2

I got out of bed and looke
d out of the wingo and saw
nouthing and then went to
bed agan then the dog barked
and something barked and this
morning when I got up
there was fethers all over
where she was. I ~~good~~ guess that
Florence will writte. good
by from your efexinant
daughter Effie Pipe.

Letter Number 83, Page 3

Now my dear Children
I expect soon to hear of your coming
home: I pray God that you both
may commit your selves to Gods care
and keeping. by prayer and all will
be well God plants his footsteps in
the Sea and rides upon the storm
Bramley came home the 3 inst he says it
was very cold on the Ocean many Ice
bergs I understand Mrs Roberts is with
my her self home now my dear
Children with my best love wishes
and prayers to your selves and every
dear creature you leave behind you
and my dear native land.
when you leave her shores ask a blessing
to rest upon her your Mother
we all can meet C Pillar
in heaven Christ
have died for us that we might live
but if we are to proud to ask we shall
never receive

Letter Number 83, Page 4

Waupaca July 23 75

My dear Children I see Effie have not quite filed out her letter so I will just say a few words of coarse you are aware of your Son Tom Wedding next thursday and there trip to Oshkosh of coarse you think all are preparing for the great event I pray God they may be united in love to each other and God there heavenly Father or all will go wrong Daughter give me thy heart and all will be well we receive not because we ask not or ask a miss are those Weddings you have visited sanctifyed by divine grace or is the wordly gold worshiped I pray God these dear girls and there companions may give there selves to God and ask his blessing on all they do they know not how soon there Lord and Master may call for them be ready and all is well

I long to see you home all right

Letter Number 84

Date: 26 July 1875, Monday morning
Writer: Mary Stickland
Recipient: Elizabeth Stickland Pipe
Sent from: Likely, Manchester, Lancashire County, England
Sent to: Likely Post Office, Chard, Somerset County, England

Key Ideas

- Mrs. Kirkpatrick will leave for the country on Thursday, July 28, 1875. Her journey will terminate in Ilminister, Somerset.
- Mary Stickland would like Elizabeth Stickland Pipe to meet Mrs. Kirkpatrick as Elizabeth Wall Stickland Bartlett says Whitelackington, Somerset, is near Ilminster, Somerset. She wonders whether Mrs. Kirkpatrick can stay there to recover from the trip.
- Mary Stickland will send patterns of velvet and silk with her mother, Elizabeth Wall Stickland Bartlett.
- Mary Stickland is going with her husband to South Wales to visit his aging mother. Their daughter is in Cornwall on holiday.
- At the time of this writing, Mary Stickland's husband and daughter have not been identified.

Monday morning July 26th

My dear Sister [Elizabeth Stickland Pipe]

Mrs. Kirkpatrick has just sent to say she has now finally settled to leave for the country on Thursday next 28th inst. I trust you will get this soon enough to meet her and Mrs. K's

journey will terminate at Ilminster [Somerset], I think you had better meet her there as Mother [Elizabeth Wall Stickland Bartlett] says that Whitelackington [Somerset] is very near Ilminster [Somerset] and perhaps her friends you are staying with will not object to her staying the night as she will be quite worn out with her journey. Indeed I don't know how she will manage to get over such a long journey as it will be full 12 hours railway travelling, they will leave Manchester [Lancashire] a little before 7am and arrive at Ilminster [Somerset], all being well, between six and seven.

You will be able to see from the [platform] the exact time the train from Taunton [Somerset] will arrive. They will come from Bristol to Taunton [Somerset]. The fact of knowing that the parting time is now so near makes her quite sick at heart

for I feel she is too old ever to affect her to return to Manchester [Lancashire], and the knowledge of it wrings my very heart. Shall hope to write to you soon about some arrangements to be made as to her future, whether that time be long or short.

I will send you patterns of both velvet and silk by dear mother [Elizabeth Wall Stickland Bartlett]. I take a fortnight's holiday, to commence on Saturday next, my husband is in very bad health and I am anxious to see if a change

of air will do him good. Its South Wales we go to. His home and as Mrs. Barents an old [woman?] and his mother very ill he is wishful to go and have me see them. Our daughter is now in Cornwall for a holiday. I trust it will be fine on Thursday for Mother [Elizabeth Wall Stickland Bartlett] as it's so miserable when its wet. I must now close trusting you and your husband are both well as with our trusted loved to each I rest your affectionate

Sister

Mary [Stickland]

Letter Number 84, Page 1

Monday morning
July 26th

My dear Sister
Mrs Kirkpatrick
has just sent to
say she has now
finaly settled to
~~come~~ leave for the
Country on Thursday
next 29th inst
I trust you will
get this soon
enough to meet
her, and as Mrs K's

Letter Number 84, Page 2

journey will terminate
at Ilminster, I think
you had better meet
her there, as
Mother says that
Whitelackington is
very near Ilminster
and perhaps the friends
you are staying with
will not object to
her staying the night
as she will be quite
worn out with her

Letter Number 84, Page 3

journey – Indeed I don't
know how she will
manage to get over
such a long journey
as it will be fully
12 hours Railway
travelling – They
will leave Manchester
a little before 7 a.m
and arrive at
Ilminster (all being well)
between 14 & seven

Letter Number 84, Page 4

you will be able
to — I see from the
Guide the exact
time the train
from Taunton will
arrive they will come
from Bristol to
to Taunton —
the fact of knowing
that the parting
time is now so
near makes me
quite sick at
heart

Letter Number 84, Page 5

for I feel she is
too old ever to
expect her to return
to Manchester, and
the knowledge of it
wrings my boy heart.
Shall have to write
to you soon about
& some arrangements
to be made, as to
her future — whether
that time be long
or short —

Letter Number 84, Page 6

I will send you
patterns of both
velvet & silk
by ~~[illegible]~~ dear Mother
I have a fortnights
Holiday to commence
~~of~~ on Saturday next
My Husband is
in very best health
& I am anxious to
see if ~~a~~ change

Letter Number 84, Page 7

of her will do him
good, its South Wales
we go to, his home
and as his Parents
are old, & his Mother
very ill he is wishful
to go & have me
see them — our
daughter is now
in Cornwall
for a Holiday
I trust it will

Letter Number 84, Page 8

be fine on
Thursday for
Mother, as its so
miserable when
its wet. - I must
now close trusting
you & your husband
are both well,
& with our united
love to each, I rest
your ever affectionate
Sister Mary

Letter Number 84, Envelope Front

Letter Number 84, Envelope Front

Letter Number 85

Date: 5 August 1875 [envelope stamped at Neenah 5 August]
Writer: Francis Gillingham [1829-1910]
Recipient: Thomas Pipe
Sent from: Neenah, Winnebago County, Wisconsin, USA
Sent to: Winsham, Somerset County, England

Key Ideas

- Francis Gillingham visited with Mrs. Rendall and was inspired to write. Her health has improved. Francis Gillingham gives an update on their crops.
- Francis Gillingham mentions that Tom Pipe, Jr., is getting married.
- Francis Gillingham asks that the Pipes tell his parents that he is waiting for a letter.
- Francis Gillingham requests that the Pipes bring his wife (Mary L. Quartermass Gillingham) a black silk dress and a silk dress for each of the girls (Alma and Letta May). He wants full patterns since it always takes much more for "fandangos." He reminds them to bring the shawl.

Letta Gillingham, daughter of Francis Gillingham, may be wearing a silk English dress requested in this letter.

[The writing is very faded. Looks like August. Envelope is stamped Aug. 22, 1875, Chard and Taunton.]

Friend Pipe

Having delayed writing so long I am almost ashamed to write but having a few spare moments while visiting this morning with Mrs. Rendall and talking of you I made the resolve to write. Mrs. Rendall came last night, her health is much improved, the country air seems to agree with her. We are having good cool weather rather dry. Crops very good all but corn which do not look very promising. I have cut my winter wheat and finished stacking yesterday, will commence in spring in

a few days my wheat and oats is very heavy. I think I will have 2000 bushels of what 1000 of oats. My barns is all full of hay and of excellent quality. Our health is about as usual, each one able to eat their allowance. Alma [daughter, 1859-1937] is some better than when she went east last summer. Mertie [daughter Letta May, 1862-1935] just got home about the same as when she left. I see by the papers your family has increased, Tom [Pipe] has taken to him a wife Amelia Woodnorth]. I suppose you know it. Ever this I hope you have had a good time and enjoyed yourself among your friends, tell my folks I am waiting for a letter so I can write to them if you bring any goods through the custom house, and you have any money please bring my wife [Mary L. Quartermass Gillingham] a black silk

dress and a silk dress for each of the girls [Alma and Letta May], what you think the most appropriate, I leave it all with you, bring full patterns as you know it takes so much for fandangos, remember the shawl also, I am not going to write much, will talk it out when I see you which I hope will be before long. I hope your business is all fixed up satisfactory. Give my love to all enquiring friends

And accept the same yourself

From F. [Francis] Gillingham

P.S. Mind [Pay Attention to] and see all of my folks

Letter Number 85, Page 1

[illegible] Aug [illegible]

Friend Pipe

Having delayed writing so long I am almost ashamed to write but having a few spare moments while Visiting this morning with Mrs Rendall and talking of you I made the resolve to write Mr Rendell came last night [illegible] health is much improved the Country air seems to agree with her we are having good Cool weather rather dry crops very good all but corn which do not look very promising I have cut my winter wheat and finished stacking yesterday will Commence on Spring in

Letter Number 85, Page 2

a few days my Wheat and Oat
is very heavy I think I will have
2000 Bushels of Wheat 1000 of Oat
my Barns is all full of Hay and
of Excellant quality our health
is about as usal each one able
to eat their alowance Alma is
some better than when she went
East last Summer Martie I gues
got home about the same as when
she left I see by the papers you
family has Increased Tom has
taken to him a wife I suppose
you know it Ere this I hope you
have had a good time and
enjoyed yourself among your fri
tell my folks I am waiting for
a letter so I can write to them
if you bring any goods through
the Custom house And you have
any money please bring my wife
a Black Silk dress and a Silk

Letter Number 85, Page 3

dress for each of the girls
what you think the most appropriate
I leave it all with you bring
full patterns as you know it
takes so much for Sundays
remember the shawl also I am
not going to write much
will talk it out when I see
you which I hope will be fore
long I hope your Business is
is all fixed up satisfactory
give my love to all enquiring
Friends
and accept the same
yourself
Your Son
F Gillingham
P.S.
Mind and see all of my folks

Letter Number 85, Envelope Front

Letter Number 85, Envelope Back

Letter Number 86

Date: 12 August 1875
Writer: Mary Stickland
Recipient: Elizabeth Stickland Pipe
Sent from: Likely, Manchester, Lancashire County, England
Sent to: Sent to Thomas Pipe, in care of Mr. Coleman, Chard, Whitestaunton, Somerset County, England

Key Ideas

- Elizabeth Wall Stickland Bartlett was expecting Thomas and Elizabeth Stickland Pipe, but they did not come.
- Mary Stickland relays that her mother, Elizabeth Wall Stickland Bartlett, is feeble and suffering.

[Letter undated, start not included]

& I know Mother [Elizabeth Wall Stickland Bartlett] was expecting you by every train and would wait dinner, still it was impossible for you to let her know or end her suspense before 4 o'clock when I got back and when I told her you had left Manchester. She felt it very acutely, poor soul she is very feeble and suffering

as I don't know your plans of destination. I am sending this to Bardon [Farm, Somerset], please write back on receipt of this and tell me how long you intend to stay in England and give my love to your husband [Thomas Pipe] in which Mother [Elizabeth Wall Stickland Bartlett] unites and accept much yourself from us both.

From your affectionate sister Mary [Stickland]

Great haste

Letter Number 86, Page 1

& [illegible] Mother was
expecting you by every
train & would wait
dinner – till it was
impossible for me
to let her know or
end her suspense
before 4 o'clock
when I got back
& when I told her you
had left – Manchester
she felt it very acutely
poor soul she is very
feeble – & tottering.

Letter Number 86, Page 2

as I don't know your
plans of destination
I am sending this to
Gordon, Please write
to be on receipt of
this & tell me how
long you intend to
stay in England &
give my love to your
Husband in which
Mother unites & accept
much yourself from us both
from your affectionate
Sister Mary
[illegible]

Letter Number 86, Envelope Front

Letter Number 86, Envelope Front

Letter Number 87

Date: 19 August 1875
Writer: Elizabeth Jones Roberts
Recipient: Thomas Pipe
Sent from: Woodville, Calumet County, Wisconsin, USA
Sent to: Thomas Pipe, in care of Mr. Coleman, Chard, Whitestaunton, Somerset County, England

Key Ideas

- Elizabeth Jones Roberts receives a letter from Thomas Pipe stating they will be in England until the end of September. She would have gone along had she known they would have been staying until then.
- Elizabeth Jones Roberts has a friend in Liverpool, England, who would put her on board. Mrs. Bones has offered to meet her in New York. She is longing to go to England.
- Mary W. Roberts has had company: her cousin from Chicago, Miss Erskine from Racine, Wisconsin, and Mary Sessions from Waupaca, Waupaca County, Wisconsin.
- Elizabeth Jones Roberts visited her brother in Woodville, Calumet County, Wisconsin. She has not heard from Mrs. Clough.
- Elizabeth Jones Roberts says she had been to London for a short time.
- (Elizabeth Jones Roberts is widow to Robert Robert Roberts who was born in Llangollen, Denbighshire, Wales, on September 25, 1811, and died in Waupaca, Waupaca County, Wisconsin, on November 25, 1873. According to the *1870 U.S. Census*, Robert Robert Roberts held $7,000 in real estate and $45,000 in personal estate. He is buried in Lakeside Cemetery in Waupaca.)

My dear friend

I feel that you were very kind to write to me and how very glad I have been to hear from you each time. I hear about giving up going home at present as I have not seen nearly all my friends. They live at a great distance from each other. Had I known a month ago that you would have been in England till the latter end of September, I should certainly have prepared to have gone at the time you

do as it would have been a great comfort to me to have your company. I shall be able to have a friend in Liverpool [England] put me all right on board and Mrs. Bones has offered to meet me in New York, so that I hope to get on all right. I begin to feel a little longing for home and shall be anxious to get there before very long.

Mary [Roberts] has had a house full of company and no girl part of the time. Her cousin came from Chicago [Illinois] and another young lady Miss Erskine from Racine [Wisconsin] and Mary Sessions [Waupaca. Wisconsin]. The farmers have had a dreadful time

a great part of the hay is nearly spoiled. Your letter was delayed several days for I was at my brother Woodville [Calumet County, Wisconsin] near Knightons [likely family name], all accounts from Waupaca [Wisconsin] are very cheering, everything seems to be abundant and trade very good. I have not heard from Mrs. Clough.

I trust you will have a pleasant voyage home. I wonder if I told you that I had been to London for a short time. I shall be glad to hear from you if you can drop me a line before you leave, shall be at my brothers for some weeks yet. My health is very good.

I shall be at once

Respects to Mrs. Pipe [Elizabeth Stickland Pipe]

I remain your friend.

Elizth [Elizabeth Jones] Roberts

Woodvill. [Woodville, Calumet County, Wisconsin] August 19th

Letter Number 87, Page 1

My dear friend

I feel that you
were very kind to write to me
& how very glad I have been
to hear from you each time
I have about given up going
home at present as I have not
seen nearly all my friends - they
live at a great distance
from each other - had I known
a month ago that you would
have been in England till the
latter end of Sepr - I should
certainly have prepared to
have you at the time you

Letter Number 87, Page 2

do as it would have been
a great comfort to me to have
your company - I shall be able
to have a friend in Liverpool
put me all right on board
& Mr Bones has offered to meet
me in New York - so that I hope
to get on all right I begin to
feel a little longing for home
and shall be anxious to get
there before very long
Mary has had a house full
of company - and no girl part
of the time - her cousin from
Chicago & another young lady
Miss Erskine from Racine
& Mary Despious - the former
two have had a dreadful time

Letter Number 87, Page 3

a great part of the hay is
nearly spoiled Your letter
was delayed several days for
I was at my brothers - Woodalle
near Knighton all accounts from
Waupaca are very cheering
every thing seems to be abundant & trade very good I have
not heard from Mr Clough
I trust you will have a pleasant voyage home - I wonder
if I told you that I had been
to London for a short time
I shall be glad to hear from
you if you can drop me a
line before you leave shall
be at my brothers for some
weeks yet - my health is very

Letter Number 87, Page 4

good ~~I shall be at home~~
Respects to Mr Pope
I Remain your friend
Eliza R. Robert

Woodville August 19th
1875

Letter Number 88

Date: 25 August 1875 & Undated
Writer: Tom Pipe, Jr. & Amelia Woodnorth Pipe
Recipient: Thomas & Elizabeth Stickland Pipe
Sent from: Waupaca, Waupaca County, Wisconsin, USA
Sent to: Chard, Somerset County, England

Key Ideas

- Tom Pipe, Jr., tells his parents about getting married on July 28 and going on a trip to Oshkosh, Winnebago County, Wisconsin. Tom and Amelia Woodnorth Pipe returned on Tuesday and moved into the New Shop that is Perkins new building.
- Tom Pipe's buck wheat and corn crops were hit by an early frost costing him about $100.
- Tom Pipe is fixing up the Browns' old house where they will live. He is short of stamps (substitute for money) so he will not fully furnish it.
- Tom Pipe requests black beaner material for an overcoat. Tom has gained 6 pounds since he got married.
- Effie Pipe received their letter about returning late September. Elizabeth Jones Roberts intended to find a husband in England.
- Tom Pipe's wife, Amelia Woodnorth Pipe, hopes that Thomas Pipe and Elizabeth Stickland Pipe are happy that they are married. At present, they are staying with Tom's wife's parents (Paul and Sarah Woodnorth).
- Amelia Woodnorth Pipe enclosed pictures taken at Oshkosh, Wisconsin.
- Charlotte Jennings Pipe Pillar talks about going to Neenah, Wisconsin, this week for a few days.
- Sarah Woodnorth has been unwell; however, now she is better.

Waupaca, Aug 25th, 1875

Dear Father and Mother [Thomas and Elizabeth Stickland Pipe]

I thought it was about time I was writing you a letter. I suppose you have heard that we were married on the 28th July. We took a trip to Oshkosh [Winnebago County, Wisconsin], had a very pleasant time, came home Tuesday and the same day moved into the New Shop that is Perkins new building. It makes a very pleasant market to sell meat enough for to make money, but there is so much trust [purchasing on credit] that it keeps a fellow hard up most of the time, hoping that there will be better times this fall but I am afraid that they will

be close for there has been a big old frost and killed the buck wheat that is the highest share of it, also lots of the corn. It has hurt me about one hundred dollars but it can't be helped. We have got to take it as it comes.

I am now busy fixing up for housekeeping Brown old house. It will be very pleasant place to live, but we shall not furnish it much for I am too short of stamps [substitute for money] but I think we can live cosy there for we are small and the house is also, if it is so you can fetch over some black beaner for an overcoat. I wish you would and I will pay you for it when you get home. Get enough for a good big one. My wife [Amelia Woodnorth Pipe] is taking a snooze now but will enclose a few lines to you. She is very busy getting things ready for the house.

Hoping you are having a good time and enjoying yourselves. Effie [Pipe] got a letter from you today which stated that you were not coming home until the last of September. We have heard such a thing as Mrs. [Elizabeth Jones] Roberts intended getting herself a husband but I prevented taking much stock in it at least to get one in the old country, but of course I do not know much about that part of the world in regard to men. I know that this part is great and sure for young ladies or Jack [John Stickland Pipe] would not go for them. I must come to a close, hoping you are well, for we are enjoying good health and hearty as old people. I have gained 6 lbs since married man.

From your affectionate son Tom Pipe

Dear Mother [Elizabeth Stickland Pipe]

Tom [Pipe] wishes me to write a few lines to you. I hope you are pleased with Tom and myself getting married. We have been living with Father and Mother [Paul and Sarah Woodnorth] Never since, it will be just a month Sunday (the 28) since we were married and I think we shall be happy, at least I shall try to be. We are going housekeeping next week. I wish you was home to help us arrange our house.

Enclosed you will find our pictures which we had taken when at Oshkosh, Mrs. [Charlotte Jennings Pipe] Pillar talks of going to Neginah [Neenah, Winnebago County, Wisconsin] this week for a few days. She has not been very well lately. All the rest are quite well. My mother [Sarah Woodnorth] has been very sick again but is better now.

[upside down at the top]

Tom is in a hurry to send it. Mary was here yesterday to help me make a carpet. Please accept our love and your well wishes for your affections.

Lovingly Your Amellie

Letter Number 88, Page 1

Waupaca Aug 25th 1873

Dear Farther & Mother

I thought it was about time I
was writeing you a letter
I supose you heard that we were
married on the 29 of July, we took
a trip to Oshkosh had a very
pleasant time, came home Teusday and
the same day I moved into the new
shop that is Perkins new building
it makes a very pleasant market
I sell meat enought for to make
money but there is so much trust
that it keeps a fellow hard up
most of the time hopeing that there
will be better times this fall
but I am afraid that there will

Letter Number 88, Page 2

be close for there has been
a big old frost and killed the
Buckwheat that is the bigest share
of it also lots of the Corn.
it has hurt me about one hundred
Dollars but it Cant be helped, we have
got to take it as it comes.
I am now buisy fixing up for
house keeping Brown old house
it will be very pleasant place to
live but we shall not furnish it
much for I am to short of Stamps
but I think we can live Cosy there
for we are small and the house
is also, if it is so you can fetch
over some Black Beaver for a Overcoat
I wish you would and I will pay
you for it when you get home
get enought for a good big one
My wife is takeing a Snoose now
but will Enclose a few lines to
you she is very buisy getting
things ready for the house.

Letter Number 88, Page 3

hoping you are haveing a good time and Enjaying yourself Effie got a letter from you today whitch stated that you were not Comeing home untill the last of Sept we have herd such a thing as Mrs Roberts intended getting herself a husband but I havent taken much stock in it at least to get one in the old Country but of Course I do not know much a bout that part of the Wauld in regard to men, I know that this part is great and shure for the young Ladys or Jack Would not go for them I must Come to a Close hoping you are well, for we are Enjaying good health and hearty as old people I have gained Ells since married man

From your Effectionate Son

John Pipe

Letter Number 88, Page 4

Dear Mother

Tom wishes me to write a few lines to you. I hope you are pleased with Tom & myself getting married. we have been living with Father & Mother ever since, it will be just a month sunday (the 29) since we were married, and I think we shall be happy, at least I shall try to be. we are going housekeeping next week. I wish you was home to help us arrange our house. enclosed you will find our picture which we had taken when at Oshkosh. Mrs [illegible] talks of going to Neenah this week for a few days. she has not been very well lately. all the rest are quite well. my mother has been very sick again, but is better now

Tom is in a hurry to mail it. Mary was here yesterday to help me make a carpet. Please accept our love and well wishes for your safe return

Please excuse hurried writing

Your loving Millie

Letter Number 89

Date: 25 August 1875
Writer: W. Dommett
Recipient: Thomas Pipe
Sent from: Chard, Somerset County, England
Sent to: Post Office, Whitestaunton, Somerset County, England

Key Ideas

- W. Dommett asks Thomas Pipe to come into his office the next morning. He will arrange everything about the purchase. A letter from the Admiralty for him has arrived for Thomas Pipe.
- (The letter may offer proof of John Valentine Pipe's death on the *City of Glasgow* in 1854.)
- *(Return of Owners of Land 1873* has been referred to as the "modern-day *Doomsday Book.*" Both books list all property owners in England for the purposes of taxation. John Valentine Pipe is listed in *Return of Owners of Land 1873* as residing in America. He is still listed as the owner of the inherited property even though he was lost at sea in March 1854.)
- (Proof of John Valentine Pipe's death would likely be needed for Thomas and Elizabeth Stickland Pipe to sell the inherited properties.)

From Dommett & Canning solicitors, Chard, Somerset

Aug 29 Sunday 1875

Dear Sir

If you will come in tomorrow morning, I think I can arrange everything about the purchase, there is a letter from the Admiralty for you.

Yours truly

W. Dommett

Letter Number 89, Page 1

DOMMETT & CANNING,
SOLICITORS.

Chard, Somerset.

Aug 29 1875
Saturday

Dear Sir/

If you will come in tomorrow morning I think I can arrange every thing about the Minkham - there is a letter from the admiralty for you

Yrs truly
W Dommett

Letter Number 89, Envelope Front

Letter Number 90

Date: 12 September 1875
Writer: Mary Elizabeth Pipe Woodnorth, Effie Pipe Alexander & Florence Pipe McCunn
Recipient: Thomas & Elizabeth Stickland Pipe
Sent from: Pipe House, Lanark, Portage County, Wisconsin, USA [Sheridan, Waupaca County, Wisconsin, USA Post Office]
Sent to: Chard, Somerset County, England

Key Ideas

- Daughter Mary Elizabeth Pipe Woodnorth is alone this week with only three others. Charlotte Jennings Pipe Pillar is visiting people in Stevens Point, Portage County, Wisconsin.
- The county fair is going on this week.
- Tom and Amelia Woodnorth Pipe are visiting Mr. Jo Morey today.
- Mrs. Chelsey misses Thomas and Elizabeth Stickland Pipe.
- Louis Sterns came back this week. Mr. Silverthorn and Emma are visiting in Pennsylvania, USA, for two or three months. Mrs. Gus Chelsey was sick but now is better.
- Jack (John Stickland Pipe) and Mary Elizabeth Pipe Woodnorth took tea at Mrs. Chelsey's last night.
- Fred Lea and Minnie are married.

Effie Pipe Alexander continues:

- Effie Pipe Alexander is getting tired of wondering when Mother and Father (Elizabeth Stickland and Thomas Pipe) will be coming home. Florence Pipe McCunn, Elizabeth Pipe Woodnorth and she had dreams that they were all home.

Mary Elizabeth Pipe continues:

- Jack (John Stickland Pipe) says there is no sale for potatoes. Perkins and Wright have put him in horse judging and marshal of the county fair.

- Frank Beardmore and Ellis Ross married last Thursday.
- Mrs. Rendell did not come to visit.

Florence Pipe Continues:

- Florence Pipe McCunn thinks it is about time for her parents to come home.
- She is tired of telling everyone who asks that she does not know when they will return.
- Louisa has been visiting Mrs. G. Hutchinson for two weeks
- School commences on September 20.

[crosshatched]

Waupaca Sep 12/1875

Dear Father and Mother [Thomas and Elizabeth Stickland Pipe]

We received your letter yesterday of August 26, were glad to hear you are all well. We have been alone this week only four of us. Grandmother [Charlotte Jennings Pipe Pillar] is at the Points [Stevens Point, Portage County, Wisconsin] making a visit, expected her here last night but she did not come, think she will come tomorrow. We are having splendid weather again now. This week is fair week. You ought to be here, but I suppose you would think nothing of our fair now. The farmers are just commencing to dig their potatoes and cut their corn.

Tom and Amelia [Woodnorth Pipe] are at Mr. Jo Moreys visiting today. Mrs. Chelsey says if you don't come pretty soon, she don't know what she will do. She thinks she has missed you as much as anyone. <u>But I don't know</u>!

Louie Sterns came back this week. He looks pretty well. Mr. Silverthorn and Emma are at Pennsylvania [USA] visiting for two or three months. Mrs. Gus Chesley has been very sick but is some better now.

Jack and I took tea at Mrs. Chesley last night.

O dear, I can't think of a thing to write. I will leave the rest for Florence [Pipe McCunn] and Effie [Pipe Alexander] to finish out, write and tell us when you are going to start for home. Goodbye from your

Affectionate daughter

Mary [Elizabeth Pipe Woodworth]

We all join in love to all not forgetting yourselves

P.S. Fred Lea and Minnie are married. Mary [Elizabeth Pipe Woodworth]

Dear Mother and Father [Elizabeth Stickland and Thomas Pipe]

As Mary [Elizabeth Pipe] left some paper I thought I would write. When are you coming home. I am getting tired of hearing in every letter we don't know when we are coming home. Florence [Pipe McCunn] and Mary [Elizabeth Pipe Woodworth] and I [Effie Pipe Alexander] dreamt you was home and Hugo Lea and so we thought you must be coming home goodbye from

Effie [Pipe Alexander]

[other way]

Jack [John Stickland Pipe] say to tell you there is no sale for potatoes. He is cutting corn today. He said that Pirkins [Perkins] and Wright have put him in horse judge and marshall of the fair [Waupaca County Fair]. He says he is a big gun. O my, Frank Beardmore and Miss Ellie Ross were married last Thursday. There will be no young folks left here in this country when you come back, that is if you stay much longer. Jack says you can just drop a line and let us know when you are coming home. I did not see anything of that. Mrs. Rendell she did not come up here. From Mary [Elizabeth Pipe Woodworth]

School commences a week from today

Waupaca Sep 12, 1875

Dear Father and Mother [Thomas and Elizabeth Stickland Pipe]

As Mary [Elizabeth Pipe Woodworth] and Effie [Pipe Alexander] has left a little space, I thought that I would write a few words. I have begun to think that it is about time that you know when you are about to start for home. Everyone that I see is asking me when are you coming till I have got tired of telling them that I didn't know. Miss Willimans got home from NY [New York, USA] last week, where she has been visiting all summer. School commences the 20. This is fair week. John [Stickland Pipe] is one of the marshals. Louisa has been up to Mr. G. Hutchinson for two weeks and has not got home yet. Goodbye from

Florence [Pipe Alexander]

Letter Number 90, Envelope Front

Letter Number 90, Page 1

Waupaca Sept 12/87

Dear Father and Mother

We received your letter yesterday of August 26. were glad to hear you are all well. we have been alone this week only four of us Grand Mother is at the Pinks making a visit. expected her here last night. but she did not come. think she will come to morrow. we are having splendid wether as ever now. this week is fair week. you ought to be here. but I suppose you would think nothing of our fair now. the farmers are just commencing to dig their potatoes and cut their corn

Letter Number 90, Page 2

Tom and Amelia are at
Mr J Moneys visiting to day.
Mrs Chesley Says if you dont
come pretty soon. She dont know
what She will do. She thinks she
has missed you as much as any
one. But I dont know!
Louie Sterns came back this
Week. he looks pretty well.
Mr Silverthorn and Emma are
at Pennslyvania visiting. for
two or three months. Mrs Ens Chesley
has been very sick but is some
better now.
Jack and I took tea at
Mrs Chesley last night.
O dear. I cant think of a
thing to write. I will leave the
rest for Florence and Effie to
finish out, write and tell us
when you are going to Start for
home Good bye from your

Letter Number 90, Page 3

affectionate Daughter
Mary.
we all join in love to all
not for getting your selves.
P.S. Fred Lea and Minnie are
married. Mary.

Dear Mother & Father
as Mary left some papper
I thought I would write when are
you comming home I an getten
tired of hearing in every
letter wee doant now when we
are comming home Florence
Mary & I drempt you was
home and Hugo Lea and so
wee thought youmust be
comming home good by from
Effie

Letter Number 90, Page 4

To Thomas & Eliza in England 1875

Florence
Effie
Mary

Wappaca Sep 12 1875

Dear Father & Mother
as Mary & Effie ~~and~~ has left a little space I throught that I would write a fue words. I have degan to think that it is adout time that you knew when you are about to start for home every one that I sea are asking me when you are coming. tell I havegot tired of telling them that I dident know. Miss Willimans got home from N.Y. last week, where she has ben visting all sumer, School comences the 20. This is fair week ~~and~~ John is one of the morshels. Louisa has been up to Mr G. Hutchinson for two weeks and has not got home yet. good buy from Florence.

Letter Number 91

Date: 1876
Writer: William Jennings Pipe
Recipient: Thomas Pipe
Sent from: Stawell, Victoria, Borung County, Australia
Sent to: Pipe House, Lanark, Portage County, Wisconsin, USA [Sheridan, Waupaca County, Wisconsin, USA Post Office]

Key Ideas

- William Jennings Pipe served in the Police Department in Victoria, Australia, earning the distinction of Senior Constable. In 1880, he was appointed by the Governor to be a Crown Lands Bailiff in and for the colony of Victoria, Australia
- He lost money in speculation.
- William Jennings Pipe has not heard from Joseph Pipe in nine years. He was a butcher in a suburb of Melbourne, Victoria, Australia, but his business failed.
- He received a letter from John Jennings who promises to visit.
- William Pipe only knows of a few family members in Australia: Joseph Pipe, one of his sisters, and Tom Jennings.
- Many Stawell, Australia, people are mining for gold.

[crosshatched and start not included]

Poor Thomas [Jennings] has not a deal of good for himself since he has been out. I don't know if I ever told you how I was situated, and of course you know I belong to the Poha? [Police Department] they give me 8/- day and 8/- per week for house rent, fuel, and light. It is not much but it just keeps us comfortable and to tell you the truth I am not wrapped much in hard work this is unprofitable thing altogether so far as I can see. I have lost some money by speculation but have not yet given up hopes that I may get it back by the same means.

I have not seen or heard of Joseph Pipe for about nine years. He was living down in one of the suburbs of Melbourne [Australia] carrying on butchering but failed. I had a couple of letters some two or three years ago from the husband of one of the girls "Colip" [?] I think I replied to the first but not to the last one, one of them was at the Jamieson [high country region of Victoria, Australia] when I was there nine years since. Her husband died shortly afterwards and she got married again. I don't know what became of her after that. Poor Joe's [Joseph Pipe] wife used to drink indeed they were a pair of heavy sots [heavy drinkers]. Poor mother [Charlotte Jennings Pillar Pipe] writes cheerful.

We all trotting along at the same old place as when you last wrote to me, Stowell [Stawell] things have not been over bright, write me still I should not complain as I have held my own better, than the majority of the people here Stowell [Stawell] depending altogether on gold mining for its prosperity. I have a little money invested in it. I am not so far over prosperous but hope for better times of course this pretty much of a spree, one mine that I am interested in is turning out stone that is expected to go 2oz to the ton, if so it will give me £6 or £8 per month for two or three years. They will crush in a week or two and that will end the doubt. Other two or three claims that I have an interest in are not doing so well, but any day may place me for a few pounds. It has cost me from £3 to £5 every month for the last year besides the bringing in some £10 per scrit [?]. We are fairly well myself, Annie [McGregor Pipe], William [Pipe], Edwin [Pipe] and Charles McGregor. You will perceive there is a touch of "Scotch" about the last though really he is more a Pipe than the former.

I received a letter from Tom Jennings a week or two back. He seems well and promises me to come down early in July.

[other way]

[Missing part of letter. Seems to be talking about their mother, Charloette Jennings Pipe Pillar.]

though she has arrived at a ripe old age and when we can scarcely expect for her to be spared for any length of time. I trust it will please God to spare her from a lengthened illness. My dear Thomas [Pipe] it does seem to me dreadful that we should be buffeted about the world during a long lifetime and to finish up with an illness in some cases extending over many months but if such be the will of God, I suppose we must

[other way]

bow to it. I have often thought it strange that I have never met any person out here that I knew with the exception of Joseph Pipe, one of his sisters and Tom Jennings, and yet was [all?] I knew of the Pipes. Now my dearest Brother and sister [Thomas and Elizabeth Stickland Pipe] I shall draw this uninteresting epistle to a close for fear of boring you. I shall wait anxiously for a letter, your affection.

Brother

Wm. [Jennings] Pipe

Letter Number 91, Page 1

Poor Thomas has not [illegible] a deal of good for himself since he has been out. I don't know if I ever told you how I was situated? Of course you know I belong to the Police. They give me 8/- a day and 8/- per week for house rent fuel & light, it is not much but it just keeps us comfortable and to tell you the truth I am not [illegible] much in hard work it is unprofitable thing altogether so far as I can see. I have lost some money by speculation but have not yet given up hopes that I may get it back by the same means. I have not seen or heard of Joseph [illegible] for about nine years. he was living down in one of the suburbs of Melbourne carrying on [illegible] but failed. I had a couple of letters some two or three years ago from the husband of one of the girls. "Cory" I think I replied to the first but not to the last. One of them was at the Jamieson when I was there nine years since — her husband died shortly afterwards and she got married again. I don't know what became of her after that. Poor Joe's wife used to drink — indeed they were a pair of heavy sots. Poor mother writes cheerful

Letter Number 91, Page 2

We are battling along at the same old place
as when you last wrote to me, Stawell. things
have not been over bright with me still I should
not complain as I have held my own better
than the majority of the people here. Stawell is
depending all together on Gold mining for its prosperity
I have a little money invested in it. I am so
far not over prosperous but hope for better times
of course it is pretty much of a 'spec' one mine
that I am interested in is turning out stone that
is expected to go 2oz to the ton if so it will
give me £6 or £7 per month for two or
three years they will crush in a week or
so and that will end the doubt. other
two or three claims that I have an interest
in are not doing so well, but any day
may place me for a few pounds: it
has cost me from £3: to £4: every month for
the last year besides the buying in some
cases £10 per share. We are fairly well
myself, Annie, William Edwin & Charles McGregor.
You will perceive there is a touch of "Scotch"
about the last though really he is more a
Pipe than the former.
I received a letter from Tom Jennings a
week or two back, he seems well and
promises me to come down early in July

Letter Number 92

Date: 11 September 1876
Writer: Lissie Dommett Dauncey, cousin
Recipient: Cousins [Thomas and Elizabeth Stickland Pipe & children: Mary Elizabeth Pipe Woodnorth, Effie Pipe Alexander, Florence Pipe McCunn]
Sent from: Hursey, Broadwindsor, Dorset County, England
Sent to: Pipe House, Lanark, Portage County, Wisconsin, USA [Sheridan, Waupaca County, Wisconsin, USA Post Office]

Key Ideas

- Clem, Nellie (Ellen Jennings Davy), and Bill went to Kingsbury (Episcopi, Somerset) yesterday for a christening. Anna is the eighth child. John and Bessie Bond and Nellie (Ellen Jennings) Davy were sponsors.
- Polly Symes is preparing for a little stranger (baby?).
- William and Pollie Dommett Wyatt, three from Purtington, Somerset, and two from Bere Chapel, Broadwindsor, Dorset, visited for the chapel bazaar.
- William Wyatt will lease his farm. The sale is on the 21st of September. William Wyatt may then reside at Childhay, Beaminster, Dorset, on a four-hundred-acre farm which is two miles from Lissie Dommett Dauncey.
- Aunt John (An aunt is sometimes referred to by her husband's first name.) at Hellings Farm, Somerset, is better. Tilley died at Odcombe, South Somerset, near Yeovil.
- Mr. Eaton is married to Miss Fowler at Burstock, Dorset.
- Mr. Palmer has William's (William Wyatt) sale.
- Polly Dommett Wyatt is expecting her fourth child. Fanny is staying with the Dauncey family to finish school with Mabel at the quarter.
- Mr. Penney and Miss Malan are married.
- Mother wrote to Charlotte Jennings Pipe Pillar about two months ago.

- Lissie (Elizabeth) Pillar Bowron has a beautiful boy.
- Uncle and Aunt (William Jennings and Elizabeth Coleman Jennings) visited Friday. They are well at Park Farm, Dorset. Their grandson is called William Clement.
- In Letter Number 65, Lissie Dommett Dauncey is the daughter of William and Mary Ann Jennings Dommett.

Broadwindsor

Sep 11th/76

Dear Cousins

I am at last seated to answer your kind and long looked for letter. I am now rather tied to my chair with a rising on my foot. I hope it will soon be well as I am wanted so badly about the house, it being our washing week, Clem and Nellie [Ellen Jennings Davy] and Bill went to Kingsbury [Episcopi, Somerset] yesterday to a christening. No. 8 the name is Anna. John and Bessie Bond and Nellie [Ellen Jennings] Davy were the sponsors. I heard from

Polly Symes a few days ago, she is busy preparing for a little stranger. They have been here this summer. There has been a bazaar here in aid of a harmonium for the Chapel. William and Pollie [Dommett Wyatt] and three from Purtington [Somerset], two from Bere chapel [Broadwindsor, Dorset] were here, there was a concert in the evening. William Wyatt is going to lease his farm, the sale is the 21st of this month. We rather expect they will have Childhay [Farm, Beaminster, Dorset] that is about two miles from here. It is about four hundred acres. How do you like your new home. We hope you are comfortably settled.

Aunt John at Helliings [Hellings Farm, near Crewkerne Somerset] is better than she has been. I suppose you have heard of poor Tilley's death at Odcombe [South Somerset, near Yeovil]. Mr Eaton is married to a Miss Fowler of Burstock [Dorset]. Mr. Palmer has William's sale. We have had it very warm this summer. Today is the day we have had fire. We have finished harvest, gathered it in beautifully and the hay well made. Father sold his lambs at Crewkerne [Somerset] fair, two guineas each. He had the top price. Our roots are very good likely to have the prize at the ploughing match. Bell has not been very well but is better. My dear mother [Mrs. Mary Ann Jennings Dommett] has been better this summer than last. Polly Dommett Wyatt is expecting no. 4 next month. Fanny comes here to stay at the quarter to go to school with Mabel. Have you heard from William lately? We should like to know how they are all. We have had a gay wedding here. Mr. Pinney and Miss Malan. Mother [Mary Ann Jennings Dommett] wrote to Aunt [Charlotte Jennings Pipe] Pillar about 2 months ago directed it Oshkosh [Wisconsin]. We much like to hear from her soon. Father and Mother [William and May Ann Jennings Dommett] and Bill [Dommett] joins me in kindest love to each one of you. We think of Lissie [Elizabeth Pillar] Bowrons a most beautiful boy.

From your affectionate cousin

Lissie [Dommett] Dauncey

[other way]

Uncle and Aunt William [and Elizabeth Coleman Jennings] were here Friday. They are both well. They are all well at Park [Farm, Dorset] the baby is called William Clement.

Do not keep us so long without a letter again.

Letter Number 92, Page 1

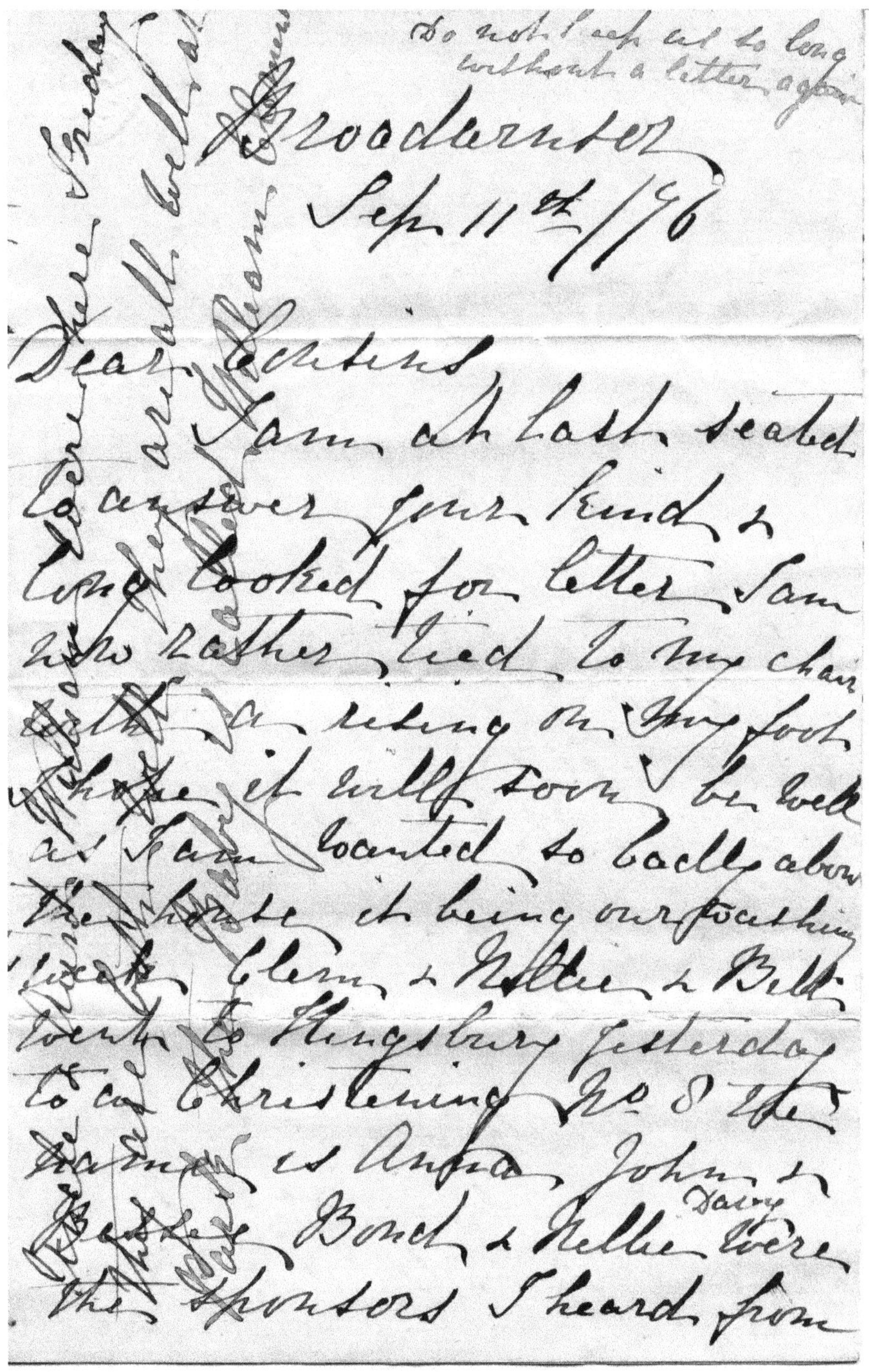

Do not keep us so long without a letter again

Broadwater
Sep 11th/96

Dear Sisters
I am at last seated to answer your kind & long looked for letter I am now rather tied to my chair with a sitting on my foot I hope it will soon be well as I am wanted so badly about the house it being our feathering week. Clem & Nellie & Belle went to Kingsbury yesterday to a Christening No 8 the name is Anna John & Daisy Bond & Nellie were the sponsors I heard from

Letter Number 92, Page 2

Polly Symes a few days ago she
& busy preparing for a little strange[r]
they have been here this summer
There has been a bazaar here
in aid of a harmonium for
the Chapel William & Pollie
& three from Purtington
two from Bere chapel were
here there was a concert in
the evening, William Wyatt
is going to leave his farm
the sale is the 21st of
this month we rather
expect they will have
Chilcot-hay that is about
two miles from here it
is about four hundred
acres How do you like your
new home we hope you
are comfortably settled

Letter Number 92, Page 3

Aunt John at Hellings is
better than she has been
I suppose you have heard
of poor Tilley's death at Odcombe
Mr Eaton is married to
a Miss Fowler of Burstock
Mr Palmer has Williams sale
We have had it very warm
this summer today is the
first day we have had fire
We have finished harvest
gathered it in beautifully
& the hay well made
Father sold his Lambs
at Crewkerne fair two
Guineas each he had
the top price Our roots
are very good likely to
have the prize at the

Letter Number 92, Page 4

Ploughing match Bell
has not been very well
but is better My dear Mother
has been better this summer
than last Polly Wyatt is
expecting No 4 next month
Fanny comes here to stay
at the Quarter to go to
School with Mabel Have
you heard from William lately
we should like to know how
they are all We have had a
gay wedding here Mr Pinney &
Miss Macan Mother wrote
to Aunt Pillar about 2 months
ago directed it Oshkosh very
much like to hear from her soon
Father & Mother & Bill joins me
in kindest love to each one
of you we think Lessie Bowron
a most beautiful boy
From your affecte Cousin
Lessie Dauncey

Letter Number 92, Envelope Front

Mrs Pipe
Sheriden
Waupaca Co
Wis

Letter Number 92, Envelope Back

Letter Number 93

Date: 2 November 1879
Writer: J.R. Kingsbury, County Judge
Recipient: Thomas Pipe
Sent from: Stevens Point, Portage County, Wisconsin, USA
Sent to: Pipe House, Lanark, Portage County, Wisconsin, USA [Sheridan, Waupaca County, Wisconsin, USA Post Office]

Key Ideas:

- The county judge gives advice to Thomas Pipe on how to take an estate inventory.
- Thomas Pipe is administrator for the D.P. Hutchinson estate, town of Lanark, Portage County, Wisconsin.

From County Judge, Portage County, Wis.,

Stevens Point Wis., Nov. 2nd, 1879

Mr Pipe

Before notifying the appraisers to come and appraise the property you should make out a description of all the lands belonging to the estate, also a list of all the personal property. It is not expected that every article of household furniture will be appraised separately. To illustrate Kitchen furniture

including cook stove $

Parlor furniture including carpet $

Cooking and glassware $

Silver ware $

So many beds and bedding $

Wearing apparel of deceased $

Family wearing apparel you will mot

You see, you are required to return inventory within three months.

I would suggest you wait at least until your threshing is done.

Then you will set apart farm products enough to furnish your family at least 6 months including pork, beef, flour, potatoes etc and make an inventory and appraisal of the value, you will also omit such an amount of hay and oats as the stock on the farm will in your judgement need, this will save you a great amount of trouble and work, no injustice to anyone.

I have made these suggestions to you to save you trouble. Many families situated as yours are at a loss to know what is right or what rights they can expect.

You see the folly of returning an amount of hay and grain for you to account for and then feed it to the stock, instead of that save out enough to feed the stock as long as you think it profitable to keep it and then account for the money you receive when it is sold.

In the meantime, I shall be glad to aid you in settling up the affairs in any way that I can.

Yours very truly

J.R. Kingsbury

County Judge

Letter Number 93, Page 1

OFFICE OF

COUNTY JUDGE.

PORTAGE COUNTY, WIS.

Stevens Point, Wis., Nov 2nd 1889

Mrs Pike,

Before notifying the appraisers to come and appraise the property, you should make out a description of all the lands belonging to the Estate, also a list of all the personal property, It is not expected that every article of household furniture will be appraised seperately, to illustrate— Kitchen furniture including Cook Stove $——
Parlor furniture including
Carpets $
Crockery & Glassware $
Silver ware $
—so many beds and bedding $
Wearing apparel of deceased $
(family wearing apparel you will omit)
You see you are required to return inventory within three months,
I would suggest you wait at least until your thrashing is done

Letter Number 93, Page 2

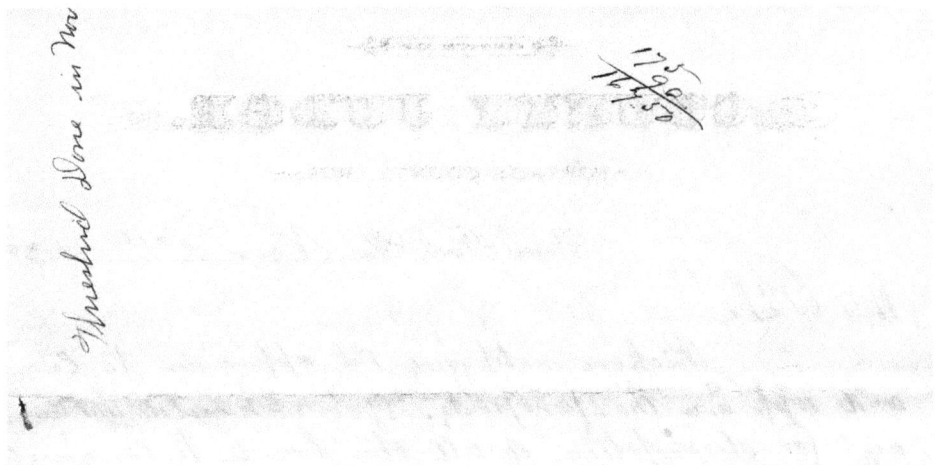

Letter Number 93, Page 3

OFFICE OF
COUNTY JUDGE.
PORTAGE COUNTY, WIS.

Stevens Point, Wis., ... 187

then you will set apart farm products
enough to furnish your family at least
6 Months including Pork, Beef, Flour, Potatoes
&c and make an inventory and appraisal
of the bal, you will also omit such
an amount of hay & Oats as the stock
on the farm will in your judgement
need, this will save you a great amt
of trouble, and work no injustice to any
one.

I have made these suggestions to you
to save you trouble, Many families situated
as yours are at a loss to know what is right
or what rights they can exercise.
You see the folly of retaining an amount of
hay & grain for you to account for and then
feed it to the stock, instead of that save
out enough to feed the stock as long as
you think it profitable to keep it and
then account for the money you receive
when it is sold, over

Letter Number 93, Page 4

In the mean time I shall be glad to aid you in settling up the affairs in any way that I can.

Yours very truly

J. R. Kingsbury
County Judge

Letter Number 94

Date: 30 November 1880
Writer: E.S. Donaldson, M.D.
Recipient: Estate of Thomas Pipe
Sent from: Waupaca, Waupaca County, Wisconsin, USA
Sent to: Pipe House, Lanark, Portage County, Wisconsin, USA [Sheridan, Waupaca County, Wisconsin, USA Post Office]

Key Ideas:

- Dr. Donaldson sends his last bill to the estate of Thomas Pipe.
- Dr. Donaldson visited Thomas Pipe as counsel on September 16, 1880.

Estate of Thos Pipe $500

Receipt Nov. 30, 1880

Waupaca Nov. 30, 1880

The Estate of Thos Pipe

To ditto E.S. Donaldson Dr.

1880 Sept. 16 For visit as counsel $500

Received payment

E.S. Donaldson, M.D.

This painting of Thomas and John Valentine Pipe's birth village, Donyatt, Somerset, features The Blessed Virgin Mary Church and Donyatt Bridge. The brothers' grandfather, James Pipe, in his will proved 18 October 1834, left their father John Pipe £5. The will describes James Pipe's property which includes, in part, "all that house by the river side near Donyatt Bridge called the Bucking House. All within the parish of Donyatt." (See Appendix F.)

DONYATT PARISH CHURCH, 1874

Charles Leaver (fl. 1867-1883)

Oil on canvas, 36 x 54 in.

By courtesy of Ivor and Joan Weiss, Kelvedon, near Colchester, Essex.

Charles Leaver was a painter of landscapes and rural subjects and seems to have specialised in 'church in snow' scenes, in each of which he frames the church with bare, frosty trees set against a wintry sky. Little is known about Leaver's life. It is known that he was based at Harbourne in Birmingham and frequently exhibited at the Royal Birmingham Society of Arts, but the settings of his pictures suggest that he travelled a good deal in the British Isles.

Donyatt parish church, near Ilminster in Somerset, dates from the fifteenth century, though its font and the stone base of its pulpit probably once stood in an earlier church on the site. Donyatt's curious name may be a corruption of 'Donna's Gate' or 'Donna's Gap' ('Donna' was possibly once the lord of the manor), or the name may derive from 'Dene-yatt', as the village lies in the Ile Valley, or Dene, and 'Yatt' was the Old English word for 'gateway'.

In common with some other Somerset churches, the one at Donyatt features an open parapet, pairs of buttresses clasping the tower, and, in the belfry section, windows with elaborate, perforated tracery rather than the more usual louvre design. The pinnacle crowned by a weather vane was removed during recent re-building work. Within the church is a Jacobean pulpit and the original Tudor pews. These would have been there when Henry VIII visited Park Manor, which stood nearby in the thirteenth-century Royal Forest of Neroche but has long since been demolished. The almshouses to the left of the picture were built in 1625 with local stone, which was probably brought from the same quarry as the stone used for the church.

C.M.B.

Letter Number 94, Page 1

Estate of
Thos. Pipe
$5.00

Letter Number 94, Page 2

Waupaca, Nov 30, 1880
The Estate of Thos. Pipe
To Dr. E. S. Donaldson Dr.

1880			
Sep.	6	To 1 Visit & Counsel	$5.00

Received payment
E. S. Donaldson M.D.

Chapter 9

Lanark, Portage County, Wisconsin
1883 - 1914

Chapter 9 includes letters from 1883 to 1914 while Elizabeth Stickland Pipe is living at The Pipe House in the town of Lanark, Portage County, Wisconsin, with her son William Edwin Pipe and his wife Mary Agnes Messer Pipe. One letter is written by William Edwin Pipe to Thomas Messer before William Edwin married his daughter, Mary Agnes Messer. Three letters are about William Edwin and Mary Agnes Messer Pipe's growing family. One letter is from Stevens Point, Wisconsin, where the John Stickland and Elizabeth Johnson Pipe family live. Mary Elizabeth Pipe Woodnorth and her husband Frank Woodnorth write Elizabeth Stickland Pipe to announce their marriage. Mary Elizabeth Pipe Woodnorth also writes to an unknown recipient. One letter is a tribute to William Edwin Pipe in the form of a poem from an attorney in Manitowoc, Wisconsin. Two letters are to Grandmother Elizabeth Stickland Pipe from her granddaughters, Florence and Ethel McCunn, who are living in Scotland and England, respectively. Both girls ask Grandmother Elizabeth Stickland Pipe where she originated in England. Both express an interest in traveling to their grandmother's homeland to visit any remaining family and friends. Included at the end of this chapter is a hand-written list of deaths in the Jennings/Bond family from 1837 to 1872. Elizabeth Stickland Pipe died in January 1916 at the age of 91.

(L-R) Mary Agnes and William Pipe, Thomas Messer, Mary Niven Messer, and Edwin Pipe standing behind his parents, Elizabeth and John (Jack) Stickland Pipe.

Letter Number 95

Date: 9 April 1883
Writer: William Edwin Pipe
Recipient: Thomas Messer
Sent from: Pipe House, Lanark, Portage County, Wisconsin, USA [Sheridan, Waupaca County, Wisconsin, USA, Post Office]
Sent to: Oxford Junction, Jones County, Iowa, USA

Key Ideas:

- William Edwin Pipe, son of Thomas and Elizabeth Stickland Pipe, writes Thomas Messer with a request to allow his daughter, Mary Agnes Messer, to stay at the Pipe House three or four months longer for her continued good health.
- William Edwin Pipe marries Mary Agnes Messer on November 29, 1883, in Oxford Junction, Jones County, Iowa.

Sheridan April 9th, [18]83

Mr. Messer

Dear Sir

Although a stranger I take the liberty to write to you asking you for your daughter Aggie [Mary Agnes Messer], undoubtedly it will be hard for you to give your consent as we have never met, if it was not so far I would come and see you. If it would not be asking so much, I would like to have Aggie [Mary Agnes Messer] stay here three or four month[s] longer, health is much better than it was last fall. Hoping to receive a favourable answer.

Respectively yours

Wm. [Edwin] Pipe

Letter Number 95

183

Sheridan april 4th

Mr Messer
Dear Sir
Although a stranger I take the liberty to write to you asking you for your daughter Aggie undoubtfuly it will be hard for you to give your consent as we have never met if it was not so far I would come and see you if it would not be asking to mutch I would like to have Aggie stay here three or four month longer her helth is mutch better than it was last fall, Hopeing to receive a favorible answer
respectively yours
Wm Pipe

Letter Number 96

Date: 6 September 1883
Writer: Mary Elizabeth Pipe Woodnorth & Frank Woodnorth
Recipient: Elizabeth Stickland Pipe
Sent from: Kirby House, East Water and Mason streets
Milwaukee, Milwaukee County, Wisconsin, USA
Sent to: Pipe House, Lanark, Portage County, Wisconsin, USA
[Sheridan, Waupaca County, Wisconsin,
USA, Post Office]

Key Ideas

- Mary Elizabeth Pipe Woodnorth writes to her mother, Elizabeth Stickland Pipe, with the news she is in Milwaukee with Frank Woodnorth. They are now married.
- Mary Elizabeth hopes that her mother is not too surprised or upset.
- She notes they were married in a church.
- Mary Elizabeth feels she is old enough to make her decision. She hopes they can still get along.
- Mary Elizabeth will pick up her belongings on Sunday. She will write to her brother William Edwin Pipe in a few days.

Frank Woodnorth continues

- Frank says he would have liked Elizabeth Stickland Pipe's sanction on their marriage.
- He says he is to blame, not Mary Elizabeth.
- Frank hopes that he and Elizabeth Stickland Pipe can be friends. If Elizabeth cannot, he hopes she can be friends with Mary Elizabeth Pipe Woodnorth.

Kirby House,

A Kirby Proprietor

Cor. [Corner] E. Water and Mason Sts.

Office on First floor

Milwaukee Sep[t.] 6th, 1883

My dear Mother

I think you will not be surprised to find that I am in Milwaukee. Perhaps I have done wrong in not telling you more or rather talking to you more about my getting married, but I spoke to you twice on the subject and you seemed so indifferent and even the last time told me not to talk to you. So, what could I do. It was a very different way than I wanted to do. Although we were married in the church, I would ten times rather have been married at home and had you all there, but I could see there was no use wishing any such thing. So done the next best thing. Am sorry to have you all feeling so bad, but think I am old enough to know what I wanted to do. Of course, I am the one

that has got to live with Frank, and not the rest of the family. If I ever regret the day "as you have said I would," I shall be the one to suffer the consequences. If you think I have disgraced the family and don't want to have anything to do or ever say to me, of course I will try not to trouble you. But if you think and look at it as a great many do, and think it all right, I shall be very much better pleased. I know you all think that everyone thinks it was absurd for me to do as I have, but there has a great many talked to me on the subject and some, especially one, a very old friend of yours, had a long talk with me to my surprise, and told me to go ahead if I felt so disposed. She thought it the best thing I could do and thought I never should be sorry. Of course, Frank has been a rough fellow, but she says he has changed for the better, and I think no one needs to say a word. For your [Mary Elizabeth Pipe's] own brothers, some of them are not the very best. I understand, perhaps you will think the last is not a quotation, but it is. We leave here tomorrow morning for Oshkosh. The next day for Waupaca and I think Sunday I shall come and get my things, if nothing happens. I shall write to Will [William Edwin Pipe] in a few days, all for this time, love to all.

From Mary [Pipe Woodnorth]

[Frank Woodnorth continues]

Milwaukee 9-6-[18]83

Mrs. Pipe

Madame

At last Mary and I are married. I would have liked your sanction, but as you are so much opposed to it, I persuaded Mary to do as she did. If there is any wrong done, I am the only one to blame. I would like you to be friends with us, and if you can't with me you can still be friendly with Mary, for she is still your daughter. I do not expect that you will feel that way yet, but as time passes I hope that you will see that we have done right, for I know that I will make Mary happy.

Hoping that you will be friends with Mary. I have the honour still to be.

Frank S. Woodnorth

Letter Number 96, Page 1

Milwaukee 9-6-83.
Mrs Pipe
Madam.
At last Mary & I are married. I would have liked your sanction, but as you were so very much aposed to it. I persuaded Mary to do as she did. If there is any wrong done. I am the only one to blame. I would like you to be friends with us. and if you cant with me. you can still be friendly with Mary. for

Letter Number 96, Page 2

she is still your daughter I do not expect that you will feel that way yet. but as time passes I hope that you will see that we have done right. for I know that I will make Mary happy. Hopeing that you will be friends with Mary. I have the honor still to be

Frank S Woodworth

Letter Number 96, Page 3

WAKE ME UP WHEN KIRBY DIES.

KIRBY HOUSE

A. KIRBY, Proprietor.

Cor. E. Water and Mason Sts.

OFFICE ON FIRST FLOOR.

Milwaukee, Sep 6 1883.

My Dear Mother,

I think you will not be surprised to find that I am in Milwaukee. perhaps, I have done wrong in not letting you know; or rather talking to you more about my getting Married. but I spoke to you twice on the subject. and you seemed so indifferent, and even the last time told me not to talk to you. so what could I do? it was a very different way than I wanted to do, altho we were married in the church. I would ten times rather have been Married at home. and had you all to there. but I could see there was no use wishing any such thing. so done the next best thing. am sorry to have you all ~~thus~~ feeling so bad. but think I am old enough to know what I wanted to do. of course I am the one that

Letter Number 96, Page 4

have got to live with Frank, and not
the rest of the family. if I ever
regret the day "as you said I would"
I shall be the one to suffer the conce
quences. if you think I have disgraced
the family, and dont want to have any
thing to do, or even say to me, of course
I will try not to trouble you. but if
you it think and look at it as a great many
do, and think it all right I shall be very
much better pleased. I know you all think
that every one thinks it was absurd for me
to do as I have, but there has a great many
talked to me on the subject in the matter, and
some, especially one a very old friend of yours. had
a long talk with me. to my surprise, and told
me to go ahead if I felt so disposed she thought
it the best thing I could do. and thought I
never should be sorry. of course Frank has been
a rough fellow, but she says but he has have changed
for better, and I think no one needs to say a word
for your own brothers some of them are not the
very best. I understand, perhaps you will think
the last is not a quotation, but it is. We leave
here tomorrow morning for Oshkosh. the next day
for Waupaca. and I think Sunday for I
shall come and get my things. if nothing
happens. I shall write to Will in a few
days. all for this time love to all
from Mary -

Letter Number 97

Date: 22 March 1887 [Births support 1887, not 1884]
Writer: Thomas Messer
Recipient: William Edwin Pipe
Sent from: Oxford Junction, Jones County, Iowa, USA
Sent to: Pipe House, Lanark, Portage County, Wisconsin, USA [Sheridan, Waupaca, Waupaca County, Wisconsin, USA, Post Office]

Key Ideas:

- Thomas Messer is asking whether Aggie (Mary Agnes Messer Pipe) should bring the baby (Mae Elizabeth Pipe born October 23, 1884) home in March or in fall.
- (Mae Elizabeth Pipe stayed with Thomas and Mary Niven Messer when William Edwin and Mary Agnes Messer Pipe's second child, Mina Margaret Pipe, was born on September 18, 1886.)
- Mae Elizabeth Pipe is nicknamed Toots.
- Grandma Mary Niven Messer will bring Baby Aggie (likely Mae Elizabeth Pipe) home if she can stay.
- An explanation from a descendant in Letter Number 99 tries to clarify which baby stayed with Thomas and Mary Niven Messer. Mina Margaret Pipe, who was born in 1886, likely stayed with her mother, Mary Agnes Messer Pipe. The Messer grandparents likely took care of Mae Elizabeth Pipe who is at the time about two years old.

Oxford [Oxford Junction]

Dear Will [William Edwin Pipe]

We have a dispute here and you are the only one that can settle it, Aggie [Mary Agnes Messer Pipe] is ?? to bring the baby [Mae Elizabeth Pipe born 1884] home with her since she has seen her away Pa and Ma want her to stop to next fall. She has got to be such a nice little girl it is hard to part with her, but it is all left to you. If she come now or next fall

Aggie [Mary Agnes Messer Pipe] has got the best of it, but if you say she has got to stay, we will keep her to fall, and Grandma [Mary Niven Messer] will bring her up to you. It will be lonesome without her now. She is such a good little girl [Mae Elizabeth Pipe] laughing all the time when she is awake, so it is all left to you if baby has to come home now or next fall, it is very cold here at present. No sign of spring yet.

I suppose ?? given you all here.

No more at present

From your [Thomas] Messer

Letter Number 97, Page 1

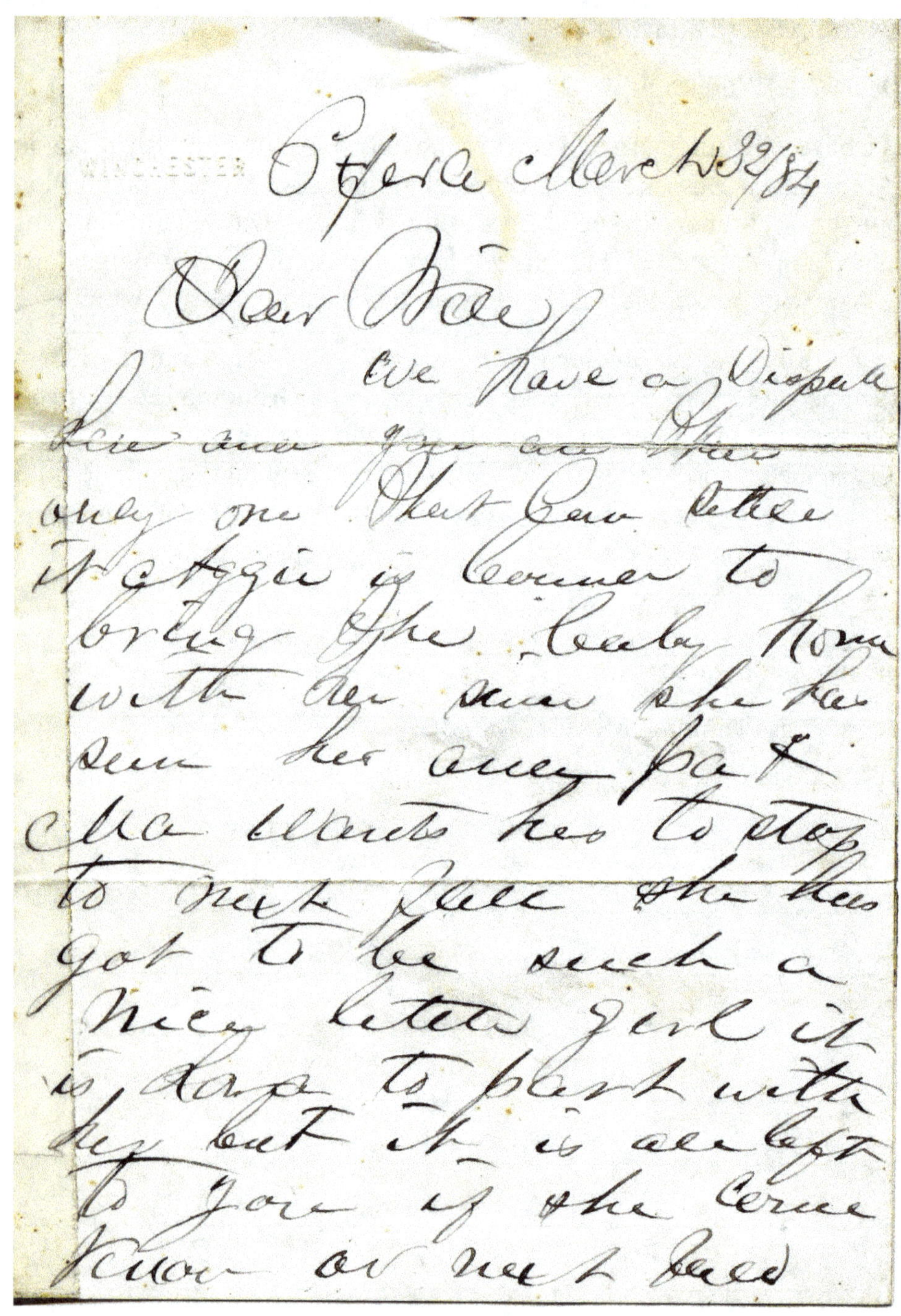

Oxford March 22/84

Dear Wife

We have a Dispute here and you are the only one that can settle it. Aggie is coming to bring the baby home with her since she has seen her aunty. Pa & Ma wants her to stop to next Fall she has got to be such a nice little girl it is hard to part with her but it is all left to you if she come soon or not bess

Letter Number 97, Page 2

Aggie has got the best
of it here but if you
say she has got to
stay we will keep her to
Lou and Grandma
will bring her up to
you it will be lonesome
without her I know
she is such a good
little girl laughing
all the time when
she is awake so it is
all left to you if
baby has to come
home now or next
fall it is very cold
weather here at present
no signs of spring

Letter Number 97, Page 3

Letter Number 98

Date: 22 March 1887 [Births support 1887, not 1884]
Writer: Thomas Messer
Recipient: William Edwin Pipe
Sent from: Oxford Junction, Jones County, Iowa, USA
Sent to: Pipe House, Lanark, Portage County, Wisconsin, USA [Sheridan, Waupaca County, Wisconsin, USA, Post Office]

Key Ideas

- This is a transcription of Letter Number 97 by a descendant.

Dexter [Oxford Junction] March 22, 1884

Dear Will

We have a dispute her and you are the only one that can settle it. Aggie is to bring the baby home with her since she has seen her only – wants her to stop to next fall. She has got to be such a nice little girl it is hard to part with her, but it is all left to you if she cries. Or next Aggie has got the best of it here but if you say she has got to stay we will keep her to

And grandma will bring her up to you it will be lonesome without her

She is such a good little girl laughing all the time she is awake, so it all left to you if baby has to come home - or next fall. It is very cold weather here

No sign of spring

[This letter appears to be a transcript by someone trying to decipher the difficult handwriting of the letter]

Letter Number 98, Page 1 - Transcription

Cerue cries Cervel Cruel Dexter

March 22 1884

Dear Will

We havea despute

here and you ae the only one

that can settle it. Aggie is

bring the baby home with her

since she has seen her only ——

—— wants her to stop to next

fall? she has got to be such

a nice little girl it is hard

to part with her but it is all

left to you if she cries

or next

Aggie has got the best of it her

but if you say she has got to stopy

we will keep her to

Letter Number 98, Page 2 - Transcription

and grandma is ~~to~~ will bring her
up to you it will be lonesome
without her
She is such a good little girl
laughing all the time she
is awake so it is all left
to you if baby has to come home
or next fall
It is very cold weather here
as No sign of spring

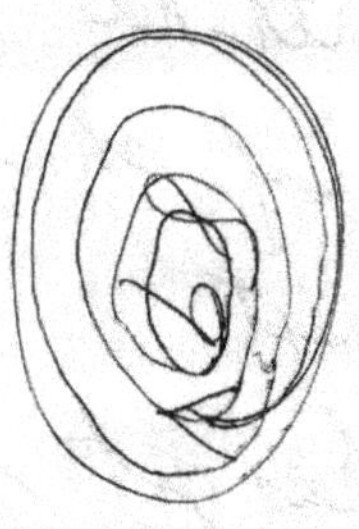

Letter Number 99

Date: 31 August 1887
Writer: Thomas Messer
Recipient: Mary Agnes Messer Pipe & Margaret Messer Jeffers
Sent from: Oxford Junction, Jones County, Iowa, USA
Sent to: Pipe House, Lanark, Portage County, Wisconsin, USA [Sheridan, Waupaca County, Wisconsin, USA, Post Office]

Key Ideas

- An explanation from a descendant states: "From Grandpa (Thomas) Messer to daughters, Aunt Maggie (Margaret Ann Messer) and Grandma (Mary Agnes Messer Pipe). She (Mary Agnes Messer Pipe) brought Tods (Toots is Mae Elizabeth Pipe born 1884.) back when Mina (Margaret Pipe) was born or a year old."
- (Margaret Ann Messer married George Jeffers on April 5, 1894.)
- Grandpa Thomas Messer says that the Methodist Hall had a crown festivity in the Hathway House.
- Grandpa Thomas Messer asks whether Totes (Toots or Mae Elizabeth Pipe) talks yet.
- Tilly Ollesen has moved beside her mother. Sissie Nivens is going to be married.
- (According to the Wisconsin Historical Society, the Grand Army Home in King, Waupaca County, Wisconsin, was established in 1887 for Union veterans and their wives and family members. Local community members likely visited the site when it opened.)
- Janet Niven McCunn Cameron is the Grandmother Cameron whose death is reported in Letter Number 100.

From Grandpa [Thomas] Messer to [daughters] Aunt Maggie [Margaret Ann Messer Jeffers] and Grandma [Mary Agnes Messer Pipe]. She [Mary Niven Messer] brought Tods [Toots or May Elizabeth Pipe] back when Mina [Margaret Pipe] was born or a year old.

Oxford July 31, 1889

Dear Agi [Mary Agnes Messer Pipe] and Maggie [Margaret Annie Messer Jeffers]

Yours we received over, was happy to hear you arrived all safe and found them all well, it is about the same here as it has been all summer, that over dry, we had a few cool days but did not last long. We had a rain storm Friday night but all right again and no damage. You will see by the papers what has been going on since you

left. The Methodist Hall a nice crown festivity in the Hathway house right over. I think they are pretty well Ma [Mary Niven Messer] says you are not tell her half enough about the children, does Totes [Toots or May Elizabeth Pipe] talk, know ever if there is not said within fifty miles so as you can get a sand pile for her and how is the little baby [Mina Margaret Pipe] getting along, is she walking yet, Tilly Ollesen moved up beside her mother, now have been up to see Gran Arme [Grand Army Home] yet? Ma [Mary Niven Messer] wants to know if is so that Sissie Nivens is going to be married, this fall, how is Cameron [Janet Niven McCunn Cameron] getting along or do you

go and visit them, how does George Shaw get along, is he as pushing as ever. Have you heard any more from Mr. Niven, we are happy to know you are going to get a girl at last, hoping you will get along with her good. We will send you the paper over, you will see the rest of news.

No more at present

From your G [Thomas Messer]

Letter Number 99, Page 1

From grandpa Messer to Aunt Maggie + Grandma Pipe. she brot Lots back when Mina was born or a year old

Oxford July 31/187

Dear Agga & Maggie

Yours we received and was happy to hear you arrived all safe and found them all well it is about the same here as has it has been all summer hot and dry we had a few cool days but did not last long we had a rain storm Friday night but all right again and no damage done you will see by the papers thats has been going on since you

Letter Number 99, Page 2

left. the Methodist had
a Ice Cream festivaly in
the Hathway house night
and i think they done
pretty well Ma says you
are not tell her half
Enough about the Children
dos Lotie talk know
and if their is not sand
with in fifty miles so as
you can get a sand pile
for her and how is the
little Baby geting along.
is she walking yet Tilly
Olesen is moveed up beside
her mother know have
been up to se Gran Anne
yet Ma wants to know
if is so that Lissie Niven
is going to be Married
this fall how is Cameron
geting along or do you

Letter Number 99, Page 3

go and visit them how
does George Shaw get along
is he as pushing as Ever
have you hard any more
from Dr Niven we are
happy to hear you are going
to get a girl at last
hoping you will get along
with her good we will
send you the paper and
you will se the news of
news

No more at present
[illegible]
[illegible]

Letter Number 99, Page 4

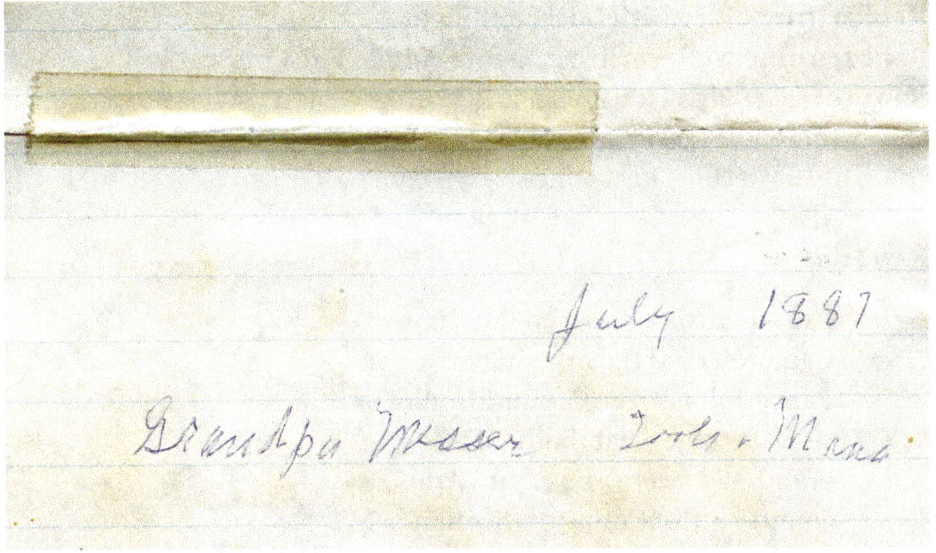

July 1887

Grandpa Messer Tols. Mass.

Letter Number 100

Date: 1 January 1902
Writer: Florence McCunn
Recipient: Elizabeth Stickland Pipe
Sent from: 37 Rose Street, Dunfermline, Fife County, Scotland
Sent to: Pipe House, Lanark, Portage County, Wisconsin, USA [Sheridan, Waupaca County, Wisconsin, USA, Post Office]

Key Ideas:

Florence McCunn (right) with her sister, Ethel

- Grandma Janet Niven McCunn Cameron died the other day.
- Papa, John Niven McCunn, said it is strange that both of their grandmas were born in "this country" (McCunn in Scotland and Stickland in England).
- Florence asks Grandma Elizabeth Stickland Pipe, "Now what part of England did she come from? Have you any friends there?" John Niven McCunn has offered to take Florence McCunn to see any remaining friends or relatives of Elizabeth Stickland Pipe.
- Florence McCunn and brother Walter McCunn have been invited to seven Christmas holiday parties.
- Florence McCunn says Dunfermline is a historic Scottish town with ruins of the place of King Malcolm and Queen Margaret. The old abbey where they worshipped is still standing.
- Florence McCunn sends a photograph of her sister Ethel McCunn and herself.

---

7 Rose Street

Dunfermline

1st Jan 1902

Dear Grandma [Elizabeth Stickland Pipe]

This is the first day in the year 1902. New Year's Day is a great day with the people in Scotland. Last night a good many people did not go to bed till two or three o'clock this morning. They sat up to see the New Year come in as they call it. When the clock struck one. They all

wished each other a happy New Year. The other day before we had heard of the day of the death of Grandma [Janet Niven McCunn] Cameron which we were all very, very sorry to hear of, papa [John Niven McCunn] said it a strange thing that both of our Grandmas were born over in this country [McCunn in Scotland and Stickland in England]. Now what part of England did you come from?

Have you any friends there? Papa [John Niven McCunn] says that if you tell me he will take me there to see

the place someday, and look up your friends that is if you have any that you know are still there. This Christmas Walter [McCunn] and I have been invited to seven parties this Christmas holidays now. We have a fortnight, but it is nearly finished now. This winter we have had three weeks of frost and snow. Which is pretty good for Scotland. But is all away now. However, it is early in the winter, and we have a good

chance to have some more yet. Dunfermline is a historical town. It has the ruins of the palace of King Malcom [Malcolm] and Queen Marget [Margaret]. Opposite the ruins is the old Abbey where they worshipped. There are services still held in the Abbey. How is Toots [May Elizabeth Pipe]? I hope you are all well. I will send you a snapshot of Ethel [McCunn] and myself. I wish you all a very happy New Year

Your loving

Granddaughter

Florence McCunn

Letter Number 100, Page 1

37 ROSE STREET,
DUNFERMLINE.

1th Jan. 1902

Dear Grandma,

This is the first day in the year 1902. New Year's day is a great day with the people in Scotland. Last night a good many people did not go to bed till two or three oclock this morning. They sat up to see the New Year come in as they call it. When the clock struck one. They all

Letter Number 100, Page 2

wished each other
a happy New Year.
The other day before
we had heard of
the death of Grandma
Cameran which we
were all very very
sorry to hear of, papa
said it is rather
a strange thing that
both of our Grandmas
were born over in
this country. Now
What part of England
did you come from?
Have you any friends
there? Papa says that
if you tell me he will
take me there to see

Letter Number 100, Page 3

the place some day,
and look up your
friends that is if you
have any that you
know are still there.
This christmas Walter
and I have been
invited to seven parties.
We are having our
christmas holidays
now. We have a fortnight
but it is nearly
finished now. This
winter we have had
three weeks of frost
and snow. Which is
pretty good for Scotland
But is is all away
now. However it is
early in the winter
and we have a good

Letter Number 100, Page 4

chance to have some more yet. Dunfermline is a historical town. It has the ruins of the palace of King Malcum and Queen Marget. Opposite the ruins is the old Abbey where they worshipped. There are services still held in the abbey. How is Toots? I hope you are all well. I will send you a snap-shot of Ethel and myself. I wish you all a very happy New Year.

Your Loving
Granddaughter
Florence McCunn

Letter Number 100, Envelope Front

Letter Number 100, Envelope Front

Letter Number 101

Date: After 21 May, 1903 [After Mary Elizabeth Pipe married Oliver Anderson
Writer: Mary Elizabeth Pipe Woodnorth
Recipient: Unknown
Sent from: Unknown
Sent to: Unknown

Key Ideas

- Mary Elizabeth Pipe Woodnorth has looked for Oliver and Toots (May Elizabeth Pipe) Anderson all last week.
- She is going to Mrs. (Margaret Ann Messer) Jeffers.
- Mary Elizabeth Pipe Woodnorth leaves for a church guild meeting.
- She asks whether Lizzie (Elizabeth Johnson Pipe) is with the unknown recipient of the letter.
- Mary Elizabeth Pipe Woodworth says it is too bad the church in Stevens Point burned. It was a nice church.
- She adds Eugene Townsend's wife died suddenly and is to be buried today.

[Letter undated]

I thought it strange she did not go before. I think she will be back as soon as

possible. Luan [?] hasn't come back yet, think she is still in R [?]. We looked for Oliver and Toots [Oliver and Mae Elizabeth Pipe Anderson] all last week, wonder why they did not come. I am going to Mrs. Jeffers this time to a guild meeting so will close. Hoping you are all well

And with my love, Mary

Is Lizzie [Elizabeth Johnson Pipe, wife of John Stickland Pipe] with you now. It was too bad the church at the point [Stevens Point, Wisconsin] was burned. It was such a nice one.

Eugene Townsend's wife is to be buried today, died very sudden.

Letter Number 101

I thought it strange she did
not go before. I think she will
be back as soon as possiable. Dean
hasent come back yet. think she
is still in R. we looked for
Olive and Toots all last week.
wonder why they did not come.
I am going to Mrs Jeffers. this
p.m. to a guild meeting so will
close. hopeing you are all well.
and with love. Mary.
is Lizzie with you now.
it was to bad the church at
the point was burned. it was
such a nice one.

Ezra Townsends wife is to be buried
to day. died very sudden.

Letter Number 102

Date: 15 October 1912
Writer: Ethel McCunn
Recipient: Elizabeth Stickland Pipe
Sent from: 16 Ferndale Grove, Frizinghall, Bradford, West Yorkshore County, England
Sent to: Pipe House, Lanark, Portage County, Wisconsin, USA [Sheridan, Waupaca County, Wisconsin, USA, Post Office]

Key Ideas:

- Ethel says she lost Mamma (second wife of John Niven McCunn) on September 26. Mamma was in bed since September 15. Ethel McMunn was not told how serious the situation was because she could not be home. After she found out, she went home for ten days.
- Florence McCunn and John McCunn were the only family members in the house at the time of their mother's death. The little ones were at school, Harold McCunn was at college, and Papa, John Niven McCunn, was at the office.
- Ethel explains that her father, John Niven McCunn, has had trials losing his first wife, Florence Pipe McCunn. (Florence Pipe McCunn is the daughter of Thomas and Elizabeth Stickland Pipe. She is also granddaughter of Charlotte Jennings Pipe Pillar.) Now, his second wife has died.
- Ethel McCunn remembers seeing her mother, Florence Pipe McCunn, only two or three times.
- Florence McCunn will be the housekeeper for the family.
- Ethel McCunn asks from what part of England her grandma (Elizabeth Stickland Pipe) originated.

---

16 Ferndale Grove

Frizinghall

Bradford

England

My dear Grandma [Elizabeth Stickland Pipe]

It is a very long time since I wrote to you and although I have often intended to do so, it has always been put off. Now that we are in such great trouble I must do it. It has made me fear that if I put it off, I may lose you too before it is done. Mamma [second wife of John Niven McCunn] was taken from us on the 26th of Sept. She had only been in bed from the 15th. I had taken a post here leaving home on the 16th. When they wrote me from home, they did not tell me how ill she was because they knew how anxious it would make me especially as I could not be at home and I have a very responsible

post. It was a great shock to get the wire saying she was gone. I went home for ten days. Not even the Drs. expected anything so sudden. That very morning they thought she was ever so much better, and they all went off to their various duties feeling brighter than they had since she went to bed. Florence [McCunn] and John [McCunn] were the only members of the family in the house at the time. The two little ones were at school. Harold [McCunn] at college and Papa [John Niven McCunn] at the office. It was haemorrhage [hemorrhage]and came on while Florence [McCunn] was feeding her. Poor dear she did get a shock and was quite upset for a day or two. The Drs. had to give her something to let her sleep. Poor Papa [John Niven McCunn] has had his trials I don't think anything could be harder to bear. First to lose our own Mamma [Florence Pipe McCunn] that we hardly can remember and now this one that was so good to us all. I can only remember my own mother as I saw her on two or three occasions. Once outdoors and twice in the house. Her face I cannot recall but her figure is very clear to me and the way she moved about. Florence [McCunn] will be housekeeper, I think. I have my art training and would like to use it if they can spare me from home. I am just down here for three months introducing a new system of Art Needlecraft into a large girls' school. After Xmas I want to stay at home and study for six months. Both for the sake of being at home with the others for a while and for the benefit of my work. I should very much like to know to what part of England you belonged. I asked Papa [John Niven McCunn], but he could not tell me. Well, I must say good night. With much love

Your affectionate grandchild Ethel

["McCunn, Grandmother (granddaughter) to Elizabeth (Stickland Pipe)" written in later]

Oct 15th, 1912

Letter Number 102, Page 1

16 Ferndale Grove,
Frizinghall,
Bradford.
England.

My dear Grandma,

It is a very long long time since I wrote to you and although I have often intended to do so it has always been put off. Now that ~~we are in such great trouble I must do~~ it. It has made me fear that if I put it offe I may loose you too before it is done. Mamma was taken from us on the 26th of Sept. She had only been in bed from the 15th. I had taken a post here leaving home on the 16th. When they wrote me from home they did not tell me how ill she was because they knew how anxious it would make me especially as I could not be at home and I have a very responsible

Letter Number 102, Page 2

my own mother as I saw her on two or three occasions. Once out doors and twice in the house. Her face I can not recall but her figure is very clear to me and the way she moved about. Florence will be housekeeper I think. I have my art training and would like to use it if they can spare me from home. I am just down here for three months introducing a new system of Art Needlecraft into a large girls school. After Xmas I want to stay at home and study for six months. Both for the sake of being at home with the others for awhile and for the benefit of my work. I should very much like to know to what part of England yo belonged. I asked Papa but he could not tell me. Well I must say Good-night. With much love.

Letter Number 102, Page 3

Your affectionate grandchild,

Ethel. McCrum

Oct 15th 1912.

Grandmother to Elizabeth

Letter Number 102, Page 4

post. It was a great shock to get the wire saying she was gone. I went home for a days. Not even the Drs. expected anything so sudden. That very morning they thought she was ever so much better + they all went off to their various duties feeling brighter than they had since she went to bed. Florence & John were the only members of the family in the house at the time. The two little ones were at School, Harold at college + Papa at the office. It was hemmorage and came on while Florence was feeding her. Poor dear she did get a shock + was quite upset for a day or two. The Drs. had to give her something to let her sleep. Poor Papa has had his trials I don't think any thing could be harder to bare. First to loose our Mamma that we hardly can remember and now this one that was so good to us all. I can only remember

Letter Number 102, Envelope Front

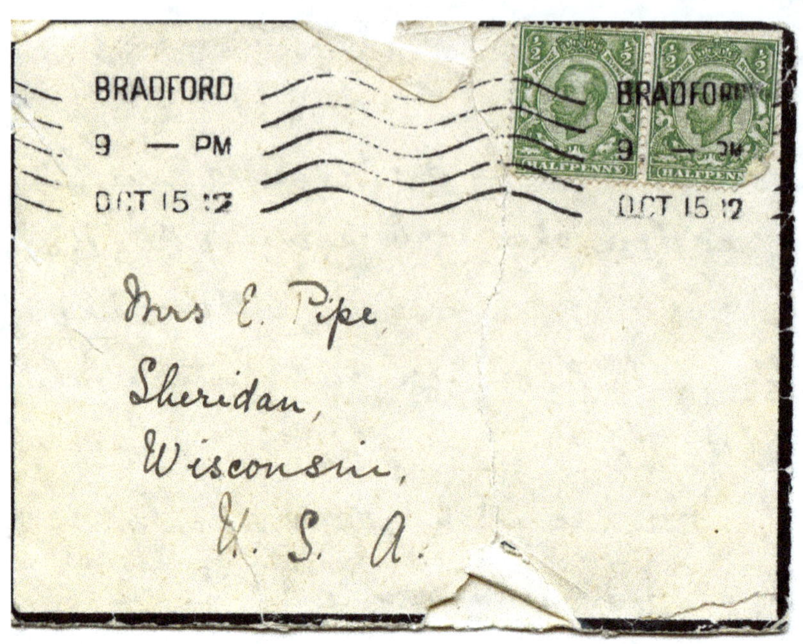

Letter Number 102, Envelope Back

Letter Number 103

Date: 1 January 1914
Writer: Elizabeth Johnson Pipe
Recipient: Mary Agnes Messer Pipe
Sent from: 413 Normal Avenue, Stevens Point, Portage County, Wisconsin, USA
Sent to: Pipe House, Lanark, Portage County, Wisconsin, USA [Sheridan, Waupaca County, Wisconsin, USA, Post Office]

Key Ideas:

- Lizzie (Elizabeth Johnson Pipe) is the wife of recently deceased John Stickland Pipe. (John Stickland Pipe is the son of Thomas and Elizabeth Stickland Pipe. Charlotte Jennings Pipe Pillar is his grandmother.)
- (Mary Agnes Messer Pipe married William Edwin Pipe, son of Thomas and Elizabeth Stickland Pipe. Charlotte Jennings Pipe Pillar is William Edwin Pipe's grandmother.)
- Lizzie asks whether Bessie is Mary Elizabeth Bowron, daughter of Elizabeth Pillar Bowron. (Bessie is also the granddaughter of Charlette Jennings Pipe Pillar.)
- Lizzie states that she has had dinner with Frank Pipe's wife, Ida Goff Pipe, and their daughter Mabel Pipe. Mabel has a sprained ankle.
- (John Stickland Pipe died March 23, 1913. His recent death is likely the reason Christmas does not feel like the usual holiday to her.)

Stevens Point

Jan 1st, 1914

Dear Aggie [Mary Agnes Messer Pipe]

Your card received for which I thank you. I did not send out any cards this Christmas at all, it did not seem like Xmas at all to me. I had dinner and supper with Ida [Goff, Frank Pipe's wife] and Mabel [Frank and Ida Pipe's daughter]. Mabel [Frank and Ida Goff Pipe's daughter] has been laid up with a sprained ankle, and I am now suffering with a sore foot. I had thought some of spending New Year with you. I received your letter a while ago but was unable

[to] accept your kind invitation then and I expect it will be some cold weather after this so I cannot leave the coole stowe [coal stove] how are you all, in mother's house if so give her my love. I received the announcement of the marriage of Mary Elizabeth Bowron is that Bessie. I did not know she was nicknamed.

Love and best wishes for a happy New Year for you all

Lizzie

413 Normal Ave.

Letter Number 103, Page 1

Stevens Point
Jan 1st 1914

Dear Aggie
Your card received
for which i thank you I did
not send out many cards this
Christmas at all it did not seem
like Xmas at all to me I had
dinner and supper with Ida
and Mabel, Mabel has been laid
up with a sprained ankel,
and I am now suffring with
a sore foot. I had thought
some of spending New Years
with you, I received your letter
a while ago but was Mabel

Letter Number 103, Page 2

exept your Kind inviatation
then and I Expect it will
be some cold weather after
this so I can not leave the
coble stove, how are you all
is mother home if so give her
my love, I received the anounce-
ment of the marriage of
Mary Elizabeth Bowron
is that Bessie, I did not
Know she was nicknamed
love and best wishes for
a happy New Year for you
all

Lizzie

413 Normal ave

Letter Number 103, Envelope Front

Aunt Lizzie
to Grandma

U.S. POSTAGE
2 CENTS 2

STEVENS POINT
JAN 2 -14
9— [illegible] AM
WIS.

Mrs W. E. Pipe
Sheridan
Wisconsin

Letter Number 104

Date: 19 August 1914
Writer: Isaac Craite, Attorney and Couselor at Law
Recipient: William Edwin Pipe
Sent from: South Eighth Street, Manitowoc
Manitowoc County, Wisconsin, USA
Sent to: Pipe House, Lanark, Portage County, Wisconsin, USA
[Sheridan, Waupaca County, Wisconsin,
USA, Post Office]

Key Ideas

- William Edwin Pipe apparently helped Isaac Craite when he ran out of gas. The poem was written as a thank you to William Edwin Pipe.

A token of friendship, - a calabash pipe
Smoke it, smoke it, to your like
Gasoline we got, even on a hike
A kind act was by W.E. Pipe.

The 8th Mo. On the 17th, - Sabbath day
Car stopped, want move, there to stay
Driver mumm, all silent, nothing to say
Friendly man, help, -to- morrow make hay.

Christianity shown by little acts
Monuments measured by deeds in the past
Down the hill all rolling very fast
But remember brothers, -we'll meet at last.

AMEN

Letter Number 104, Page 1

ISAAC CRAITE

ATTORNEY AND COUNSELOR AT LAW

ROOMS 12 AND 14 WILLIAMS BLOCK TELEPHONE RED 177

MANITOWOC, WIS.,

A token of friendship,- a calabash pipe
Smoke it, smoke it, to your like
Gasoline we got, even on a hike
A kind act was by W.E. Pipe.

The 8th Mo. on the 17th,-Sabbath day
Car stopped, want move, there to stay
Driver mumm, all silent, nothing to say
Friendly man, help,-to-morrow make hay.

Christianity shown by little acts
Monuments measured by deeds in the past
Down the hill all rolling very fast
But remember brothers,-we'll meet at last.
AMEN.

Letter Number 104, Envelope Front

ISAAC CRAITE
ATTORNEY AND COUNSELOR AT LAW
PHONE RED 177
ROOMS 12 AND 14, TEITGEN'S BLOCK
SOUTH EIGHTH STREET
MANITOWOC, WISCONSIN

MANITOWOC AUG 19 5-30P 1914 WIS.

Mr. W.E. Pipe,
Sheridan, Wisconsin

Letter Number 105

Date: 1870s or later
Writer: Unknown
Recipient: Future generations
Sent from: Unknown
Sent to: Pipe House, Lanark, Portage County, Wisconsin, USA [Sheridan, Waupaca County, Wisconsin, USA, Post Office]

Key Ideas

- The author of this death record is unknown. Likely Charlotte Jennings Pipe Pillar provided the information about her family line.
- Relationship titles of grandparents, aunts, uncles, and cousins, may support Thomas Pipe as the writer of this record; however, as common in the letters, people were sometimes called by their relationship name.
- A close analysis of handwriting could possibly identify the writer.

Death record, on headed paper of Thomas Pipe proprietor of Fulton Meat Market 187-

Grandfather died [Appendix C]	July 11th 1837	age 68 years
Grandmother ditto	Dec 20th 1843	age 75 years
Uncle John Bond [Appendix E]	Feb 28th 1854	age 80 years
Aunt Bradley [Appendix E]	October 17th 1866	age 88 years
Cousin Lovdy[?] B	March 29th 1868	age 58 years
Cousin John Bond	November 21st 1862	ditto marks
Uncle Edwin Jennings	February 10th 1871	age 71 years
Aunt Edwin Jennings	February 13th 1870	age 58 years
Cousin Mary Ann Jennings	October 1872	age [28 years]
Uncle John Jennings	December 2nd 1872	age 69 years
Uncle Thomas Jennings	December 12th 1872	age 67 years

[backside]

Marked in pencil “Death Record”

Letter Number 105, Page 1

Appleton Post Print.

STATEMENT.

Waupaca, Wis., ...187

M ....

To THOMAS PIPE, Dr.,

Proprietor of the

Fulton Meat Market.

The Highest Cash Price Paid for Fat Stock.

Interest Charged on all accounts running over Thirty Days.

Grandfather	Died	July 11th	1837	Age	68 years
Grandmother	"	Dec 20th	1843	Age	75 years
Uncle John Bond	"	Feby 28	1854	Age	86 years
Aunt Beadle	"	October 17	1866	Age	88 years
Cousin Emily B	"	March 29	1868	Age	58 years
Cousin John Bond	"	November 21	1862	"	. . .
Uncle Edwin Jennings	"	Feby 10	1871	Age	71 years
Aunt Edwin Jennings	"	Feby 13	1870	"	58 "
Cousin Mary Ann Jennings	"	October	1872	"	
Uncle John	"	December 2	1872	"	69 "
Uncle Thomas	"	December 12	1872	"	67 "

Letter Number 105, Page 2

Conclusion

The Pipe family letter collection of 105 letters spanning 63 years and four generations is a firsthand account of one immigrant family's life in America. In many ways, their story is the story of many immigrants during this time.

One difference, however, is that their story is told with their own pens and in their own words. Each life event is reported as it happens in their lives. Doubts and fears about the future are expressed in the moment. Joys and celebrations that warm the writer's hearts are shared in the reader's presence. The family's life events become shared experiences with the reader.

Another important difference with the Pipe family's immigration story is the transactional nature of many of the letters. The Stickland family farms continue to operate as businesses after Elizabeth Stickland Pipe unexpectedly inherits those properties in Yarcombe and Membury, Devon, England, even though she is living in America. Readers overhear discussions about building repairs, prices of crops, and all-important weather conditions on which farmers' lives are dependent. Comparisons are made between the cost of goods and services in England and America. Even the international exchange rate between England and America plays a factor in their financial decision making.

In Letters Number 100 and 102, Florence and Ethel McCunn, respectively, express curiosity about their grandmother Elizabeth Stickland Pipe's family origins. Did Grandmother Pipe answer their questions with a written account of her life? Did the girls travel with their father, John Niven McCunn, to Yarcombe to visit remaining friends and family? Today, their descendants may never know whether Grandmother Pipe answered her granddaughters' questions. However, they will know where Elizabeth Stickland Pipe was from. The Pipe family letter collection answers this question and others in detail.

The Pipe family letter collection provides Yarcombe historians with information and insights into the lives of their earlier residents and farmers. The collection also provides Wisconsin historians with a detailed account of one of their earliest families to settle in Wisconsin. Perhaps, most importantly, the Pipe family letter collection invites the reader to get to know Pipe family members on a personal level. Through reading the letters, the reader develops a personal relationship with individual family members as they reveal themselves in their own words.

Appendix A

The will of John ***STICKLAND***
Dated 25 February 1806 and proved 22 June 1810

THE NATIONAL ARCHIVES via Ancestry

PREROGATIVE COURT OF CANTERBURY

PROB 11/1512/370

Will of John Stickland

Dated 25th February 1806

Proved 22nd June 1810

I John Stickland of Yarcombe in the county of Devon yeoman being of sound mind

and perfect memory do this twenty fifth day of February in the year of our lord one

thousand eight hundred and six make and publish this my last will and testament in

manner following that is to say

I give unto my wife Betty the sum of £50 to be paid her in one year next after my decease

Also I give unto my said wife such part and articles of my household goods and

furniture as she shall select and choose within one year next after my death not

exceeding in value the sum of £50 according to the estimation of the same by my herein after named trustees

And I devise give and bequeath unto my son John Stickland his heirs and assigns

for ever all my message and lands which I have in fee simple within the parish of

Yarcombe aforesaid or elsewhere

And I constitute and ordain my friends Robert Spiller of Underdown and Henry Spiller

of Knightshayne within the said parish of Yarcombe yeomen and Robert Smith of

Stockland in the county of Dorset tallow chandler to be guardians and trustees of my

said son John and of my said messuages and lands for and on behalf of my said son

John during his minority to let protect and manage the same as in their discretion

they think best for his advantage maintenance and education

And I give and bequeath unto my two daughters Mary and Elizabeth the sum of

£300 each to be paid them on their respective attainment to the age of 21 years with

interest for the same from my decease until their arrivals to that age after the rate of

4.5% which interest or such part thereof as my hereinafter named trustees and

executors in trust shall think proper it is my will shall be applied from time to time

towards the maintenance and education of my said daughters Mary and Elizabeth

during the minority but in case either of them my said daughters shall happen to

marry before her attainment to the age of 21 years it is my desire that my executors

in trust may if they think fit immediately on such marriage pay the said legacy of

£300 to such of my said daughters or both of them so married together with such

interest as may then remain and endure for the same

And in case my said wife shall happen to be with child at the time of my decease I

then give unto such my posthumous child or children as she shall be afterwards

delivered of the sum of £250 to be paid such child or children at the age of 21 years

for interest for the same after the land and in manner so directed touching the said

Page 2

legacies of £300 given to each of my said daughters Mary and Elizabeth which said

two legacies so given to them in case my said wife shall happen to have such my

posthumous child or children and the same live to the age of 21 years shall in that

case be reduced from £300 down to £250 each, nor shall my said two daughters

Mary and Elizabeth be entitled to claim during the minority of such my posthumous

child or children only such legacies of £250 each with interest therefore after the rate

and manner before mentioned

Al the rest and remainder of my leasehold lands stock goods monies chattels and

personal estate whatsoever and wheresoever, after payment of my just debts funeral

expenses and before mentioned legacies I give and bequeath unto my said friends

Robert Spiller Henry Spiller and Robert Smith and the survivor of them his executors

administrators and assigns upon trust and for the following intents and purposes,

that is to say it is my will and I direct my said trustees to protect manage and dispose

of all my said residuary estate in the best way and manner they and the survivor of

them in their discretion can during the minority of my two sons Thomas and Robert

Stickland and to apply from time to time the rents interests and profits of the same

or such part thereof as my said trustees or the survivor them think proper towards

the decent and frugal maintenance and education of my said two sons Thomas and

Robert during their minority and on the attainment of the eldest of them to the age of

21 years it is my will that my said trustees shall then pay make assign and deliver

over unto such eldest of my said sons one full just moiety of all my said residuary

effects and the accumulated profits of the same, if any then remaining in the hands

and care of my said trustees or either of them for the use and benefit of the eldest of

my said two sons for ever

And on the attainment of the youngest of my said two sons to his age of 21 years I

then order my said trustees to pay assign and deliver over unto him the other moiety

of my residuary estate and effects with the accumulated profits of the same, if any,

then remaining in the custody of my said trustees or either of them for the sue of my

said two sons for ever

And in case either of my said two sons Thomas or Robert shall happen to die during

his minority and leave no legitimate issue I then give the survivor of them all my said

residuary estate and effect to be paid assigned and delivered over to him by my said

trustees on his attainment to the said age of 21 years save only that my said trustees

shall first pay thereout the sum of £20 unto each of my then surviving children,

except my said son John, in addition to the legacies which I have here-inbefore given

to them

And further it is my will if both my said sons shall happen to die and leave no

legitimate issue during their minority that then all my said residuary estate and

effects shall devolve and be paid by my said trustees in equal and like shares unto all my then surviving children on their respective attainments to the full age of 21

years 'and in case my said daughters Mary, Elizabeth or any posthumous child or

children shall happen to die in their minority and leave no legitimate issue and not

have been paid their respective legacies hereby given to them as I have before

directed, it is then my will that the legacy and legacies given to such decease

Page 3

daughter or daughters posthumous child or children shall devolve and be paid in

equal and like shares unto all my surviving children, except my said son John

Stickland, on their several attainments to the age of 21 years

Further it is my will and direction that my said trustees and the survivor of them his

executors administrators and assigns shall and will confide the care maintenance of

all my children during their minority unto my said wife Betty and also the direction

and superintendence of their education unless my said wife shall be her misconduct

or imprudence give my said trustees good and sufficient reason to take the care

maintenance and education of my children out of her management and power for the

security and advantage of my said children

And I hereby constitute and ordain my said friends Robert Spiller Henry Spiller and

Robert Smith joint executors in trust of this my will during the minority of said two

sons Thomas and Robert Stickland and on their attainment to the full age of 21 years

I then appoint my said two sons Thomas and Robert to be thenceforth join executors

of this my will

Also it is my will and I hereby legally authorise my said trustees and executors in

trust to pay retain and reimbursee themselves and each of them from time to time

out of my said trust estate for all their or either of their necessary trouble and

reasonable expenses in the proper execution of this my last will and the fulfilment of

my aforesaid trusts and that my said trustees and executors in trust shall not be

answerable or responsible for any more of my monies property and estate than they

or either of them shall actually receive or be in possession of, nor for any loss that

shall happen in the execution of this my will and my aforesaid trusts except the same

occur their or either of their wilful neglect or default, nor shall the one of them be

answerable or responsible for the acts and deeds of the other of them but each of

them for his own acts and deeds

In witness whereof I the said John Stickland have to the first sheet of this my last

will and testament containing two sheets of paper set my hand and to the last sheet

thereof my hand and seal the day and year first above written

Signed: John Stickland

Signed sealed published and declared by the said testator, the above erasure being

first made, as and for this last will and testament in the presence of us who at his

desire in his presence and in the presence of each other have subscribed our names

as witnesses thereto: the mark of George Flood, the mark of James Vincent and Wm

Kite

Proved at London 22 nd June 1810 before the judge by the oaths of Robert Spiller and

Henry Spiller and Robert Smith the executors till Thomas Stickland and Robert

Stickland the sons or either of them shall attain the age of 21 years having been first

sworn by common duly to administer

Citation:

Prerogative Court of Canterbury and Related Probate Jurisdictions: Will Registers. Digitized images. Records of the Prerogative Court of Canterbury, Series PROB 11. The National Archives, Kew, England; Ancestry.com. *England & Wales, Prerogative Court of Canterbury Wills, 1384-1858* [database on-line, images 826-828]. Provo, UT, USA: Ancestry.com Operations, Inc., 2013. entry for John Stickland.

Transcribed by ST Moore

Appendix B

The will of Robert ***STICKLAND***
Dated 19 February 1831 and proved 19 March 1832

THE NATIONAL ARCHIVES

PREROGATIVE COURT OF CANTERBURY

PROB 11/1797/393

Will of Robert Stickland

Dated 19th February 1831

Proved 19th March 1832

This is the last will and testament of me Robert Stickland of Yarcombe in the county

of Devon yeoman

In the first place I give and bequeath the sum of £1,000 unto my cousin Thomas

Smith of Clayhidon in the said county of Devon yeoman and Robert Spiller of

Painshayne in the parish of Yarcombe aforesaid yeoman their executors

administrators and assigns to be paid within one year next after my decease with

interest after the rate of 4% from my death until so paid

Upon and for the trust intents and purposes and with under and subject to the

powers and declarations hereinafter expressed concerning the same, that is to say

upon trust that they the said Thomas Smith and Robert Spiller and the survivor of

them and the executors administrators and assigns of such survivor do and shall as

soon as they or he conveniently can lay out and invest the same in their or his

names or name in the purchase of parliamentary stocks or funds of Great Britain or

on good and sufficient real security or securities with full power from time to time to

vary the same at their or his discretion

And do and shall during the natural life of my dear mother Elizabeth Stickland as

from time to time received pay all the interests dividends and proceeds of the said

sum of £1,000 unto her my said mother Elizabeth her agent or assigns for her own

absolute use and benefit

And from and after the decease of my said mother Elizabeth upon trust that they the

said Thomas Smith and Robert Spiller and the survivor of them or the executors

administrators or assigns of such survivor do and shall pay transfer and assign the

sum of £500 part of the said sum of £1,000 unto my brother Thomas Stickland if he

be then living otherwise unto and amongst all his then surviving children if more than

one in equal and similar shares and portions but if only one such child then the

whole to that one

And also from and after the death of my said mother upon trust to pay transfer and

assign the sum of £200 part of the said £1,000 unto John the son of my said brother

Thomas and £100 unto Elizabeth his daughter if they have then respectively attained

the age of 21 years otherwise on their respective attainments to that age and in the

interim from the death of my said mother until he my said nephew and niece shall

attain their said ages of 21 years it is my will that the interest and proceeds of the

said legacies of £200 and £100 shall be paid unto my said brother Thomas or his

representative towards the education and maintenance of my said nephew and niece

Page 2

And further it is my will and I declare if either of them my said nephew or niece shall

happen to die during his or her minority and leave no legitimate issue that then the

legacy of him or her so dying without issue hall devolved and be paid unto and

amongst all the then surviving children of my said brother Thomas if more than one

in similar shares, but if only one survivor then the whole to that one

And upon further trust to pay transfer and assign upon and from the death of my said mother the remaining sum of £200 part of the said sum of £1000 unto my brother

John Stickleand as a vested legacy provided always and it is my will and I do hereby

direct that it shall and may be lawful to an for my said trustees and each of them and

every of their executors and administrators by and out of the said trust money

hereinbefore mentioned to deduct and reimburse himself of themselves and to allow

to each other from time to time all such costs damages journeys charges and

expenses as they every or either of them shall be put unto pay or sustain by reason

of any of the trusts hereby in them reposed or in the execution thereof or by reason

of any other matter or thing relating thereto as between solicitor and client

And that none of my trustees shall be answerable for any more money than what

they shall respectively receive nor be charged or chargeable for the receipt or

receipts of the other of them but each for his own receipt acts deeds wilful defaults

only nor shall they or either of them be accountable for any involuntary loss or losses

of all or any part of the said trust money but shall be saved harmless in respet of all

acts and things done by them or either of them in the execution of the trusts hereby

in them reposed and also stand indemnified of and from all such involutary loss and

losses unless the same happen through their or his wilful neglect or default

And I give my said brother Thomas the sum of £100 to be paid my within one year

net after my decease

All the rest residue and remainder of my stock goods monies securities for money

mortgages in fee otherwise chattels and personal estate whatsoever, charged in the

first place with the payment of all my just debts funeral and testamentary expenses

and before mentioned legacies thereout, I give and bequeath unto my said brother

John Stickland his executors administrators and assigns and him my said brother

John I constitute and appoint executor of this my will

In witness whereof I have to the first sheet of this my last will and testament

containing two sheets of paper set my hand and to this the second and last sheet my

hand and seal this 19 th day of February in the year of our lord 1831

Signed: Robert Stickland

Signed sealed published and declared by the said Robert Stickland the testator as

and for his last will and testament in the presence of us who at his request and in his

presence and in the presence of each other have subscribed our names as witnesses the words 'all or such involuntary loss and losses' having been first

interned

Wits: Martha Pitts, Robt Spiller, Wm Kite

Probate granted to John Stickland brother and sole executor

Citation:

Prerogative Court of Canterbury and Related Probate Jurisdictions: Will Registers. Digitized images. Records of the Prerogative Court of Canterbury, Series PROB 11. The National Archives, Kew, England; Ancestry.com. *England & Wales, Prerogative Court of Canterbury Wills, 1384-1858* [database on-line, images 708-709]. Provo, UT, USA: Ancestry.com Operations, Inc., 2013. entry for Robert Stickland.

Transcribed by ST Moore

Appendix C

*The will of John **JENNINGS**, of Birch Oak in the parish of Membury Devon yeoman Dated 9 May 1837 and proved 7 February 1838*

THE NATIONAL ARCHIVES

PREROGATIVE COURT OF CANTERBURY

PROB 11/1890/425

Will of John Jennings of Birch Oak in the parish of Membury Devon yeoman
Dated 9th May 1837

Proved 7th February 1838

I John Jennings of Birch Oak in the parish of Membury in the county of Devon yeoman do make ordain publish and declare this to be my last will and testament in manner following, that is to say

First I give and bequeath unto **my grandson John Pipe son of my daughter Charlotte now the wife of John Pipe** the sum of o£10 of lawful money current in England to be raised out of all and every of my effects and paid to him on his attainment of age of 21 years by my executrix hereafter named

Also I give and bequeath to **my daughter Charlotte Pipe** and to each of her children that shall be living at the time of my death one decent suit of mourning the same to be ordered and selected and paid for from and out of my effects by my executrix

And whereas **my two sons Edmund Jennings and Thomas Jennings** and my said **daughter Charlotte wife of the said John** Pipe have been already provided for as to the part or share of my property which would have been theirs had no such provision for them been made therefore my will is and I hereby order and direct that no further provision for them shall be made from and out of my live and dead stock and other my effects nor shall they or either of them be entitled to ay part or share or proportion thereof

Also I give and bequeath unto **my wife Mary Jennings and my other three children namely John William and Mary Ann Jennings** all and every my household goods money book debts live and dead stock farming utensils and all other my effects of what kind and nature soever and wheresoever to hold the same to her my said wife for and during the term of her natural life with impeachment of waste except willful or malicious waste subject nevertheless to the payment of the said sum of £10 to **my said grandson John Pipe** here before given and all other expenses that may be lawfully incurred in and towards the fulfilling the purposes of this my will and all other my just debts funeral and testamentary expenses

And from and immediately after the death of my said wife Mary then I give and bequeath the same household goods money book debts live and dead stock farming utensils and all other my effects unto my said three children namely John William and Mary Ann Jennings the same to be divided among and between them in equal portions share and share alike and for the purpose of effecting such distribution in the manner and for the purposes aforesaid

And for carrying this my will into effect in all respects I hereby authorise and empower my brother in law John Bond of Ilton in the county of Somerset gentleman and my son Edmund Jennings of the same place yeoman their executors or administrators to the fulfilment in all respects of the contents of this my will

And for this purpose I hereby empower them the said John Bond and Edmund Jennings their executors or administrators with the consent of my said wife and three children namely John William and Mary Ann Jennings to call in and compel payment of any monies that may be due unto me at the time of my death

And I hereby further authorise and empower the said John Bond and Edmund Jennings to take an inventory of all and every of my effects al and every of my effects at the time of my death or as soon as conveniently can be afterwards and to inspect into and look to the same when and as often as is necessary during the lifetime of my said wife and to see that the same is not diminished in value by any fraud or wilful waste and t pay himself and themselves all reasonable expenses her or they may be at or put to in the discharge of the trusts hereby in him and them reposed

And I hereby constitute ordain and appoint my said wife Mary Jennings sole executrix of this my last will and testament

In witness whereof I the said John Jennings the testator have to this my last will and testament set my hand and seal the 9th day of May 1837

Signed: John Jannings

Signed sealed published and declared by the said testator the interlineations being first made in the presence of us who in his presence at his request and in the presence of each other have subscribed as witnesses:

John Dommett, John Hayes

Proved at London 7th February 1838 before the judge by the oath of Mary Jennings widow the relict and sole executrix to whom administration was granted having been first sworn by commission duly to administer

Citation:

Prerogative Court of Canterbury and Related Probate Jurisdictions: Will Registers. Digitized images. Records of the Prerogative Court of Canterbury, Series PROB 11. The National Archives, Kew, England; Ancestry.com. *England & Wales, Prerogative Court of Canterbury Wills, 1384-1858* [database on-line, images 828-829]. Provo, UT, USA: Ancestry.com Operations, Inc., 2013.entry for John Jennings.

Transcribed by ST Moore

Appendix D

*The will of John **STICKLAND***
of Yarcombe co Devon yeoman
Dated 28 February 1848 and proved 30 July 1850

THE NATIONAL ARCHIVES

PREROGATIVE COURT OF CANTERBURY

PROB 11/2117/70

Will of John Stickland of Yarcombe co Devon yeoman
Dated 28th February 1848

Proved 30th July 1850

This is the last will and testament of me John Stickland of Yarcombe in the county of Devon yeoman

First I charge all my real and personal estate of what nature or kind soever with the payment of all my debts funeral expenses and legacies as well such as I hereby give and also such as I may hereafter give by any codicil or codicils to this my will

I do appoint Robert Spiller of Pounds Farm in the parish of Yarcombe aforesaid yeoman and Robert Smith of Dunkeswell in the county of Devon yeoman my trustees and executors of this my will

I give unto **my dear wife Ann Stickland** the sum of £1,000 to be paid to her within twelve calendar months after my decease and as hereinafter mentioned I also give and bequeath to my said wife all my household goods plate glass furniture and other effects in and upon the dwelling house outhouses and premises where I now live or which I might occupy at my decease together with all my dairy goods farming utensils horses waggons carts agricultural implements cider and casks with the live and dead stock upon the farms which I may occupy at my decease

I direct that my wife shall be at liberty to continue in the occupation of any dwelling house land and premises which I may occupy at my decease for twelve calendar months hereafter without paying any rent for such occupation

And I also direct that in the event of my death happening at a time when it will not be practicable for my said wife conveniently to remove the crops in ground during the twelve calendar months aforesaid it shall be lawful for my said wife to continue in the occupation of such dwelling house land and premises for such additional time as may be necessary for her to do so, she paying such sum by way of rent for such additional occupation as my trustees shall in their and his discretion think fit

I direct that the fixtures in and upon the dwelling house in which I reside and particularly the ancient back in the fire place in my general siting room dated 1554 together with the cider press and apple mill and things which are generally considered fixtures shall remain attached to the freehold of the premises

I also direct my trustees for the time being of this my will to pay the legacy of £1,000 hereinbefore given to my wife out of any moneys due to me at my decease upon bonds notes debts or other personal securities, except mortgages for terms of years. And in the event of such personal securities being insufficient to pay the said legacy I direct that my wife shall be at liberty to elect to take any mortgage belonging to me not exceeding a security for £1,000 either in a discharge of such legacy or to make up the deficiency of such personal security and in the event of my wife's declining of such mortgage and there should be no such personal securities as aforesaid sufficient to discharge the said legacy owing to me then I direct that my said trustees to pay the said legacy out of my general personal estate

I give to **my niece Elizabeth the wife of John Pipe of Mem**bury in the county of Devon yeoman the sum of £300 to be paid to her within twelve calendar months from my decease

I give to **my niece Mary Stickland** the sum of £300 to be paid to her with twelve calendar months after my decease

I give to **Dan Pym of Buckland St Mary** in the county of Somerset yeoman the sum of £100 and in the event of his dying before me I direct that the legacy so given to him shall be divided equally amongst his children and the issue of any deceased child of the said Dan Pym such issue to take his or her parents share

I give to **Page Shire the elder of Buckland** aforesaid the sun of £100 and in the event of his dying before me I direct that the legacy so given shall be divided equally amongst his children and the issue of any decease child of the said Page Shire, such issue to take his or her parents share

I give to **Sidney Doble Levi Doble and Edwin Doble** sons of Robert Doble of Buckland aforesaid yeoman the sum of £19 19s each

Also I give to **Temperance Greedy the wife of James Greedy of Curland** in the county of Somerset yeoman and **Edith Wyatt the wife of Walter Wyatt o**f Buckland St Mary aforesaid yeoman the sum of £19 19s each

I give to my executors **Robert Spiller and Robert Smith** the sum of £50 each for their trouble in the execution of the trusts of this my will

I give and bequeath unto the said Robert Spiller and Robert Smith their executors administrators and assigns all estate vested in me as trustee for any person or persons upon trust to hold the same upon the trusts thereof

I do charge all that and those my estate and estates farms lands hereditaments and premises called **Much Hill Farm in the parish of Yarcombe** aforesaid occupied by Joel King, **Combes's Pithayne** and **the allotment in Mannings Common in Yarcombe** aforesaid now in my own occupation **Whithorns otherwise Bardscombe** situate at Membury aforesaid and now in my own occupation and also **Peacross** in Membury aforesaid occupied by John Dening with the annual sum of £30 to my nephew John Stickland during his life

And I direct such annual sum to be paid to my said **nephew John Stickland** by quarterly payments in each year during his life the first quarterly payment to be made at the expiration of three calendar months next after my decease

And I give power to my said **nephew John Stickland** to recover the annuity when in arrears for more than twenty eight days and all costs and charges of such recovery by distress and sale in like manner as rack rents are recoverable by law

And as to all my said estates called **Much Hill Farm Combes's Pithayne with the allotment on Mannings Common Whithorns otherwise Bardscombe and Peacross** I give devise and bequeath the same unto the said Robert Spiller and Robert Smith their heirs executors administrators and assigns upon the trusts and to and for the several uses and intents and purposes hereinafter expressed and declared concerning the same, that is to say

To the use and behoof of my **nephew Thomas Stickland son of my late brother Thomas Stickland** and his assigns for and during the term of his natural life without impeachment of waste except voluntary waste in houses and other buildings and from and after the determination of that estate to the use and behoof of the said Robert Spiller and Robert Smith their heirs and assigns during the natural life of my said nephew Thomas Stickland upon trust to preserve and support the contingent uses and estates hereinafter limited from being defeated or destroyed and for that purpose to make entries and bring actions as the case shall require but nevertheless to permit and suffer my said nephew Thomas Stickland and his assigns to hold and enjoy the said premises and to receive and take the rents issues and profits thereof to his and their own use and benefit during the term of his natural life

And from and after the death of my said nephew Thomas Stickland to the use of the first and every other son of his body lawfully to be begotten severally and successively according to their several securities in tail general and in default of such issue to the use of all and every the daughters and daughter of the body of my said nephew Thomas Stickland lawfully to be begotten to be divided between them if more than one in equal shares as tenants in common and the heirs of the respective bodies of all and every such daughters and daughter issuing and if there shall be but one such daughter then to the use of such only daughter and the heirs of her body lawfully issuing and in default of such issue of my said nephew Thomas Stickland then as to my said estates called Combe Pithayne and the allotment in Mannings Common Whitehorns otherwise Boundscombe and Peacross to the use and behoof of my said niece Elizabeth Pipe and her assigns for and during the term of her natural life without impeachment of waste except as aforesaid and from and after the determination of that estate to the use of the said Robert Spiller and Robert smith and their heirs for and during the natural life of my said niece Elizabeth Pipe upon trust to support the contingent uses hereinafter limited from being defeated or destroyed and for that purpose to make entries and bring actions as the case shall require

But nevertheless to permit and suffer **my said niece Elizabeth** Pipe and her assigns during her life to receive and take the rents and profits of the same hereditaments for her and their own use and benefit and from and after the decease of my said niece Elizabeth Pipe to the use of all and every the children and child of my said niece Elizabeth Pipe lawfully to be begotten who being a son or sons shall attain the age of 21 years or die under that age leaving issue of his her their body or being a daughter or daughters shall attain the said age or marry under that age with the consent of her or their guardian for the time being to be equally divided between or amongst them if more than one in equal shares as tenants in common, and if there shall be but one such child then to the use of that one or only child

And in default of such issue of my said niece Elizabeth Pipe then to the use of **my niece Mary Stickland** her heirs and assigns for ever

And as to my said estate called **Much Hill** I give and devise the same in default of such issue of my said **nephew Thomas Stickland** to the use and behoof of such issue of **my said niece Mary Stickland** and her assigns for and during the term of her natural life without impeachment of waste except as aforesaid and from and after the determination of that estate to the use of the said Robert Spiller and Robert Smith and their heirs for and during the natural life of my said niece Mary Stickland upon trust to support the contingent uses hereinafter limited from being defeated or destroyed and for that purpose to make entries and bring actions as the case shall require but nevertheless to permit and suffer my said niece

Mary Stickland and her assigns during her life to receive and take the rents and profits of the same hereditaments for her and their own use and benefit

And from and after the decease of my said niece Mary Stickland to the use of all and every children and child of my said niece Mary Stickland lawfully be begotten who being a son or sons shall attain the age of 21 years or die under that age leaving issue of his or their body or being a daughter or daughters shall attain the said age or marry under that age with the consent of her or their guardian for the time being to be equally divided between or amongst them if more than one in equal shares as tenants in common and if there shall be but one such child then to the use of that one or only child

And in default of such issue of my said niece Mary Stickland then to the use of my niece Elizabeth Pipe her heirs and assigns for ever

And as to all the rest residue and remainder of my residuary real and personal estate and effect of what nature kind or quality soever and wheresoever situate subject to the payment of my debts funeral expenses and in legacies I give devise and bequeath the sae and every part thereof unto and to the use of my **said nephew Thomas Stickland** his heirs executors administrators and assigns for his and their own absolute use and benefit

And I hereby expressly declare that my will to be that any sale mortgage or charge on any other disposition in the way of anticipation which **my said nephew John Stickland** in regard to his annuity or which **my said Thomas Stickland or my nieces Elizabeth Pipe and Mary Stickland** or either of the in regard to any estate or interest for life which they or either of them may at any time take in any part of my real and personal estate shall make or attempt or agree to make of the said annuity or estates for life respectively shall to all intents and purposes be absolutely void

And I do hereby declare that any legacies hereinbefore by me given to ay person who may be married women shall be paid to them for their separate use and benefit independently and exclusively of any husband or husbands to whom they may be married and without being in anywise subject to their debts claims or demands and that the receipts of the married women respectively notwithstanding their respective covertures shall be good and effectual discharges for the same

And I do hereby declare that the receipt or receipts of the said Robert Spiller and Robert Smith or the survivor of them or the executors or administrators of such survivor for any sum or sums of money payable to them or him or by virtue of the trusts I this will shall be a sufficient and effectual discharge or sufficient or effectual discharges for the same respectively or so much thereof respectively as in such receipt of receipts thereof respectively shall be expressed or acknowledged to so received, and that the person or persons not whom they same shall be given his her or their executors administrators assigns shall not afterwards be answerable or accountable for any losses misapplication nor non-application or be obliged or concerned to see to the application of the money therein mentioned and acknowledged to be received or any part thereof provided always and I hereby declare that if the trustees appointed for this my will or be appointed under the present provision of any of them or their or any of their executors administrators and assigns shall die or be desirous of being discharged from or refuse or decline or be incapable to act in the trusts thereby in them reposed as aforesaid before the same shall be fully executed then and in every such case it shall and may be lawful to and for the said trustees or the surviving or continuing trustee appointed under this my will whether they or he shall accept the trusts thereof or shall renounce the same or for the trustees or for the surviving or continuing trustee to be appointed under this present provision or the executors or administrators of such last surviving or continuing trusteed by any deed or deeds instrument or instruments in writing to be by them him or her sealed and delivered in the presence of and attested by two or more credible witnesses from time to time to nominate and appoint any fit person or persons to be a trustee or trustees in the room or place of the trustee or trustees so dying or desiring to be discharged or becoming unwilling or incapable to act as aforesaid, and that when and so often as any new trustee shall be nominated and appointed as aforesaid all the trust estates monies and premises or such of them as shall then be subject to the trusts and provisions as aforesaid which shall have vested in such trustee or trustees so dying desiring to be discharged or becoming unwilling or incapable to act as aforesaid shall be thereupon with all convenient speed conveyed assigns or transferred so and in such manner as that the same shall and may be loyally and effectually vested in the person or persons so to be appointed as aforesaid either solely or jointly with the surviving or continuing trustees or trustee as occasion shall require, to the use and upon and for the trusts intents and purposes hereinbefore expressed or declared or such of them as shall be then subsisting undetermined and capable of taking effect and the person or persons so to be appointed as aforesaid I shall have and be entitle to exercise the same powers and authorities as if he or they had been appointed a trustee or trustees of this my will provided always and I do hereby further declare that the trustees of this my will hereby appointed and to be appointed as aforesaid and each and every of them his heirs executors and administrators shall be charged and chargeable for such monies only as they respectively shall actually receive by virtue of the trusts hereby in them reposed notwithstanding their or any of their giving or jointly in giving any receipt or receipts for the sake of conformity

And I direct that none of them shall be answerable or accountable for any banker or broker with who the said trust monies and premises shall be place for safe custody or for any default tor neglect of the others or other of them or for involuntary losses

And also that it shall and may be lawful for them with and out of the monies which shall come to their respective hands by virtue of the trusts aforesaid to retain and reimburse themselves respectively and also to allow their respective co-trustees or co-trustee all costs charges damages expenses and fees to counsel for advice which they or any of them shall or may sustain expend or disburse in or about the execution of the aforesaid trusts or in relation thereto

In witness whereof I have to the first eight sheets of this my last will and testament affixed my hand and to the ninth and last sheet thereof my hand and seal this 28th day of February 1848

Signed: John Stickland

Signed by the said John Stickland the testator as and for his last will and testament in the presence of each of us present at the same time who at his request in his presence and in the presence of each other have hereunto subscribed our names as witnesses the erasures and alterations against which we have placed our initial having first bee made

Signed: H. Dommett solicitor, Chard

H. Kinsman his clerk

Proved at London 30th July 1850 before the judge by the oaths of Robert Spiller and Robert Smith the executors to whom administration was granted having been first sworn by commission duly to administer

Citation:

Prerogative Court of Canterbury and Related Probate Jurisdictions: Will Registers. Digitized images. Records of the Prerogative Court of Canterbury, Series PROB 11. The National Archives, Kew, England; Ancestry.com. *England & Wales, Prerogative Court of Canterbury Wills, 1384-1858* [database on-line, images 72-74]. Provo, UT, USA: Ancestry.com Operations, Inc., 2013. entry for John Stickland.

Transcribed by ST Moore

YARCOMBE PARISH

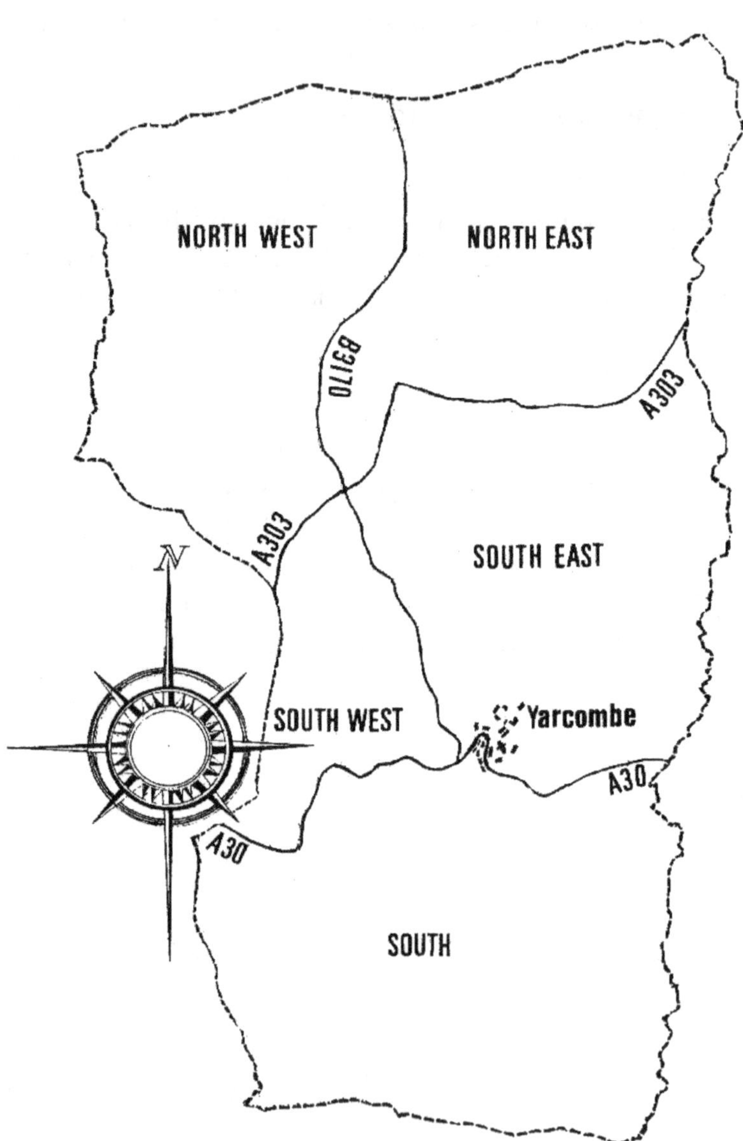

Yarcombe Parish map is found on page 29 of Ruth Everitt's 1999 From Monks to the Millennium. The "Gazetteer" shows the parish in 5 geographical areas. Everett's book can be found on the Yarcombe Home page at http://www.yarcombe.net/Ancestral-Searches.html.

SOUTH EAST

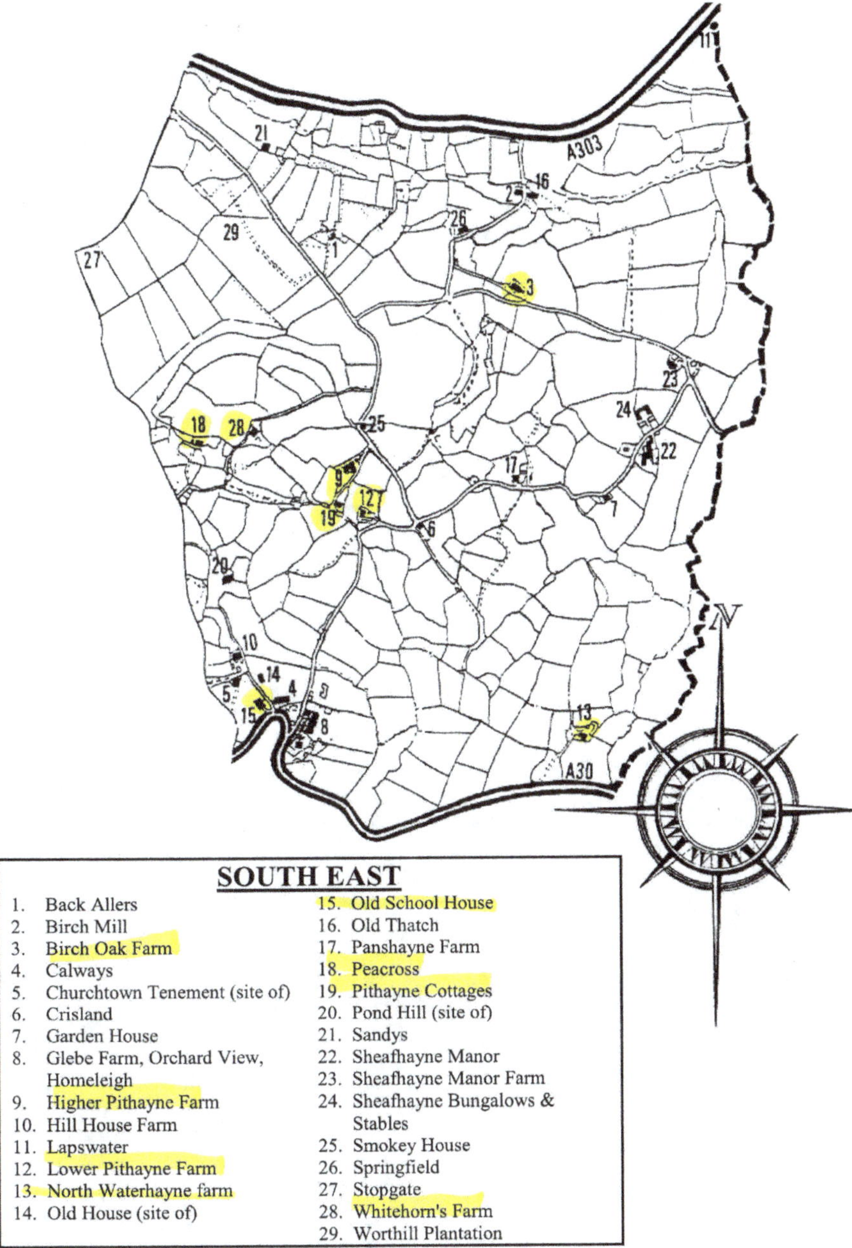

Many of the farms mentioned in the letter collection are located on the Southeast Yarcombe map. The highlighted names and locations show the proximity of these properties. The map is found on page 68 in Everett's book.

Appendix E

*The will of John **BOND** of Atherstone, gent.*
Dated 20 January 1854 and proved 18 May 1854

THE NATIONAL ARCHIVES

PREROGATIVE COURT OF CANTERBURY

PROB 11/2190/391

Will of John Bond of Atherstone gent
Dated 20th January 1854

Proved 18th May 1854

This is the last will and testament of me John Bond of Atherstone in the parish of Whitelackington in the county of Somerset gentleman

I give to my **nephew William Bond son of my last brother William** £350

I give to my **niece Letitia the wife of George Wakely** £150

I give to my **niece Elizabeth Bond daughter of my late brother Isaac Bond** £150

I give to my **niece Harriet the wife of Joseph Hayne** £150

I give to my niece **Mary Ann Dommett daughter of my late sister Mary Jennings** £150

I give to my nephew **John Jennings son of my said late sister Mary Jennings** £200

I give to my **nephew William Jennings another son of my said late sister Mary Jennings** £100

I give to **nephew Thomas Jennings another son of my said late sister Mary Jennings** £100

I give to **nephew Edwin Jennings another son of my said late sister Mary Jennings** £400

I give to my **niece Charlotte another daughter of my said late sister Mary Jennings** £50

I give to **my nephew Nicholas Bradley son of my sister Ann Bradley** £100

I give to my **nephew Edmund Bradley another son of my said sister Ann Bradley** £100

I give to my **niece Mary the wife of James Wyatt** £100

I give to my **niece Ann the wife of Frederick Bond** £500

I direct all the previous pecuniary legacies to be paid within one year next after my decease and with interest after the rate of four pounds per centum per annum from the time of my death to the time of the payment of the same respectively

I direct the legacies of such of the said pecuniary legatees as at the time of the actual payment thereof respectively shall be married women to be paid into their respective proper hands in order that the same may be enjoyed and disposed of as their separated property free form marital control and for which legacies their respective receipts shall be discharges

I give to **Edwin Francis Jennings the son of Edward Jennings by his late wife Fanny whose maiden name was Fanny Stephens**, £500 when he shall attain the age of 21 years and I direct that the said legacy shall not vest in him nor be paid unless he shall attain that age, but if the said Edwin Francis Jennings should die under the age of 21 years then one moiety of the said sum of £500 shall on his death be paid to his father the said Edwin Jennings and the other moiety thereon shall lapse to or for the benefit of my nephew John Bond the executor of this my will and if the said Edwin Francis Jennings shall be under the age of 21 years at the time of my decease then I direct that a sum equal to the interest of £500 at the rate of four pounds per centum per annum commencing from the time of my decease shall during the minority of the said Edwin

Francis Jennings or if he shall die under the age of 21 years until his death be paid and applied by my executor in such manner as he in his discretion shall think fit in or towards the maintenances education and bringing up of the said Edwin Francis Jennings

I hereby direct that in case any or either of my legatees hereinbefore named shall at the time of my decease be indebted to me in any sum or sums of money secured by bond or promissory note that the legacy given to each legatee so being indebted or so much of such legacy as shall be equal to the amount due on his or other said bond or note may be retained by my executor and applied in discharge or in part discharge of the amount due on the bond or note of the legatee from whom the same shall be retained

I also give to my said **nephew Thomas Jennings** my gig and the horse which at the time of my decease shall be used in bearing the same and also all my wearing apparel

I also give to my said **niece Ann the wife of Frederick Bond** my phaeton

I give my print "Thomas Oldaker" and my silver cup inscribed "E Abraham Esq: to **John Bond** as a token of respect / set/ to my nephew John Bond son of my said late brother Isaac Bond, for his sue and after his decease to my said nephew Frederick Bond and after the survivor of them **to John Bond son of my said nephew Frederick Bond**

I give to each of my friends Mrs Chapman, wife of William Coward Chapman, Miss Eliza Buncombe, Mrs Stephens wife of John Stephens, Mrs Budge the wife of Mr Geroge Budge, Miss Rebecca Stephens and Mrs Grabham wife of James Grabham a mourning ring of the value of £2

I give to each of my male and female farm labourers above the age of 21 years who shall have worked for me for one whole year next immediately before my decease £1 to be paid as soon after my decease as may be

I give to each domestic servant who shall be living with me at the time of my decease a suit of mourning

I desire and request my executor to erect as soon after my decease as conveniently may be a substantial tomb to the memory of myself and family in the church yard of Ilton in the said county of somerset and enclose and fence in the said tomb with iron palings

I give all my cash monies securities for money all terms and interest to which hi shall be entitled in any messuages lands or tenements as lessee or assign at the time of my decease and all the rest residue and remainder of my goods chattels estate and effects of what nature or kind soever they may be unto my said **nephew John Bond son of my said late brother Isaac Bond** who is now living and has lived for many years with me for his own soe and absolute use and benefit subject to repayment and discharge of all the aforesaid legacies as above specified and to the payment of my debts funeral and testamentary expenses and I give all estates which now are or herein may become and be at the time of my decease vested in me upon any trusts or by way of mortgage unto my said nephew John Bond his heirs executors and administrators respectively subject to the equities and upon the trusts affecting the same respectively

And I also give to my **said nephew John Bond** his heirs and assigns all real estates and interest which I have hereafter purchase or acquire and I appoint my said nephew John Bond whole and sole executor of this my will

I revoke all former wills by me made

In witness whereof I have to this my will contained in two sheets of paper set my hand and sealed, to wit my hand at the bottom of the first sheet and my hand and seal to this last sheet the 30th day of January 1854

Signed: John Bond

In witness contained in this and the previous sheet of paper was signed and sealed by the above hand John Bond the testator and by him declared to be his will in the presence of us present at the same time who at his request in his presence and in the presence of each other have hereunto set our names as witnesses

William Denman, John Rutter

Proved at London 18th May 1854 before the worshipful Samuel Fowkes Warnbey doctor of laws and surrogate by the oath of John Bond the nephew the sole executor to whom administration was granted having been first sworn duly to administer'

Citation:

Prerogative Court of Canterbury and Related Probate Jurisdictions: Will Registers. Digitized images. Records of the Prerogative Court of Canterbury, Series PROB 11. The National Archives, Kew, England; Ancestry.com. *England & Wales, Prerogative Court of Canterbury Wills, 1384-1858* [database on-line, images 325-326]. Provo, UT, USA: Ancestry.com Operations, Inc., 2013. entry for John Bond.

Transcribed by ST Moore

Appendix F

*Estate Duty copy of will of James **PIPE***
of Donyatt, yeoman
Dated 11 September 1833 and proved 18 October 1834

SOMERSET HERITAGE CENTRE

DD/ED/1834/206.

Estate Duty copy of will of James PIPE of Donyatt, yeoman.

Dated 11 Sep 1833.

Proved: 18 Oct 1834

To son James Pipe annuity of £10 a year for life chargeable upon my dwelling house

and appurtenances called Wheadons now in my occupation with powers of distress

and entry for recovery thereof to be paid half yearly the first payment to made in the

six calendar months next after my decease

To son John Pipe £5 to paid within 12 months of my decease

To daughter Elizabeth Pipe for her life my dwelling house and garden called Lesseys

with the orchard and close of pasture or meadow called Home Close, one close of

pasture land called The Drying Close or Yarnhay, and also all that house by the river

side near Donyatt Bridge called the Bucking House, all within the parish of Donyatt

After death to her children

If Elizabeth dies without children then to my grandson James Pipe, son of my son

Joseph Pipe forever

To daughter Elizabeth Pipe all my household goods and furniture

To sons Joseph Pipe and Edward Pipe 20s each to be paid within one month after

my decease

Residue to son Orlando Pipe and daughter Mary Pipe

Friend Ralph Horsey of Taunton gent to make inventory of all my goods and chattels

Son Orlando and daughter Mary Pipe to be joint executors

Signed: Jas Pipe

Wits: Richard Cannicott, Mary Lang, John Cannicot

Probate granted to Orlando Pipe and Mary Pipe spinster both of Donyatt

Value of estate under £800

Will of James Pipe, Page 1

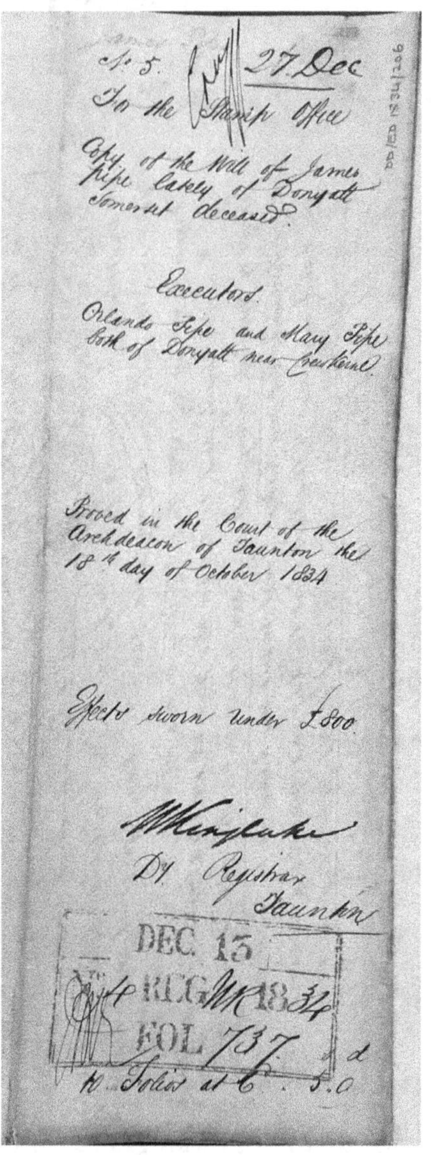

No. 5. 27 Dec

To the Stamp Office

Copy of the Will of James Pipe lately of Donyatt Somerset deceased.

Executors.

Orlando Pipe and Mary Pipe both of Donyatt near Crewkerne.

Proved in the Court of the Archdeacon of Taunton the 18th day of October 1834

Effects sworn under £800

Dy Registrar Taunton

DEC 13

REG 1834

FOL 737

10 Folios at 6 . 5.0

Citation:

Estate Duty copy of will of James PIPE of Donyatt, yeoman, Somerset Heritage Centre, Somerset, England.

Transcribed by ST Moore.

Will of James Pipe, Page 2

my estate and effects be taken and made within one month after my inter-
ment - And I hereby request authorise and empower my good friend Ralph
Horsey of Taunton Gentleman to see to the making of such inventory and
valuation of my said estate and effects so given and devised to my said
children Orlando and Mary and that an equal division be made thereof between
them and of the third part of my household goods and furniture so as aforesaid
given to my said daughter Elizabeth and in all other respects to see to and
assist in the execution of this my will and that he shall reimburse himself
out of my said estate and effects so as aforesaid given to my said children
Orlando and Mary all costs and expences he may incur in the execution of
the trust hereby in him reposed - And I do hereby constitute and appoint my
said son Orlando Pipe and my said daughter Mary Pipe joint executor and
executrix of this my will And I hereby revoke all other wills by me at any
time heretofore made and do declare this present writing contained in two
sheets of paper to be my last will and testament - In witness whereof I
have hereunto set my hand & seal to wit my hand to the first sheet and
my hand and seal to this last sheet the day and year first above written -
—— Jas Pipe (LS) —— Signed sealed published and declared by
the said James Pipe the testator as and for his last will and testament
in the presence of us who in his presence and in the presence of each other
have subscribed our names as witnesses thereto — Richd Cannicott ——
— Mary Lang —— John Cannicott ——

This and the foregoing sheet contain a true copy of the original will
the same having been examined therewith this ninth day of December
1834 by us -

[illegible] Lovelace

Jno Chorley Junr

Appendix G

*Deed of Confirmation between Mrs. Elizabeth **PIPE** and Sir Francis George Augustus Fuller Elliot **DRAKE** Dated 1874*

Deed of Confirmation

Dated 1874

Mrs Elizabeth Pipe

To

Sir Francis Geo A. F E. Drake baronet

This Indenture made the [blank] day of [blank] one thousand eight hundred and seventy four **between Elizabeth Pipe** of Greece in the county of Monroe in the state of New York in the United States of America widow of the one part and **Sir Francis George Augustus Fuller Elliott Drake** of Nutwell Court Woodbury in the county of Devon baronet of the other

Whereas by an indenture dated the [blank] day of [blank] one thousand eight hundred and seventy three and made between Thomas Pipe and Elizabeth his wife therein after referred to by and comprehended in the designation of "The Lessors" of the one part and the said Sir Francis George Augustus Fuller Elliott Drake who was thereinafter referred to by and comprehended in the designation of "The Lessee" of the other part

It is witnessed that for the consideration therein mentioned they the said Thomas Pipe and Elizabeth his wife **did** and each of them **did** by the now reciting presents demise and to farm let unto the said lessee

<u>All those</u> messuages or dwelling houses commonly called or known as "Whitehorns" situate in the parish of Membury within the county of Devon and "Pithayne" within the parish of Yarcombe in the said county of Devon with the barns stables outhouses yards gardens and appurtenances thereto respectively belonging

<u>And also</u> all those several closes or pieces of land arable meadow and pasture or orchard land or ground adjoining or lying near or contiguous thereto respectively and then or theretofore held and enjoyed therewith and containing together sixty three acres or thereabouts, be the same more or less

<u>And also</u> all that allotment or close of land situate in and forming part of Mannings Common in the parish of Yarcombe aforesaid heretofore in the

[page 2] occupation of George Bondfield [Bonfield] deceased and then and late of Susan Bondfield [Bonfield] deceased his widow and containing by estimation three acres more or less with their and every of their appurtenances

<u>And also</u> the exclusive right of shooting and sporting over the same except all timber and trees whatsoever and all mines minerals gravel pits and quarries thereon

<u>To hold</u> the same, subject as thereinafter mentioned, unto the said before lessee his executors administrators and assigns for the term of ten years from the twenty fifth of March then last under the yearly rent of one hundred pounds payable on the four usual quarterly days of payment without deduction except Property Tax and the further yearly rent of fifteen pounds by equal quarterly payments on the days therein aforesaid for every acre and so in proportion for every less quantity than an acre of the Meadow ground thereby demised with the said lessee should plough up or convert into tillage without the previous consent in writing of the lessors their heirs and assigns

<u>And</u> by the indenture now in recital the said lessee for himself his executors administrators and assigns covenanted with the lessor their his and her heirs and assigns that the lessee would during the said term duly pay the said rent thereby reserved as and when the same respectively became due

<u>And also</u> to pay all rates and taxes in respect of the demised premises

And to keep the same premises in sufficient repair on being allowed rough timber and two pounds per hundred for reed except the main walls and roof of the farm house and buildings and outer doors thereof which were

[page 3] to be kept in repair by the lessors and also the barn of Whitehorns which it was thereby agreed might be let down and also except injury by accidental fire

And at the expiration of the term to so deliver up the same to the lessors their heirs or assigns

And that it should be lawful for the lessors their heirs or assigns and their his or her agents at all reasonable times during the said term to enter upon the demised land view and examine the condition thereof and to leave notice of any wants of reparation which the said lessee his executors administrators or assigns would within three months after every such notice repair and make good accordingly

And also to use and manage the demised premises in a good and husbandlike manner and in a due and regular course of husbandry

And also should not carry off any hay straw or manure from the said premises but in and upon the same would spend use lay and employ all the hay straw swedes turnips mangoldwurzels [beets] fodder dung soil muck manure and compost that should from time to time arise come grow or be made in and upon the same premises

And also should leave upon the demised premises all the manure that should be produce thereof during the last year of the said term without requiring any recompense for the same

And not to break up or convert into tillage any of the meadow or pasture lands

And that it should be lawful for the lessors their heirs or assigns at Michaelmas next before the expiration of the said term to enter upon and plough up all such parts of the said demised lands as should the preceding year have been sown with winter corn or grain

And it is by the now reciting indenture provided and agreed

[page 4] that if the said rents thereby reserved or any part thereof should be unpaid for twenty one days after any of the said days whereon the same ought to have been paid, although no formal demand thereof

should have been made, or in case of the breach or non-performance of any of the covenants and agreements therein contained by the said lessor their executors administrators or assigns then that it should be lawful for the said lessors their heirs or assigns attorney or agent into the demised premises to re-enter

And by the now reciting indenture the said Thomas Pipe for himself his heirs executors and administrators and for the said Elizabeth his wife her heirs executors administrators covenanted with the said lessee that he and they paying the rents and observing performing and keeping the covenants thereinbefore on his and their parts contained should peaceably hold occupy and enjoy the demised premises with their appurtenances for the said term and to keep the buildings of the premises in repair except in such matters as were thereinbefore covenanted and agreed to be demised and performed by the said lessee

And it was thereby declared and agreed that the yearly rent thereinbefore reserved was so reserved and should be taken and be in the proportions and manner following, that is to say the yearly sum of eighty five pounds as and for the annual value of the hereditaments thereby demised and that the sum of fifteen pounds the balance of the said yearly rent as consideration for the omission from the now reciting demise of the usual reservation

[page 5] to lessors of the right of hunting shooting and sporting over the demised premises

And whereas the hereinbefore recited indenture was executed by William Jennings in the names and as the attorney of the said Thomas Pipe and Elizabeth his wife and it has since been made known to the said Sir Francis George Augustus Fuller Elliott Drake that the marriage of the said Elizabeth Pipe with the said Thomas Pipe was informal and void and he has requested and it has been arranged and agreed that the said Elizabeth Pipe should confirm the said least in manner hereinafter mentioned and enter into the covenants hereinafter contained

Now this indenture witnesseth that in pursuance of such request and arrangement and agreement and in consideration of the premises and of ten shillings now in hand paid by the said Sir Francis George Augustus Fuller Elliott Drake to the said Elizabeth Pipe the receipt whereof she does acknowledge, **she** the said Elizabeth Pipe **Doth** by these presents demise lease and to farm let unto the said Sir Francis George Augustus Fuller Elliott Drake

All and singular the said messuage farm and lands and all and every the hereditaments described comprised or referred to in the hereinbefore recited indenture with their and every of their appurtenances

To hold the same unto the said Sir Francis George Augustus Fuller Elliott Drake his

[page 6] executors administrators and assigns for the residue of the said term of ten years if she the said Elizabeth Pipe shall so long live nevertheless upon the conditions and subject to the provisos and agreements contained in the hereinbefore recited indenture

And the said Elizabeth Pipe for herself her heirs executors and administrators doth hereby covenant agree and declare with the said Sir Francis George Augustus Fuller Elliott Drake his executors administrators and assigns that the said hereinbefore recited indenture of lease shall be deemed and taken to be good valid and effectual to all intents and purposes for all the residue of the said term of ten years if the said Elizabeth Pipe shall so long live

And that during such term she the said Elizabeth Pipe her heirs executors or administrators shall and will uphold the same

And that the said Sir Francis George Augustus Fuller Elliott Drake his executors administrators and assigns paying the said yearly rent of one hundred pounds hereinbefore mentioned to be reserved in and by the hereinbefore in part recited indenture of lease and duly performing the same indenture on his and their parts to be performed shall

[page 7] and may peaceably and quietly hold possess and enjoy the said premises during the said term thereby granted without any eviction or disturbance by the said Elizabeth Pipe her heirs or assigns or any person or persons lawfully or equitably claiming by from or under her

In witness whereof the said parties to these presents have hereunto set their hands and seals the day and year first above written

Signed sealed and delivered

By the above named Elizabeth Pipe

In the presence of

A.B.

Add address and description, (with title)

C.D.

Add address and description

After enquiry Mrs Pipe to please place her finger on the seal and say "I deliver this as my act and Deed"

Citation:

Privately held by Elizabeth Pipe Hansen [ADDRESS FOR PRIVATE USE,] Amherst, Wisconsin, 2025.

Transcribed by ST Moore

Deed of Confirmation, Cover

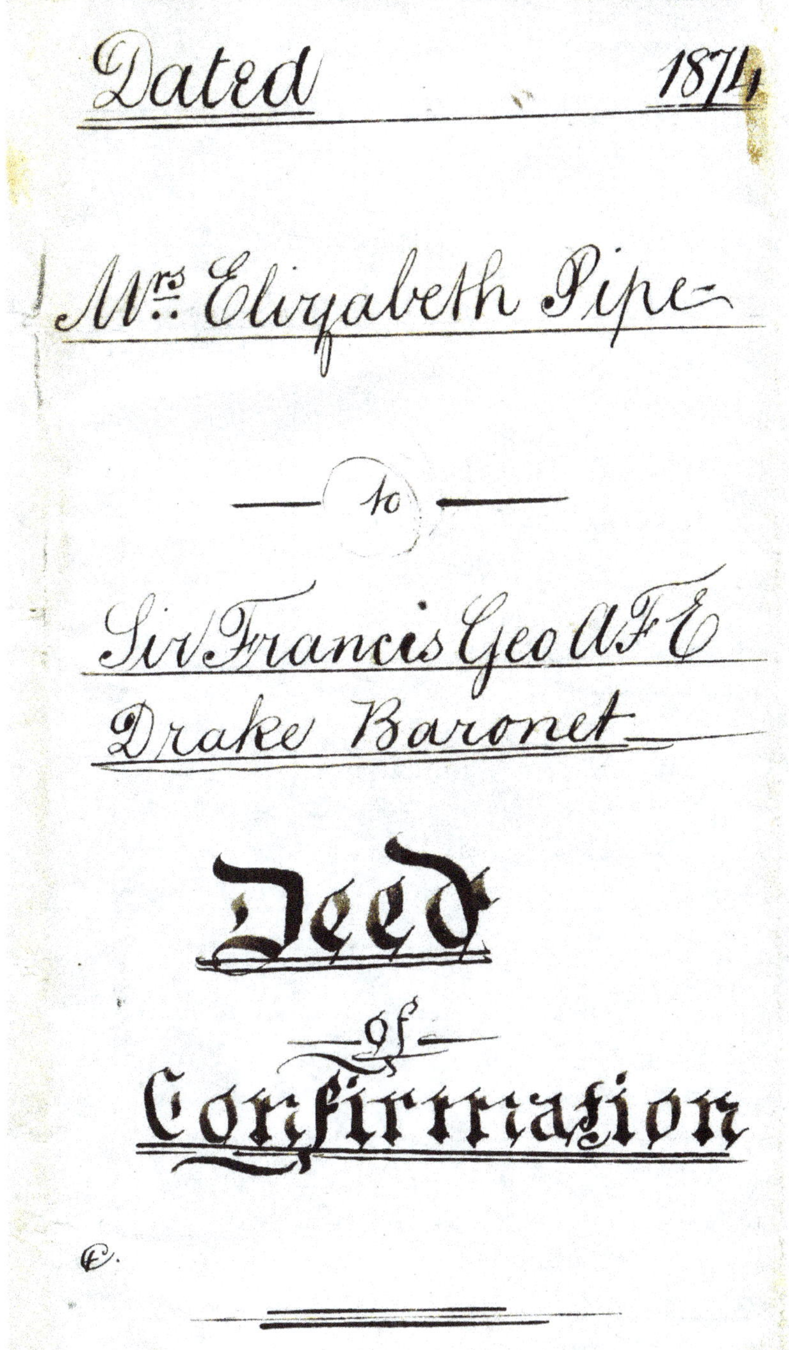

Dated 1874

Mrs Elizabeth Pipe

to

Sir Francis Geo A F E Drake Baronet

Deed of Confirmation

Deed of Confirmation, Page 1

This Indenture made the day of One thousand Eight hundred and Seventy four **Between Elizabeth Pipe** of Greece in the County of Monroe in the State of New York in the United States of america Widow of the one part and **Sir Francis George Augustus Fuller Elliott Drake** of Nutwell Court Woodbury in the County of Devon Baronet of the other part **Whereas** by an Indenture dated the day of One thousand eight hundred and seventy three and made between Thomas Pipe and Elizabeth his Wife thereinafter referred to by and comprehended in the designation of "The Lessors" of the one part and the said Sir Francis George Augustus Fuller Elliott Drake who was thereinafter referred to by and comprehended in the designation of "The Lessee" of the other part **It is witnessed** that for the considerations therein mentioned they the said Thomas Pipe and Elizabeth his wife **Did** and each of them **Did** by the now reciting presents demise and to farm let unto the said Lessee **All those** Messuages or Dwellinghouses commonly called or known as "Whitehorns" situate in the parish of Membury within the County of Devon and "Pithayne" within the parish of Yarcombe in the said County of Devon with the Barns Stables Outhouses Yards Gardens and appurtenances thereto respectively belonging **And also** all those several closes or pieces of Said arable Meadow and pasture or Orchard land or ground adjoining or lying near or contiguous thereto respectively and then or theretofore held and enjoyed therewith and containing together Sixty three acres or thereabouts (be the same more or less) **And also** all that allotment or close of land situate in and forming part of Mannings Common in the parish of Yarcombe aforesaid heretofore in the

Deed of Confirmation, Page 2

occupation of George Bondfield deceased and then
and late of Susan Bondfield deceased his Widow
and containing by estimation three acres more or
less with their and every of their appurtenances
and also the exclusive right of shooting and
sporting over the same except all timber and trees
whatsoever and all mines minerals Gravel pits and
quarries thereon To hold the same (subject as
thereinafter mentioned) unto the said Lessee his
executors administrators and assigns for the term of
Ten Years from the twenty fifth of March then last
under the yearly rent of One hundred pounds
payable on the four usual quarterly days of
payment without deduction except property Tax
and the further yearly rent of fifteen pounds by
equal quarterly payments on the days therein
aforesaid for every acre and so in proportion for
every less quantity than an acre of the Meadow
ground thereby demised which the said Lessee
should plough up or convert into tillage without
the previous consent in writing of the Lessors their
Heirs and assigns And by the Indenture now in
recital the said Lessee for himself his executors
administrators and assigns Covenanted with the
Lessors their his and her Heirs and assigns that
the Lessee would during the said term duly pay
the said rents thereby reserved as and when the
same respectively became due and also to pay
all rates and taxes in respect of the demised
premises and to keep the same premises in
sufficient repair on being ~~being~~ allowed rough
Timber and Two pounds per hundred for Reed
except the main walls and roof of the Farm House
and Buildings and outer Doors thereof which were

Deed of Confirmation, Page 3

to be kept in repair by the Lessors and also the Barn
at Whitehorns which it was thereby agreed might
be let down and also except injury by accidental fire
and at the expiration of the term to so deliver up
the same to the Lessors their Heirs or assigns and
that it should be lawful for the Lessors their heirs or
assigns and their his or her agents at all reasonable
times during the said Term to enter upon the demised
and view and examine the condition thereof and to
leave notice of any wants of reparation which the said
Lessee his Executors administrators or assigns would
within three months after every such Notice repair
and make good accordingly and also to use and
manage the demised premises in a good and eee
husbandlike manner and in a due and regular
course of husbandry and also should not carry off
any hay straw or manure from the said premises
but in and upon the same would spend use lay
and employ all the hay straw Swedes turnips eee
mangold Wurtzell fodder dung soil muck manure
and compost that should from time to time arise come
grow or be made in and upon the same premises
and also should leave upon the demised premises
all the manure that should be produced thereon
during the last year of the said term without eee
requiring any recompense for the same and not to
break up or convert into Tillage any of the Meadow
or pasture Land and that it should be lawful
for the Lessors their heirs or assigns at Michaelmas
next before the expiration of the said Term to enter
upon and plough up all such parts of the said eee
demised Lands as should the preceding year have
been sown with Winter Corn or Grain and it is
by the now reciting Indenture provided and agreed,

Deed of Confirmation, Page 4

that if the said rents thereby reserved or any part ee
thereof should be unpaid for Twenty one days after
any of the said days whereon the same ought to
have been paid (although no formal demand thereof
should have been made) or in case of the Breach or
nonperformance of any of the Covenants and eeee
agreements therein contained by the said Lessee his
executors administrators or assigns then that it should
be lawful for the said Lessors their heirs or assigns
attorney or agent unto the demised premises to eee
reenter **and** by the now reciting Indenture
the said Thomas Pipe for himself his heirs eeee
executors and administrators and for the
said Elizabeth his wife her heirs executors
and administrators covenanted with the said Lessee that he
and they paying the rents and observing eeee
performing and keeping the Covenants thereinbefore
on his ~~and their~~ and their parts contained should
peaceably hold occupy and enjoy the demised
premises with their appurtenances for the said
Term **and** to keep the Buildings of the premises
in repair except in such matters as were
thereinbefore covenanted and agreed to be done
and performed by the said Lessee **and** it was
thereby declared and agreed that the yearly rent
thereinbefore reserved was so reserved and should
be taken and be in the proportions and manner
following that was to say the yearly sum
of eighty five pounds as and for the annual
value of the hereditaments thereby demised
and that the sum of fifteen pounds the
balance of the said yearly rent as a eeee
consideration for the omission from the now
reciting demise of the usual Reservation

Deed of Confirmation, Page 5

to Lessors of the right of hunting shooting
and Sporting over the demised premises
And Whereas the hereinbefore recited
Indenture was Executed By William Jennings
in the names and as the attorney of the said
Thomas Pipe and Elizabeth his Wife and it
has since been made known to the said
Sir Francis George Augustus Fuller Elliott Drake
that the marriage of the said Elizabeth Pipe
with the said Thomas Pipe was informal
and void and he has requested and it has
been arranged and agreed that the said
Elizabeth Pipe should confirm the said Lease
in manner hereinafter mentioned and
enter into the Covenants hereinafter contained
Now this Indenture Witnesseth that in
pursuance of such request and arrangement
and agreement and in consideration of
the premises and of Ten shillings now in
hand paid by the said Sir Francis George
Augustus Fuller Elliott Drake to the said
Elizabeth Pipe the receipt whereof ~~she doth hereby~~
she doth hereby acknowledge She the said
Elizabeth Pipe Doth by these presents
demise and to farm let unto the said
Sir Francis George Augustus Fuller
Elliott Drake All and singular the said
Messuage Farm and Lands and all and
every the hereditaments described comprised
or referred to in the hereinbefore
recited Indenture with their and every
of their appurtenances To hold the same
unto the said Sir Francis George
Augustus Fuller Elliott Drake his

Deed of Confirmation, Page 6

executors administrators and assigns for
the residue of the said Term of Ten years
if she the said Elizabeth Pipe shall so
long live nevertheless upon the conditions and
subject to the provisoes and agreements eee
contained in the hereinbefore recited eeee
Indenture **And** the said Elizabeth Pipe
for herself her heirs executors and eeee
administrators **Doth** hereby Covenant agree
and declare with the said Sir Francis ee
George Augustus Fuller Elliott Drake ee
his executors administrators and assigns
That the said hereinbefore recited Indenture
of Lease shall be deemed and taken to be
good valid and effectual to all intents
and purposes for all the residue of the
said Term of ten years if the said eeee
Elizabeth Pipe shall so long live **and that**
during such term she the said Elizabeth
Pipe her heirs executors or administrators
shall and will uphold the same **and
that** the said Sir Francis George Augustus
Fuller Elliott Drake his executors eeee
administrators and assigns paying the said
yearly rent of **One** hundred pounds hereinbefore
mentioned to be reserved in and by the
hereinbefore in part recited Intenture of Lease
and duly performing the **several** Covenants
contained in the same Indenture on his
and their parts to be performed shall and

Deed of Confirmation, Page 7

may peaceably and quietly hold possess and enjoy the said premises during the said term thereby granted without any eviction or disturbance by the said Elizabeth Pipe her heirs or assigns or any person or persons lawfully or equitably claiming by from or under her In Witness whereof the said parties to these presents have hereunto set their hands and seals the day and year first above written

Signed Sealed and delivered by the above named Elizabeth Pipe in the presence of

Elizabeth Pipe+

A. B.

of &c

add address and description (with Title)

C. D.

of &c

add address and description

+after signing Mrs Pipe will please place her finger on the seal and say "I deliver this as my act and Deed"

Indexes

Origin & Destination	Letter Number
Hursey, Burstock, Beaminster, Dorsetshire County, England	65,66,67,70
Kirby House, Milwaukee, Milwaukee County, Wisconsin, USA (Corner of East Water & Mason Streets)	96
London, England	38,44
Manchester, Lancashire County, England	81,84,86
Manitowoc, Manitowoc County, Wisconsin, USA (South Eighth Street)	104
Neenah, Winnebago County, Wisconsin, USA	75,85
New York, New York, USA (111 Broadway)	74
North American Hotel, State Street, Rochester, Monroe County, New York, USA	14,17
North Greece, Monroe County, New York, USA	4
Northay Farm, Whitestaunton, Chard, Somerset County, England	1,2,3,4,5,6,7,8,13,14, 15,16,17,18,19,22,23, 24,25,26,27,28,29, 30,31,32,33,34,35, 36,37,39,40,41,42, 43,45,46,47,48,49, 50,51,52,53,54,55, 56,57,58,59,60,61,62
Oxford Junction, Jones County, Iowa, USA	95,97,98,99
Pipe House, Lanark, Portage County, Wisconsin, USA [Sheridan, Waupaca County, Wisconsin, USA, Post Office]	73,78,83,90,91,92, 93,94,95,96,97,98, 99,100,102,103,104, 105
Rochester, Monroe County, New York, USA	1,2,3,5
Stawell, Victoria, Borung County, Australia	77,91
Stevens Point, Portage County, Wisconsin, USA	93
Stevens Point, Portage County, Wisconsin, USA (413 Normal Avenue)	103
Stoford near Yeovil, Somerset County, England	16

Origin & Destination	Letter Number
Taunton, Somerset County, England (Stamp Office)	12
Thorncombe, Dorset County, England	75
Unknown	101,105
Vinland, Winnebago County, Wisconsin, USA	10,11,20,22,23,24, 25,26,27,36
Waupaca, Waupaca County, Wisconsin, USA	37,38,39,40,41,42, 43,44,45,46,47,48, 49,50,51,52,54,55, 56,57,58,59,60,61, 62,63,64,65,66,67, 68,69,70,71,72,79, 88,94
West Liverpool, Lancashire County, England (8 Gloucester Street)	15
Whitestaunton, Somerset County, England (Post Office)	89
Winsham, Somerset County, England	85
Woodville, Calumet County, Wisconsin, USA	87
Yarcombe, Devon County, England	9

Writer & Recipient	Letter Number
Alexander, Effie Pipe	83,90,92
Bartlett, Elizabeth Wall Stickland	16
Chapman, Mr.	14,17
Coleman, Mr.	86,87
Craite, Isaac (Attorney and Counselor at Law)	104
Dauncey, Lissie Dommett	92
Davy, Mary Ann Jennings	47,55,65
Dommett & Canning	69,71,76
Dommett, H.	72
Dommett, Mary Ann Jennings	11
Dommett, W.	68,69
Donaldson, E. S. (M.D.)	94
Future, Generations	21,105
Gillingham, Francis	75,85
Francklyn, Charles	74
Jeffers, Margaret Messer	99
Jennings, Edwin	11
Jennings, Elizabeth Coleman	8,14,16,19,22,23,24, 26,27,28,29,31,33, 35,36,40,41,43,46, 49,51,52,54,55,58, 60,62,63,64,65,66, 67,70
Jennings, John	11,20
Jennings, Thomas	11
Jennings, William	1,2,3,4,5,6,7,11,14, 15,17,18,19,23,25, 27,30,32,33,34,35, 36, 37,39,40,41,42, 45,46,47,48,50,51, 52,53,54,56,57,59, 60,61,66,67,70,76
Kenny, John	15
Kingsbury, J. R. (County Judge)	93

Writer & Recipient	Letter Number
Kite, Thos.	12
McCunn, Ethel	102
McCunn, Florence	100
McCunn, Florence Pipe	90,92
Mead, H.C.	74
Messer, Thomas	95,97,98,99
Pillar, Charlotte Jennings Pipe	11,36,83
Pipe, Amelia Woodnorth	88
Pipe, Elizabeth Johnson	103
Pipe, Elizabeth Stickland	4,7,8,14,17,19,22,24, 26,28,29,31,33,35, 38,41,46,48,51,55, 56,58,59,60,61,63, 65,66,68,70,71,72, 77,78,79,80,81,83, 84,86,88,90,92,96, 100,102
Pipe, John Valentine	4,7,9,10,13
Pipe, Mary Agnes Messer	99,103
Pipe, Thomas	10,18,20,23,24,25, 26,27,28,29,30,31, 32,33 33,34,35,37, 39,40,41,42,43,44, 45,46,47,48,49,50, 52,53,54,55,56,57, 58,59,60,61,62,63, 64,65,66,67,69,70, 73,75,76,77,78,79, 80,82,83,85,87,88, 89,90, 91,92,93
Pipe, Thomas (estate)	94
Pipe, Tom Jr.	79,88
Pipe, William Edwin	95,97,98,104
Pipe, William Jennings	6,38,44,77,91
Poll, Alfred	82

Writer & Recipient	**Letter Number**
Rendell, Giles	73
Roberts, Elizabeth Jones	87
Scranton, Edwin	1,2,3,5
Spiller, Robert	9
Stickland, Anna	80
Stickland, Mary	81,84,86
Unknown	21,101,105
Woodnorth, Mary Elizabeth Pipe	78,90,92,96,101
Woodnorth, Frank	96
Wyatt, William	12,13

Acknowledgements

Over the years, Pipe descendants cared for over 105 family letters in this collection, along with several dozen framed portraits and over 100 family pictures. I especially thank the Marjorie Pipe Johnson, Marlene Anderson Sannes, and Elizabeth Pipe Hansen families. They are the guardians of these family treasures. Undoubtedly, earlier descendants found their ancestors' handwriting too difficult to read and understand. However, the letters were not discarded. These family caretakers protected ancestral voices that now have been brought back to life. Once again, their voices are heard.

I especially thank Susan Moore from Somerset, England, who professionally transcribed each letter to preserve local dialect as much as possible so that each letter writer would be heard as authentically as possible. Susan graciously met with Marlene Anderson Sannes, her daughter Sara Sannes Franson, her granddaughter Oakley, and me while we were in England to discuss, among other things, the letter collection and her transcription of the letters.

I thank Robert John Mittelstaedt who funded, in part, the transcription costs so that future generations, like himself and his daughter Madeline, will be able to read and understand the lives of their ancestors. His legacy will resonate for generations to come.

I thank Miranda Gudenian, editor of *Yarcombe Voices*, a village magazine, and Steve Horner, a local historian, for kindly helping us locate local historical sources for Yarcombe and neighboring villages. They have worked tirelessly over the years to preserve the memory of Yarcombe history, especially the Drake estate. This collection of letters builds on their work. Today, the Yarcombe Home Page website welcomes others to join its continuing research.

I thank churchwarden Geoffrey Berry for coordinating the restoration of the Stickland tombstone in St. John the Baptism Churchyard in Yarcombe. His assistance unlocked generations of Stickland family history in Yarcombe. Sarah-Jane at The Belfrey at Yarcombe, a boutique hotel, surpassed our expectations for hospitality and local information. We thank you for making our time in Yarcombe feel like a visit home! I extend special thanks to Alex from Unique Devon Tours, who made local connections, drove us safely through the hedgerows, and guided us through our ancestral villages. I thank the Parris and Meyrick families, current occupants of Birch Oak Farm and Higher Pithayne Farm, respectively, for taking time to visit with Pipe family descendants.

Several Pipe descendants read earlier versions of this book and offered valuable feedback. They include Judy Mittelstaedt Anderson, Ida Mae Rosin Frizzell, Marlene Anderson Sannes, and Robert John Mittelstaedt. Their first-hand knowledge of family matters was essential to understanding key ideas in the letters.

Pipe descendants Marlene Anderson Sannes and Judy Mittelstaedt Anderson funded various aspects of the project, especially the portrait restoration and tombstone restoration in Yarcombe. I thank Bill Casper, owner of The Hang Up Gallery of Fine Art in Neenah, Wisconsin, and Charles Dunning, a freelance photographer at Landmark Vistas in Neenah, for restoring the Pipe family portraits. As a result of their expert work, portraits are included in this book. Their work enables readers to see some of the people who wrote letters so many years ago.

I want to thank Mary Diehl and Joan Kuss, newly found descendants of Mary Ann Pipe Sinclair, who shared family pictures, Bible pages, and two letters written by Mary Ann and her brother, Edwin Pipe, in the later 1830s in England. Their mother, Charlette Jennings Pipe Pillar, kept the items as remembrances of her children.

I thank Susan Chapman for helping me scan the letter collection and for her meticulous work on the database that created the indexes for letter writers and recipients along with their locations. Any errors are mine. I am grateful to Susan for the many hours of encouraging and inspiring conversation.

I am indebted to Mike Dauplaise, president of M&B Global Solutions, for his expertise in publishing and book design. He makes his work seem easy and simple. I know it is anything but that! Thank you, Mike, for your valuable suggestions. Jeff Ash has worked tirelessly editing this manuscript. In addition, his research into my research has added a depth of understanding I would not have without his help.

I give a special thanks to Joshua Ranger, university archivist at the University of Wisconsin-Oshkosh, for his assistance in researching the town of Vinland, Winnebago County, Wisconsin. The Wisconsin Historical Society and its local affiliates, especially the Winneconne Historical Society and the Waupaca Historical Society, especially Waupaca Railroad Depot manager Mike Kirk, provided a foundation of original documents and family stories that others can build on as more records become available online.

I am also indebted to the town of Vinland chair, board and clerk for allowing me to research town records, especially Brooks Cemetery, where at least seven Pipe ancestors are buried, including Charlotte Jennings Pipe Pillar. Special thanks to Julie Maxwell who has helped organize and scan town records.

Because of the efforts of the people mentioned and others too numerous to mention, descendants and others interested in local history in both England and Wisconsin will get to know on a personal level many of the people who came before them.

About the Author

Dr. Joan Naomi Steiner

Joan Naomi Steiner was born and raised on her grandfather's farm in Calumet County, Wisconsin. She graduated from Chilton High School. She earned her doctorate at New York University and her Master of Science in Teaching English and Bachelor of Science degrees from the University of Wisconsin-Stevens Point.

Dr. Steiner's professional career includes teaching high school students for twenty-five years and administrating in school districts for seventeen years. She has also taught at the university level and worked as a consultant for more than forty school districts in Wisconsin.

Dr. Steiner has known the Pipe family descendants for most of her life. Recently, her son invited her to visit his cousins, who inherited the Pipe family portraits and letter collection. Her research has uncovered not only records, but also family history told by ancestors in their own words.

Dr. Steiner has also written *A German Bohemian Immigration: The Population Shift from Western Bohemia to Calumet County, Wisconsin,* which has been translated into German and Czech languages. Dr. Steiner's website is a database of findings and a repository for records and resources for immigrants from Great Britian, Germany, and today's Czech Republic. You can find it at https://germanbohemianwisconsin.com/.

Select Bibliography

Chard History Group. *Chard in 1851*. Publication No. 5 of Chard History Group: Chard. Somerset, England: The society, 1975.

Bishop, Zachary. *The Waupaca Chain O' Lakes.* Arcadia Publishing: Charlestown, South Carolina, 2020.

Bodley, Hugh, editor for The Devonshire Association. *Poor Relief in Devon: Two A-Level Personal Studies*. Devenish & Company: Bath, England, 1991.

Clark, Thomas G. *Let Glasgow Flourish: The Disappearance of the SS City of Glasgow*. Distinctive Press: Monee, Illinois, 2019.

Everitt, Ruth. *From Monks to the Millenium: A History of Yarcombe Parish*. 1999.

Garfield, Simon. *To the Letter: A Celebration of the Lost Art of Letter Writing*. Penguin Group: New York, 2013.

Great Britain. Local Government Board. *Return of Owners of Land 1873*. Her Majesty's Stationery Office: London, 1875.

Higginbothan, Peter. *Workhouse Encyclopedia*. The History Press: Cheltenham, Gloucestershire, England, 2012.

Higginbothan, Peter. *Life in a Victorian Workhouse from 1834 to 1930*, Pitkin Publishing: Andover, Hampshire, England, 2011.

Horn, Pamela. *The Victorian Country Child.* Alan Sutton Publishing Limited: Stroud, Gloucestershire, England, 1990.

Huddy, Frank and Jeff Farley. *Chard and its Villages Through Time.* Amberley Publishing: Stroud, Gloucestershire, England

Jefferies, Richard. *The Toilers of the Field.* Double 9 Books. Daryaganj, New Delhi, 2025.

Leider, David. *The Story of Waupaca and its Railroads.* Wisconsin Historical Society: Madison, Wisconsin, 1998.

Martin, E.W. *The Shearers and the Shorn: A Study of Life in a Devon Community*. Routledge & Kegan Paul Ltd: London, 1965.

Moore, Susan T. *Family Feuds: An Introduction to Chancery Proceedings*. The Foundation of Family History Societies: Alden Group: Oxford, England, 2003.

Moore, Susan T. *Tracing your Ancestors through the Equity Courts: A Guide for Family & Local Historians.* Pen & Sword Books LTD: Barnsely, South Yorkshire, England, 2017.

Morris, John. *Doomsday Book: A Survey of the Counties of England,* 9:1. Phillimore & Co. LTD: London, 1985.

Nelson, Wendell. *The House by the Side of the Road.* Olde Keene Store Publishers: Stevens Point, Wisconsin, 2017.

Nesbit, Robert C. *Wisconsin A History.* The University of Wisconsin Press: Madison, Wisconsin, 1989.

New York Genealogical and Biographical Society. *New York Family History Research Guide and Gazetteer*: New York, 2015.

Richardson, Ruth. *Death, Dissection and the Destitute.* Penguin Books: London, 1988.

Sellman, Roger R. *Devon Village Schools in the Nineteenth Century.* David and Charles: Newton Abbot, Devon, England, 1967.

Shakespeare, Liz. *Fever: A Story from a Devon Churchyard.* Letterbox Books: Littleham, Devon, England, 2005.

Stanes, Robin. *A History of Devon.* Phillimore & Co. LTD. Chichester, Sussex, England, 1986.

Sturm, Jr., John. *Stretching Waters: A Historical Guide to the Chain O'Lakes, Waupaca, Wisconsin.* Killarney House, 1992.

Tapster, Donald. *The Parish Church of St. John the Baptist Yarcombe Devon.*

New York Genealogical and Biographical Society, *New York Family History Research Guide and Gazetteer*, (The New York Family Genealogical and Biographical Society: New York, 2015) 480.

Waupaca County Wisconsin Map 1874. Privately held by Joan Naomi Steiner [ADDRESS FOR PRIVATE USE,] Neenah, Wisconsin, 2025.

Wisconsin Historical Society, Patricia Hermansen, *Indian Legend Map, Chain O'Lakes Region, Waupaca,* 97618.

www.ingramcontent.com/pod-product-compliance
Lightning Source LLC
Chambersburg PA
CBHW070904130626
46555CB00001B/13

* 9 7 9 8 9 8 6 5 7 0 9 4 5 *